A Book Of

ENTERPRISE PERFORMANCE MANAGEMENT

For
MBA Semester - III
As Per Pune University's New Syllabus
Effective from June 2013

Jayant Oke
M.A., M.M.S.

Anil Agashe
M.A.

Dr. Satish Inamdar
LLB, M.Com, Ph.D. CA, ICWA, CS

N2148

ENTERPRISE PERFORMANCE MANAGEMENT

ISBN 978-93-5164-042-4

First Edition : August 2014

© : Authors

The text of this publication, or any part thereof, should not be reproduced or transmitted in any form or stored in any computer storage system or device for distribution including photocopy, recording, taping or information retrieval system or reproduced on any disc, tape, perforated media or other information storage device etc., without the written permission of Authors with whom the rights are reserved. Breach of this condition is liable for legal action.

Every effort has been made to avoid errors or omissions in this publication. In spite of this, errors may have crept in. Any mistake, error or discrepancy so noted and shall be brought to our notice shall be taken care of in the next edition. It is notified that neither the publisher nor the authors or seller shall be responsible for any damage or loss of action to any one, of any kind, in any manner, therefrom.

Published By :
NIRALI PRAKASHAN
Abhyudaya Pragati, 1312, Shivaji Nagar,
Off J.M. Road, PUNE – 411005
Tel - (020) 25512336/37/39, Fax - (020) 25511379
Email : niralipune@pragationline.com

Printed By :
Repro Knowledgecast Limited,
Thane

DISTRIBUTION CENTRES
PUNE

Nirali Prakashan
119, Budhwar Peth, Jogeshwari Mandir Lane
Pune 411002, Maharashtra
Tel : (020) 2445 2044, 66022708, Fax : (020) 2445 1538
Email : niralilocal@pragationline.com

Nirali Prakashan
S. No. 28/27, Dhyari,
Near Pari Company, Pune 411041
Tel : (020) 24690204, Fax : (020) 24690316
Email : bookorder@pragationline.com

MUMBAI
Nirali Prakashan
385, S.V.P. Road, Rasdhara Co-op. Hsg. Society Ltd.,
Girgaum, Mumbai 400004, Maharashtra
Tel : (022) 2385 6339 / 2386 9976, Fax : (022) 2386 9976
Email : niralimumbai@pragationline.com

DISTRIBUTION BRANCHES

NAGPUR
Pratibha Book Distributors
Above Maratha Mandir, Shop No. 3, First Floor,
Rani Jhansi Square, Sitabuldi, Nagpur 440012,
Maharashtra, Tel : (0712) 254 7129

JALGAON
Nirali Prakashan
34, V. V. Golani Market, Navi Peth, Jalgaon 425001,
Maharashtra, Tel : (0257) 222 0395
Mob : 94234 91860

BENGALURU
Pragati Book House
House No. 1, Sanjeevappa Lane, Avenue Road Cross,
Opp. Rice Church, Bengaluru – 560002.
Tel : (080) 64513344, 64513355,
Mob : 9880582331, 9845021552
Email:bharatsavla@yahoo.com

KOLHAPUR
Nirali Prakashan
New Mahadvar Road,
Kedar Plaza, 1st Floor Opp. IDBI Bank
Kolhapur 416 012, Maharashtra. Mob : 9855046155

CHENNAI
Pragati Books
9/1, Montieth Road, Behind Taas Mahal, Egmore,
Chennai 600008 Tamil Nadu, Tel : (044) 6518 3535,
Mob : 94440 01782 / 98450 21552 / 98805 82331, Email : bharatsavla@yahoo.com

RETAIL OUTLETS
PUNE

Pragati Book Centre
157, Budhwar Peth, Opp. Ratan Talkies,
Pune 411002, Maharashtra
Tel : (020) 2445 8887 / 6602 2707, Fax : (020) 2445 8887

Pragati Book Centre
Amber Chamber, 28/A, Budhwar Peth,
Appa Balwant Chowk, Pune : 411002, Maharashtra,
Tel : (020) 20240335 / 66281669
Email : pbcpune@pragationline.com

Pragati Book Centre
676/B, Budhwar Peth, Opp. Jogeshwari Mandir,
Pune 411002, Maharashtra
Tel : (020) 6601 7784 / 6602 0855

PBC Book Sellers and Stationers
152, Budhwar Peth, Pune 411002, Maharashtra
Tel : (020) 2445 2254 / 6609 2463

MUMBAI
Pragati Book Corner
Indira Niwas, 111 - A, Bhavani Shankar Road, Dadar (W), Mumbai 400028, Maharashtra
Tel : (022) 2422 3526 / 6662 5254, Email : pbcmumbai@pragationline.com

Preface ...

It is indeed our pleasure and privilege to offer this book on "Enterprise Performance Management" to our beloved readers and students.

Over the years, Enterprise Performance Management has emerged as an imperative for all the corporate organisations, particularly as the business environment has become more and more competitive. Further, the corporates cannot afford only to work out strategy, without it being realised on the ground. The reality is that in today's world, performance has become a survival condition.

The dictum is said to be Deliver or Be Delivered, Execute or Be Executed and Perform or Perish.

Hence, corporate managers have to be familiar with the basics of Enterprise Performance Management as it would facilitate the corporate to gain, retain and sustain competitive advantage and ensure survival, success and prosperity.

This book has been written in a lucid and simple manner, with a view to facilitating understanding of the basic concepts and their applications from the decision-makers' perspective. While the syllabus has been duly covered, we have provided additional material to ensure that the students are provided with a Text Book, rather than just Summarised Notes.

We are, therefore, sure that the Readers, Teachers and our beloved Student community would find the book useful, not only from the examination point of view, but also for facilitating understanding of the concepts and their empirical / managerial applications.

We look forward to critical and constructive feedback, support and encouragement from our readers to enable us to further improve and modify the contents of this book.

We also take this opportunity to acknowledge our thanks to our publishers, M/s Nirali Prakashan, and particularly to Shri Dineshbhai Furia and Shri Jignesh Furia and their entire staff for their patience and active co-operation.

Pune

Jayant Oke
Anil Agashe
Satish Inamdar

Syllabus ...

1.
- **1.1 Performance Management:** Concept, Need, Linkages with Strategic Planning, Management Control and Operational Control.
- **1.2 Performance Evaluation Parameters:** Financial – Responsibility Accounting – Concept of Responsibility Centers, Revenue Centre, Expense Centre – Engineered and Discretionary Costs-Committed Costs, Profit Centre, Investment Centers. ROI, ROA, MVA, EVA – DuPont analysis. (Numericals Not expected – Interpretation only) Limitations of Financial Measures.
- **1.3 Performance Evaluation Parameters:** Non-financial Performance measures – Balanced Scorecard, Malcolm Baldrige Framework.
- **1.4 Measuring SBU Level Performance:** Concept, Need, Linkages with Enterprise Performance Management – Goal congruence. Transfer Pricing – Objective – Concept, Methods – Cost based, Market Price based and Negotiated, Applicability of Transfer Pricing.

2.
- **2.1 Capital Expenditure Control:** Concept, Need, Process Capital Budgeting, Types of Capital Expenditure decisions – pre-sanction, operational and post-sanction control of capital expenditure.
- **2.2 Tools and Techniques of Capital Expenditure Control:** Performance Index, Technical Performance Measurement, Post Completion Audit.

3.
- **3.1 Performance Evaluation Parameters for Banks:** Customer Base, NPAs, Deposits RoI, Financial Inclusion, Spread, Credit Appraisal, Investments.
- **3.2 Performance Evaluation Parameters for Retail:** ABC Analysis, Sell Through Analysis, Multiple Attribute Method, Gross Margin Return on Investment (GMROI), GMROI as Gross Margin/Average Inventory at Cost.

4.
- **4.1 Performance Evaluation Parameters for Projects:** Project Control Process: Setting base line plan, Measuring Progress and performance, comparing plan against action, Taking action, Schedule variance (time overruns), Project Cost Variance (cost overruns).
- **4.2 Performance Evaluation Parameters for Non-Profit:** Features of Non-profit organizations, fund accounting, governance, product pricing, strategic planning and budget preparations, social audit.

5.
- **5.1 Audit Function as a Performance Measurement Tool:** Financial Audit, Internal Audit, Cost Audit, Management Audit – Principles and Objectives (Audit Reports/Formats are expected to be discussed in the class from a performance measurement perspective).

Contents ...

1. Performance Management — 1.1 - 1.96

2. Capital Expenditure Control — 2.1 - 2.28

3. Performance Evaluation Parameters for Banks and Retail — 3.1 - 3.34

4. Performance Evaluation Parameters for Projects and for Non-Profit Organisations — 4.1 - 4.28

5. Audit Function as a Performance Measurement Tool — 5.1 - 5.26

- Case Studies — C.1 - C.10

- Multiple Choice Questions (MCQ's) — M.1 - M.9

Unit I

Chapter 1...

Performance Management

Contents ...

1.1 Introduction
1.2 Performance Management
    1.2.1 Concept of Performance Management
    1.2.2 Need of Performance Management
1.3 Enterprise Performance Management
    1.3.1 Meaning
    1.3.2 Performance Indicators/Measures
    1.3.3 Performance Indicators Based on 'SAVI' Framework
1.4 Theories of Organisational Control Systems
    1.4.1 Anthony's Model
    1.4.2 Activities of Management Control
    1.4.3 Anthony's Formal Control Process
    1.4.4 Factors affecting Control Process
    1.4.5 Formal and Informal Control System (GE)
    1.4.6 Informal Control Systems
    1.4.7 Design of Control System
1.5 Strategy and Strategic Management
    1.5.1 What is Strategy?
    1.5.2 Levels of Strategy
    1.5.3 Phases of Strategic Management
    1.5.4 Strategic Management Model
    1.5.5 Strategic, Tactical/Management and Operational Controls
    1.5.6 Linkages among Strategic Planning, Management Control and Operational Control
1.6 Performance Evaluation Parameters: Financial
    1.6.1 Responsibility Centres
    1.6.2 Definition
    1.6.3 Types of Responsibility Centres
    1.6.4 Revenue Centre
    1.6.5 Expense Centre

1.6.6 Profit Centre
1.6.7 Investment Centre
1.7 Performance Evaluation Parameters: Non-financial Performance Measures
1.7.1 Balanced Scorecard
1.7.2 Malcolm Baldrige Framework
1.8 Measuring SBU Level Performance
1.8.1 Definition of Strategic Business Unit (SBU)
1.8.2 Characteristics/Attributes of Strategic Business Unit (SBU)
1.8.3 Linkages of SBU with Enterprise Performance Management
1.8.4 Various Performance Measures
1.9 Transfer Pricing
1.9.1 Meaning
1.9.2 Objectives of Transfer Pricing
1.9.3 Transfer Pricing Decisions
1.9.4 Transfer Pricing and Goal Congruence
1.9.5 Example of Transfer Price
1.9.6 Pre-requisites of Transfer Pricing
1.9.7 Methods of Setting Transfer Prices
1.9.8 Applicability of Transfer Pricing
- Points to Remember
- Questions for Discussion
- Project Questions

Learning Objectives ...

- To examine the evolution of Business Environment and the meaning and need for Enterprise Performance Management (EPM)
- To understand the concept and types of Performance Indicators, with reference to EPM
- To discuss the need for Responsibility Centers
- To be aware of the different types of responsibility Centers
- To understand the functioning of each responsibility centre
- To understand the concepts of EVA and MVA
- To BSC as a tool of performance evaluation
- To learn about the relationship between the four perspectives of BSC
- To review the Baldrige Framework/Award as a tool of performance improvement / evaluation
- To analyse the need for Performance Management of a Strategic Business Unit from a Strategic Management Perspective
- To understand the concept of transfer pricing
- To study the different methods of setting transfer prices

1.1 Introduction

Today's business has become extremely competitive; indeed it has become hyper-competitive, both locally as well as globally. The world of business has never been so complex and challenging before. Never before also has it been so imperative for the world of business to be managed so clinically efficiently and effectively, to ensure survival, success and prosperity - by ensuring results and delivering performance.

Today's business organisations are at crossroads. It is felt that the old economy has gone, making way for the new economy, where organisations are moving from 'Brick' to 'Click' and from 'Physical' to 'Virtual' and from 'Local' to 'Global' organisations.

Further, earlier, the business organisations endeavoured to build competitive advantage with innovation that was difficult to imitate. Such competitive advantage, for the contemporary business organisations, has only been temporary as it is now quickly lost, because of imitation. Now, with the hyper competitive business environment, the frequency, boldness and aggressiveness of dynamic actions by competitors have resulted in creating conditions of constant change and disequilibrium. Typically, the dictum is 'what was, is not; and what will not be!"

The organisations today have to compete with other business organisations for contracts, clients and customers in the market place. And to survive and thrive in the market place, organisations must deliver the product - goods or services - to the customers that provide the best possible value for the customers, so that customers do not choose the competing organisations.

A business organisation, therefore, must be able to deliver high quality, innovative products, quickly and at a competitive price, when and where the customer wants it. And, an organisation cannot afford to deliver just one or some, but all the above as THE FOCUS NOW IS CLEARLY ON DELIVERABLES AND DELIVERY.

Business organisations and managers must –
- DELIVER OR BE DELIVERED
- EXECUTE OR BE EXECUTED, and
- PERFORM OR PERISH

There is, therefore, an urgent need for ensuring clear-cut and discernible results and performance-orientation across all levels and functions of the organisation.

Hence, there is a need for Enterprise Performance Management.

Let us, as future Business Managers/Leaders, remember that organisations that anticipate and understand the power of the Enterprise Performance Management and leverage it would be in control of the events, would occupy the centre stage and would survive and thrive.

Organisations that do not respond or take cognisance of Enterprise Performance Management and fail to leverage it, would be forced to accept changes that others initiate and would find themselves at a competitive disadvantage.

Enterprise Performance Management would enable organisations to force and forge the future and make organisations gain, retain and sustain competitive advantage to survive, succeed and prosper it today's competitive battlefield.

1.2 Performance Management

1.2.1 Concept of Performance Management

Performance management is all about improvement - synchronising improvement to create value for and from customer with the result of economic value creation to stockholders and owners. The scope of performance management is obviously very broad, which is why performance management must be viewed at an enterprise wide level.

Performance Management is a Business Process intended to ensure alignment of group and individual efforts for achievement of continuous business improvement (How and how much?).

1.2.2 Need of Performance Management

Performance Management is necessary as there is a need to:
(a) Monitor and Control Business Operations.
(b) Drive Improvement of Process efficiency.
(c) Maximise the effectiveness of the improvement effort.
(d) Achieve strategic organisational goals and objectives.

1.3 Enterprise Performance Management

1.3.1 Meaning

Enterprise Performance Management emerged when principles of Performance Management; this concept was mainly applicable to employee/process, and was applied across the enterprise and for the entire enterprise as well.

Enterprise Performance Management is also referred to as "Business Performance Management" or "Corporate Performance Management".

We would, however, use the term "Enterprise Performance Management". Further, it is also clarified that we are not looking at this from Information Technology / System perspective only and, hence, will not consider EPM to be necessarily relying on software systems only.

Enterprise Performance Management consists of *"a set of management and analytic processes, supported by technology, that enable businesses to define strategic goals and then measure and manage performance against these goals"*.

Enterprise Performance Management can also be said to be *"a set of management and analytic processes that enables the management of an organisation's performance, to achieve one or more pre-selected goals"*.

Enterprise Performance Management includes three main activities:

1. Selection of goals.
2. Consolidation of measurement information relevant to an organisation's progress against these goals, and
3. Interventions made by managers in light of this information with a view to improving future performance against these goals.

The activities stated above, are not necessarily undertaken sequentially. They can be undertaken concurrently also, if required. The activities can be taken up concurrently, with interventions by managers affecting the choice of goals, the measurement information monitored and the activities being undertaken by the organisation.

The Enterprise Performance Management core processes would include financial planning, operational planning, business modelling, consolidation and reporting, analysis and monitoring of key performance indicators, linked to strategy.

1.3.2 Performance Indicators/Measures

Enterprise Performance Management focuses upon driving strategy into strategic management across the organisation and translates strategic goals into actual results and performance.

It then follows that for Enterprise Performance Management to be effective, there has to be performance measurement and to measure the performance, there has to be effective pre-determined performance indicators/measures in place.

Without such performance indicators, an organisation would not be able to know what is happening, and also whether the strategies are actually being implemented and realised on the ground or not. However, Performance Indicators are not to be used for undertaking a post-mortem of what happened, but should be adopted as an effective instrument towards doing better in future.

In today's global, technology-driven, real-time, on-line business environment, with most organisations having flat/de-layered structures, performance indicators/measures should aim at the long-term and should be forward-thinking initiatives designed to fundamentally change the way corporations do business.

There is, therefore, an imperative need for not only performance indicators/measures but a balanced set of performance indicators/measures, capable of indicating/measuring multiple attributes of an organisation.

A performance indicator is an absolute must as it provides meaningful and comparable information with respect to the performance envisaged. As such, a performance indicator is an essential and integral constituent of a performance monitoring and evaluation system.

1.3.2.1 What is a Performance Indicator?

"Performance indicator is a measurable or tangible sign that something has been done or achieved".

"Performance indicator is a yardstick that can be used to demonstrate and ascertain that changes have or have not taken place".

1.3.2.2 Types of Performance Indicators

Let us now look at what are the various types of performance indicators.

Performance indicators could be:

1. Quantitative indicators
2. Qualitative indicators
3. Lead indicators
4. Lag indicators

1. Quantitative Indicators

Quantitative Indicators are those which are reported in terms of a specific number or percentage. Some illustrative quantitative indicators are:

(a) Number of .....
(b) Proportion of .....
(c) Amount of .....
(d) The Ratio of .....
(e) Length of distance
(f) Weight of .....
(g) Size of .....
(h) Area/Spread of .....
(i) Value of ..... etc.

2. Qualitative Indicators

Qualitative Indicators are those which measure perceptions or attitude or behaviour and tend to be qualitative or judgemental statements.

Some illustrative qualitative indicators are:

(a) Levels of .....
(b) Presence of .....
(c) Evidence of .....

(d) Quality of .....
(e) Accessibility of .....
(f) Existence of .....
(g) Sustainability of .....
(h) Improvement of .....
(i) Potential of .....
(j) Ability to (e.g. skills) .....etc.

Another category of indicators could be:
- Lead Indicators
- Lag Indicators

3. **Lead Indicators**

   Lead Indicators are value drivers.

   Many non-financial indicators can/do serve as Lead indicators in certain things.

   Some illustrative lead indicators are:

   (a) Market share
   (b) Backlog (Book-to-Bill Ratio)
   (c) New Product Development/Introduction
   (d) Product Quality
   (e) Customer Satisfaction
   (f) Employee Morale
   (g) Inventory Turn over
   (h) Bad Debt Ratio/Percentage
   (i) Safety Ratio, etc.

4. **Lag Indicators**

   Lag Indicators are measures that point to earlier plans and their execution. Financial performance are lag indicators, as they are available too late to affect future products and services.

   Some illustrative lag indicators are:
   - Net Profit
   - Gross Margin
   - ROA
   - ROE
   - ROI, etc.

1.3.3 Performance Indicators Based on 'SAVI' Framework

Performance indicators can also be based on the 'SAVI' framework, where 'SAVI' stands for Speed, Accuracy, Volume and Investment.

These performance indicators are stated as follows:

1.3.3.1 Speed Indicators
(a) Response Time Records
(b) Turn Around Time Records
(c) Cycle Time Records
(d) Project Implementation Scheduled Dates
(e) Meeting Scheduled Time Records

1.3.3.2 Accuracy Indicators
(a) Judgement-based climate or opinion surveys.
   (i) Focus Groups.
   (ii) Comment Cards.
   (iii) Telephone Surveys.
   (iv) Advisory Panels.
(b) Opinions of Community Leaders.
(c) Meeting design-specifications or passing an inspection point that ensures the product works.
(d) Customer Returns or Warranty Claims.

1.3.3.3 Value Indicators
These indicators measure the amount (number) of outputs or results from a specific activity or programme (like: number of units produced).
(a) Number of completed transactions.
(b) Percentage Market Share.
(c) Back Order details/statistics/record.
(d) Number of Failed Sales due to out-of-stock situations.

1.3.3.4 Investment Indicators
These indicators measure the amount of resources expended on a specific programme or activity or the per unit cost (cost/number of units produced).
(a) Number of Units Produced.
(b) Operating cost per unit produced.
(c) Capital cost per unit produced.
(d) Cost per customer to sales and marketing spend.
(e) Cost per unit of After Sales and Customer Support.

1.4 Theories of Organisational Control Systems

All our lives we are bound by some control system or the other. We live in a society and it is controlled by rules and regulations that actually is a control system. Since childhood we are told what to do and what not to do, we are told what is right and what is wrong this also is control. We are so used to it that we do not probably look at it as a control mechanism.

We have always thought that the first real control system was probably the Laxman Rekha that Laxman had drawn to protect Sita in Ramayana. The Rekha was not adhered to and we all know what happened after that. Sometimes we do not understand the significance of controls and therefore at times inadvertently we disregard them and the consequences can be very serious.

Some times managers disregard controls knowing fully well why they are in place. They think that by transgressing them they can achieve their targets.

All organisations are controlled internally and externally. The different laws that an organisation is subject to are external controls. What we create internally are controls in pursuance of our goals.

A system is an association of parts that are related to each other. Control system design is the process of designing the parts of the system so that the purpose of the system is attained.

The purpose of MCS is to assist the management in the coordination of the different parts of the organisation and the steering of these parts towards the overall achievement of the goals. Thus a control system is designed to bring unity out of the diverse activities of an organisation as it seeks to fulfil its overall purpose.

1.4.1 Anthony's Model

The proper domain of control system has been discussed by many authors. Anthony and Govindrajan consider strategic planning, management control and task control as three separate but interrelated processes of planning and control. They see management control as *"the process by which managers influence other members of the organisation to implement the organisation's strategies."* They believe that the domain of control systems is the successful implementation of strategy.

In the control system of Anthony, he speaks about 4 main elements.

1. **Detector or Sensor:** This is a measuring device that identifies what is actually happening in the process that is being controlled.
2. **An Assessor:** This device determines the significance of what is happening. This is done by comparing the information on what is actually happening with some standard or expectation of what should be happening.

3. **An Effector:** This device alters the behaviour if the assessor indicates the need for doing so. This device is also referred to as "Feedback".
4. **A Communication Network:** This is required to transmit information between the detector and the assessor and between the assessor and effector.

Anthony and Govindrajan point out following important aspects of a control process:

1. In control process the standards are not preset. It is rather a result of a conscious planning process. In this process the management decides what the organisation should do and a part of the control process is a comparison of actual performance with these plans. So control process requires planning. Management control involves planning and controls both.

2. Management control is not automatic. Most information is detected and collected by Managers themselves. Based on this information they try and analyse the causes of gaps that may exist between the desired results and the actual results. If the difference is substantial then they have to initiate action to bridge this gap. Such actions that may be taken require altering human behaviour.

3. Management Control requires coordination among individuals. Management Control has to ensure that all the separate parts of the organisation work in harmony with each other. This is a very important function as large organisations are divided in many units but all these units need to work towards the same goal.

4. The connection between the observed need for action and the behaviour that is required to obtain the desired action is by no means clear cut. If a manager says that costs are too high and need to be controlled, there is no automatic way to bring this about.

5. Much of the control is and has to Self control. People act in way they do not because they are always instructed to act in particular way but they act according to their own judgement of the situation that they find themselves in. It is their judgement that tells them what they need to do under the circumstances. Mangers that have the ability to anticipate changes and those who have a good analytical mind are likely to be more successful in meeting their targets.

Systems:

A system is a prescribed way of carrying out an activity or set of activities that are usually repeated.

Most systems may not be precise, so the user of the systems has to make his own judgments when unforeseen circumstances occur. A system is characterized a rhythmic, recurring, coordinated series of steps that are intended to accomplish a specified purpose.

Many management actions are unsystematic. In many situations encountered by a manger, the rules of a system are not well defined. This of course is natural as all emerging situations can never be predicted. So he has to use his best judgment in acting in a particular situation faced by him. The appropriate response is determined by the manager's skill in dealing with people. If all systems provided the correct action for all situations, there would be no need for human managers.

Management control fits between strategy formulation and task control in several respects. Strategy formulation is the systematic of the three, task control is most systematic and management control is in between. Strategy formulation focuses on the long run, task control on short run and management control in between.

Management control is the process by which managers influence other members of the organisation to implement the organisation's strategies.

Activity	Nature of end product
Strategy formulation	Goals, Strategies and policies
Management Control	Implementation of strategies.
Task Control	Efficient and Effective performance of individual tasks.

1.4.2 Activities of Management Control

1. Planning what an organisation must do.
2. Coordinating the activities of several parts of the organisation.
3. Communicating the information.
4. Evaluating the information.
5. Deciding what if any action should be taken.
6. Influencing people to change their behaviour.

The purpose of organisational control is to ensure strategies are carried out to achieve the organisation's objectives. If the manager can devise an alternate and better way of achieving this than what is stated in the plan then he should be free to use this way. Giving freedom to decision makers to achieve the desired results will make a control system more effective. In certain circumstances the manager may be required to take approval of his superior in such situations.

This process is not mechanical in nature, because it requires interaction among individuals. The goals of individual members of an organisation should be as far as feasible consistent with the goals of the organisation itself. This is called Goal Congruence.

Organisational control focuses primarily on strategy execution. Most businesses today are subject to rapid environmental changes. Management control information provides the basis for thinking about new strategies. Robert Simons calls this Interactive Controls. These controls help to bring to the notice of the managers developments that may be adverse or opportunities that may be emerging in the market place. This will help the managers to adapt to a rapidly changing environment by thinking about new strategies. Interactive controls are not a separate system; they are an integral part of the management control system.

Organisational control system encompasses both financial and non financial performance measures. This will become clear when we shall study the Balanced Score Card later.

Strategy formulation is the process of deciding on new strategies; management control is the process of deciding how to implement strategies. Strategy formulation involves only a part of an organisation. The management control on the other hand involves the whole organisation; an important aspect of the process is ensuring that the various parts are coordinated with one another.

Task control is the process of assuring that specified tasks are carried out effectively and efficiently. It is transaction oriented that is it involves the control of individual tasks.

The most important distinction between task and management control is that many task control systems are scientific, while management control can never be scientific as it involves individuals. Human behaviour can never be explained by equations. In management control managers interact with other managers; in task control either human beings are not involved at all or the interaction is between a manager and a non manager.

1.4.3 Anthony's Formal Control Process

Anthony and Govindrajan's Formal Control process is depicted in the following diagram:

This diagram is the foundation of an organisation's control process. Once a broad outline of a strategy to be followed is prepared then a strategic plan is formulated. For implementing this strategy a budget has to be prepared. There is one master budget and then annual budgets are prepared. This is required because the strategy may be implemented over a period of time. Different plans and budgets are formulated for each responsibility centre. These responsibility centre and guided and controlled by many rules and regulations that are a part of the formal control process. The performance of each responsibility centre is closely monitored and variances are duly reported to the requisite authorities for their information and for any action that may be required. Responsibility centres are rewarded if their performance is in line with goals, if not corrective measures are suggested.

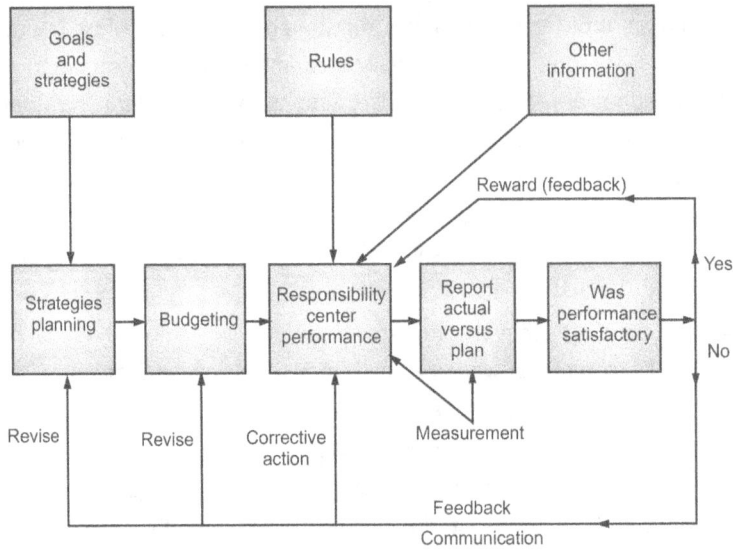

Fig. 1.1: Formal Control System
(**Source:** Management Control System-Anthony & Govindrajan)

1.4.4 Factors Affecting Control Process

William Newman considers the domain of control systems to be the control function of management and believes "Control is seen as an essential part of the management process and a part of all the managerial efforts of an organisation.

The views of Kirby and Maciariello are derived from the theory of cybernetics. In this view the entire organisation is viewed as a control system. Control is seen as characteristic or attribute of a control system: it occurs when the organisation is attaining its purpose. Purpose and the attainment of purpose are central to the work of control systems. Their definition of control system considers both the control of strategy and the control of operations. Their theory also talks about the design of the control system and therefore includes aspects of planning, organizing and leading functions of management, thus distinguishing it from other definitions.

Organisations are usually divided into subunits. They are comprised of individuals at particular locations who perform certain activities in order to fulfill a portion of the purpose of the organisation. These units are formed by using the principals of specialization and division of labour. These units themselves present other challenges to the management; the primary of these is the achievement of efficient coordination of activities between subunits. The specialized subunits of complex organisations are established with varying degrees of autonomy. Each unit has a specific objective derived from the overall purpose of the organisation and each is coordinated by another subunit in a superior-subordinate relationship.

An organisational unit is said to be effective when it meets the overall purpose of the organisation and fulfills a genuine need to society. On the other hand it is said to be efficient when it is meeting all the needs of its constituents. Effectiveness thus relates to the social purpose of the organisation, whereas efficiency relates to the personal motives of the stakeholders of the organisation. An efficient organisation achieves the purpose with minimum waste of resources. Effectiveness and efficiency are interrelated are both necessary for long term prosperity.

The control system is designed to assist executives in meeting both the overall purpose of an organisation and the requirements of its constituents. Both tasks must be met for the organisation to remain viable.

Organisations are open systems and have to deal with a set of stakeholders both internal and external.

People in an organisation have to constantly adapt and change because corporate operate in dynamically changing markets. Competitive advantage is always threatened by competition. To maintain advantage and survive in a dynamic environment control systems must facilitate innovation, adaptation and change.

Control systems are designed to favourably influence human behaviour as organisations pursue their goals and objectives. The control system designers therefore need to take into account the human behaviour. The control system designer must proceed on certain assumptions about the behaviour of human beings. Kirby and Maciariello make five assumptions about human drives. They are as follows:

1. **Basic Rationality:** Human beings are basically rational and as such are able to reason, make plans and control behaviour. Human beings are called as Rational Animals in sociology for this very reason. Normally they behave in rational manner; meaning that is some rational thought in their actions most of the time.

2. **Creativity:** A basic human instinct is the desire to be creative. All human beings are creative in something or the other. This creativity differs from person to person but it is rarely absent in human beings.

3. **Mastery:** Humans desire to manage therefore the desire to be 'in control' is innate. By nature most human beings love to control something or someone! But unless they have mastery on something this is not possible therefore most of us like to have mastery on things that we like to do.
4. **Morality:** Human beings have strong moral instincts, although these instincts may not always dominate behaviour. This is a grey area really because morality these days seem to change as per the culture of an organisation or its CEO.
5. **Community:** Human beings have strong needs and desires for human associations. Man is a social animal as well. Most of us like to be in a community. There are some who are loners but their percentage is far lesser than those who love to be in a group.

A control system is a set of formal and informal systems that are designed to assist management in steering the organisation towards the achievement of its purpose by bringing unity out of the diverse efforts of subunits and of individuals. These two systems are distinct but are also closely interrelated and sometimes they seem indistinguishable subdivisions of control systems. They are considered adaptive if the two systems are internally consistent, consistent with each other and designed to permit learning that is effective in continuously meeting the competitive challenges in the environment. However it must be understood that organisation will differ as to the extent to which their systems are formal or informal

The Formal and Informal Control Systems of GE under Jack Welch:

GE is one of the most admired companies in the world and Jack Welch is considered by many as the best manager of the 20th century! The two diagrams below will give an idea of the Formal and Informal control systems that were used by him during his time with GE.

1.4.5 Formal and Informal Control System (GE)

Formal systems make it possible for the delegation of authority at the different levels of the organisation. These systems put in place the structure, policies, and procedures that are expected to be followed by the members of the organisation. There is formal documentation of these structures, policies and procedures so that it will help the members of the organisation in performing their duties.

The formal control system has:
- Management style and culture of the organisation
- Infrastructure
- Rewards
- Coordination and integration
- Control process

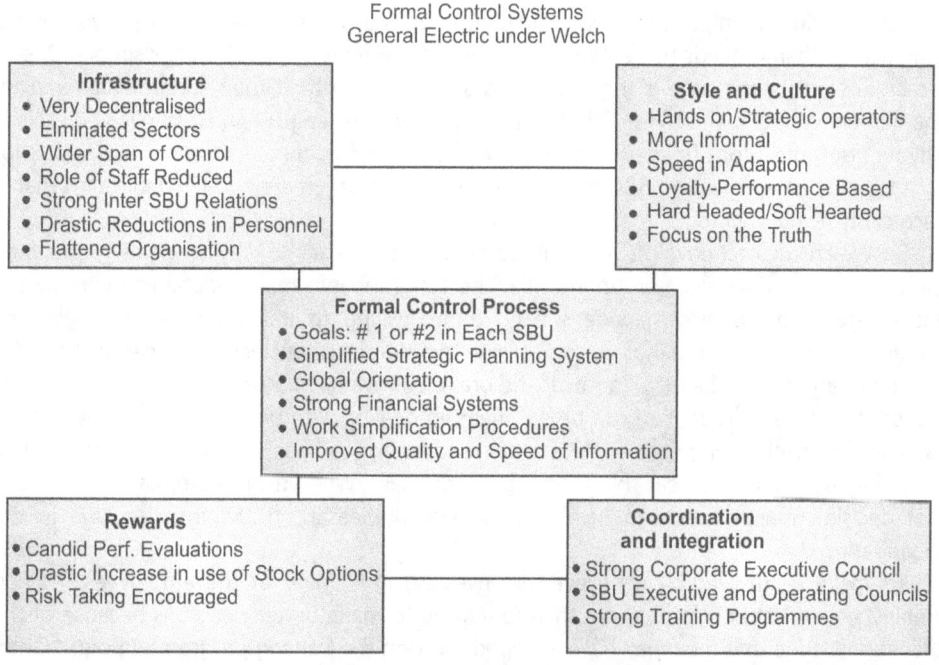

Fig. 1.2: Formal and Informal Central System

Some of the points in the above control processes are worth pondering over. Some of them are culturally alien to us in India and accepting them will require a change of mind set. The beauty of this control system is that it was first put in place, modified as required and then it came to be adopted by other organisations. This is not a theory which is normally written by some on and then somebody else tries to implement it at his cost!

Welch had a fascination of being No1 or 2 in all businesses and this position was based on market share. He would give time for his businesses to achieve this status and if they failed to so in the given time frame then he was willing to sell them off. In the later years he modified his view saying that rather than market share he should have been looking at Return on Investments as a performance measurement tool.

Welch also had seen globalisation as inevitable and therefore his control system insisted on Global orientation. Leaders with vision are always ahead of times and that is what makes them successful in the end.

He also rightly emphasized work simplification. Many times we make our work more complicated than it needs to be. We do not try and see if we can keep things simple. One of the biggest problems seen is that Managers are unable to trust their subordinates and try and do everything themselves. This makes all procedures lengthy and complicated. This is why he also puts a lot of belief in decentralization. Therefore the creation of SBUs with a lot of autonomy being given to SBU heads which helps him to create a flat organisation that is necessarily result oriented.

So Welch tries to develop new culture which emphasizes loyalty to goals rather than personalities. This is not common in India. The culture is informal. Adaptability is rewarded and encouraged. Today's manager's need to be willing to unlearn because unless one unlearns learning newer things becomes extremely difficult. Business also has to be done with head and not by heart ruling over the brain. You cannot be soft hearted in the fiercely competitive market place. You can be soft hearted dealing with people to an extent. For the same reason truth is emphasized. Managers tend to like to hear what they are comfortable with. They do not like to hear things that are unpleasant. When truth is emphasized it means that decision makers need to be ready to hear unpleasant truths from anyone in the organisation.

To make all this work he believed in investing in training of the employees. Trained employees are better informed are therefore likely to make better decisions because of the sheer knowledge that they may have acquired through the training programs. In our country there are companies like L & T who believe in this philosophy and seem to be benefiting from this activity.

He also believes in strong corporate and SBU level executive councils who control an organisation that is decentralized but is regulated from a discreet distance.

He also put a lot of faith in candid evaluations which an extension of the role of truth that is discussed above. Another important thing is the importance given to risk taking. Businesses are risky and risks are omnipresent. One must therefore take risks to succeed. It is important that the managers must first of all be aware of the risks that they are taking. Only then they can decide which of these are worth taking. Calculated risks are to be taken. Good managers take risks which they know they can deal with they manifest. It is like the difference in the batting of Sehwag and Dravid. Sehwag takes all possible risks and succeeds because his risk perception is very different. He believes that the bowler bowls a ball that is meant to be hit. He does not consider that he will get out! Dravid on the other hand is cautious by nature and training so he does not believe in taking unnecessary risks. Mangers are also like this and also of many more shades that are in between.

1.4.6 Informal Control Systems

Every organisation will have some informal dimensions. They consist of interpersonal relationships that are not shown or rather cannot be shown on the formal organisation charts. Bernard defines the informal organisation as 'the aggregate of personal contacts and interactions and the associated groupings of people.'

Informal systems complement the formal systems in a manner similar to the way the informal organisation complements the formal organisation.

Informal control system consists of:

- Informal control process
- Infrastructure
- Management style and culture
- Coordination and integration
- Informal rewards
- GEs Informal Control System

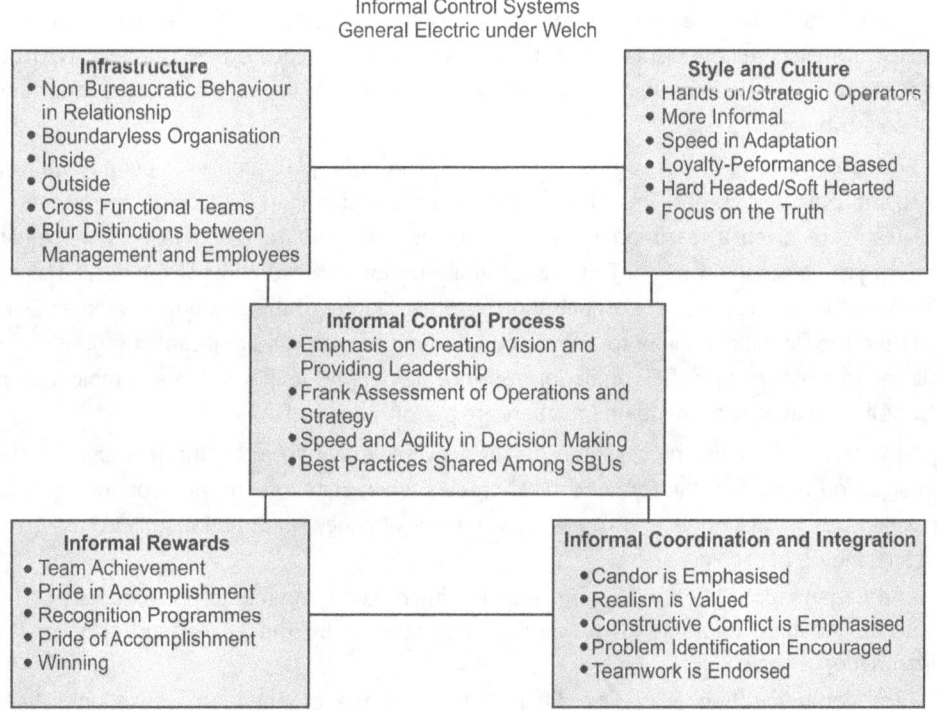

Fig. 1.3: Informal Control System

GE's informal control is also remarkable. If one looks at the control process one can see this in all the elements present there. Speed and agility in decision making today make the difference between success and failure. The need of sharing best practice across the organisation is essential because it helps the entire organisation.

There was a huge importance on destroying bureaucracy which he thought was a hindrance to quick decision making. Boundary less organisation was Welch's passion. He was fully committed to it. The old formal hierarchy was frowned upon and rightly so.

Candor and realism are a must for an open organisation. This can overcome subjectivity and makes an organisation very democratic in its functioning. Conflict is natural among individuals as they think differently. Conflicts actually bring forward many things. Conflict can actually be very constructive as many possibilities are brought to the table during discussions. This can lead to better decision making as many angles can get covered because of this. It is for the leader to encourage such arguments and bring out the best solutions after all this which then must be accepted by everybody. This can also facilitate problem identification and then on to problem solving.

Teams must enjoy their success and accomplishments. Management is a team game and successful managements display great team spirit and enjoy each other's success and help each other during failures. The dominance of world cricket by Australia for such a long time can be attributed to this.

The other feature of this success is there are plenty of replacements for people who are unable to pull their weight. Thus there is always a succession plan ready. Non performers in the team are given a reasonable chance to come good but repeated failures will mean loosing your place in the team. This is a good illustration of Head and not the heart making decisions that are good for the organisation. Another feature of this strategy is when a player gets into the side due to injury to a regular and even if he makes a significant contribution he still has to make way for the original player once he gets fit! It shows that a combination is not disturbed as long as the team members are performing.

The informal control process consists of activities engaged in by the members of the organisation outside of the formal control process when encountering non-routine decision making such as realignment of goals or when seeking new information to increase their understanding of problem areas.

An Organisational Control System requires interrelated communication structures. This structure enables information processing that can help the managers achieve the organisational goals.

The communication links, link different units of the organisation. These units have autonomy in decision making in certain fields and activities.

Because of this, the heart of the cybernetic system is Feedback. The feedback can be either positive or negative. Negative feedback gives indication of slippage in the targeted task achievements. This will prompt the managers to make a behavioral change. Positive feedback indicates that the current system is to be persisted with. A self-regulating system requires the presence of both negative and positive feedback to achieve its objectives and goals.

A management control system seeks to reduce chaos and uncertainty by bringing unity out of the diverse efforts of the various parts of an organisation. This helps the organisation in achieving its goals. Controls are used to minimise uncertainty.

We can see this quite clearly in many instances in our own country as well as in some international cases. In India we have seen even the external control systems failing or being made redundant by people like Harshad Mehta and Ketan Parekh. The regulators like RBI and SEBI come out as ones whose own control system did not stand scrutiny in these cases. Was it then an inadequate control system or was it manipulation of the control system by these persons? Later on we also saw the failure on internal control system in the cases of US 64 scheme, which had to be rescued by the Government of India and then disbanded and the way the Global Trust Bank and later The United Western Bank had to be closed down and merged with other banks. These episodes clearly show that as the internal control systems were manipulated the external control system in the form of regulators also collapsed or more likely made to look the other way for whatever reasons. In the international markets we saw the demise of Enron and WorldCom for similar reasons.

We have seen this also in many scams that have been in the news. In the coal allocation scam for example the problem seems to be that of there being no formal process for allotting mines that was followed. Thus the process may have been highly individual oriented rather than system oriented leading to serious lacunas leading to dubious allotments even to those firms who were not eligible for such allotments. This has naturally led to suspicion of corruption in the process of allotment. Auctioning of mines was recommended, but it has its own issues and a full proof system has still not evolved. However it must be mentioned here that the loss estimated by CAG is presumptive and does not take into account the impact of that cost on the final product and the price the end customer will pay if this process were to be followed.

As far as the 2 G allocation is concerned there have been procedural irregularities as is evidenced by the arbitrary change of the dates and terms and conditions of eligibility while submission of bids. The court has canceled all licenses and this may have hurt some genuine players as well. The CAG's loss estimate varies very widely as well. Again here the government says it never wanted to make money by selling spectrum and it earns its revenue as a percentage of revenue earned each by the Telecom companies and as that revenue is growing the government is making more money every year. However the lack of clear cut policy not being in place has made matters complicated is the fact.

1.4.7 Design of Control System

While designing the control system some things have to be kept in mind:
- The control system should be constructive and not punitive. The control system is designed to assist the individuals to attain their goals, and help them in the times of problematic situations. The control system is not a tool to find faults with people so that they can be punished. A good control system therefore should be fair to everyone. Many

a times we come across controls that are designed to find faults. At the traffic signal a policeman is supposed to stop people from violating the traffic rules, but what we see is he allows the violation so that he can punish and fine the offender!

- The objectives need to be measurable whenever possible. If variables cannot be measured it becomes difficult to evaluate the actions taken to achieve the results. So while designing the system it should be the endeavor to have as many measurable objectives as possible. This also helps the employees to judge their own performance. This will enable them to make corrections whenever they are necessary.
- Controls should be limited and should focus on the objectives and the key results of an activity. When we have too many controls they a lot of time is spent on paper work instead of on the core activities. This was one criticism of Sarbanes Oxley Act that came into force in US post Enron and WorldCom debacle.
- Controls need to be balanced. Many times controls designed are lopsided. They give too much importance to only some areas ignoring other areas. It is commonly observed that many control systems tend to give lot of importance to financial objectives. Some are designed solely for cost control. It must be realised that other activities of an organisation also need to be given due importance.
- A single individual should be given responsibility for achieving desired results for an objective. With this it is possible to fix responsibility on one person and hold him accountable. It also gives such a person the overall control on the task that he is responsible for.
- A successful control system seeks to identify early warning predictors of the variables that we seek to control. AWACS is an example of this. These are launched to keep an eye on enemy activities constantly, so that any possible attack can be detected at the earliest so that proper action can be taken expeditiously. It is possible to project sales by analysing the total inquiries received and the success ratio of conversion of inquiries in orders.

An acceptable range of variation from the objectives or goals should be decided in the beginning. This actually is the acceptance of the simple reality that there will be some variance between goals and actual achievements. It can never match perfectly. The accepted range of variance thus makes it clear how much deviation is acceptable.

Reports should focus upon exception to desired results and be made promptly to the person who is responsible. The exceptional things need to be investigated promptly. Due to this it is imperative that these are reported quickly. This is will make sure that these are brought to the notice of the decision maker to enable him to think of the response such a situation may demand.

The severity of a problem must be independently verified. A person who is reporting the severity may be blowing it up to protect himself. It is therefore necessary that an independent evaluation of severity is carried out before any decision is arrived at. After corrective action is initiated it needs to be monitored and compared to desired results.

An organisation has many responsibility centres and therefore the control process has to include superior-subordinate behaviour. The goals of a superior can be achieved through the achievement of goals by his subordinates. The goals of the superior are communicated to the subordinates, who in turn make necessary plans to achieve these goals. Thus the subordinates have to set their goals, in accordance with the goals of their superiors. This process depends upon the style of management and the autonomy given to managers. This process therefore may involve negotiations between the superiors and the subordinates. The feedback mechanism in the cybernetic is useful in these negotiations.

The superior's goals are more than the sum total of the goals of his subordinates. The actions of the subordinates are subject to the corrective actions of the superior's, this explains the feedback loop from the effector of the superior to the sensor of the subordinate. The feedback can lead to changes in perceptions, goals and choices.

In this kind of control process the superior meets the subordinate to review the past performance and negotiate new goals. They also discuss the objectives and targets for key variables. During this process goals are negotiated, and then the subordinates track the actual performance with these goals regularly.

The superior and the subordinate meet periodically to review the progress. They analyse the performance, and where the performance is unsatisfactory, seek to find the reasons for this and decide where the corrective action is required to be taken.

At the time of the next review session they review the effects of the corrective actions taken by them, the current performance and actions for the coming days. This is a continuous process. They also put in place an awards system that is linked to the performance and the improvement of the performance.

In this system the targets of the superior is negotiated first and then the targets of the subordinates are decided in line with these targets. The superior's targets are subject to change depending upon the result of the negotiations between the superior and his subordinates. These targets should be specific and measurable wherever possible. They should be limited in number. They should also include non-financial variables.

The goal oriented control process follows the cybernetic paradigm and it includes the essential elements of planning, decision- making and control. It must operate within the control structure and its purpose is the continuous attainment of organisational goals and objectives. This control process helps to link each organisational sub-unit to the organisation as a whole.

The very purpose of a organisational control system is to help the organisation achieve its objectives and goals. It is possible that goals of an organisation may be achieved without the achievement of maximum efficiency. It is a fact that there is always scope to improve the performance. The competitive markets make sure that companies have to strive always to improve performance. When goals are achieved and if the competition allows the achievement of the goals then there isn't much pressure to improve the performance. This may lead to under-exploitation of the environment.

This can happen in various ways. The costs may increase. Prices may not be adjusted in line with the input costs. The dividend pay out may be higher than warranted. This state of affairs is described as the organisational slack.

We find many organisations are adopting techniques like JIT, TQM, CRM, ISO certification, implementation of SAP/ERP, and Six Sigma to constantly improve their performance. The competitive pressures are the best way to keep the companies out of the organisational slack. The market will make sure that organisations will strive to be efficient always. As Jack Welch often said Excellence is no more a matter of choice but is imperative for the survival of the organisation.

The cybernetic model of the control process is an information processing or communications model. The designer of the control system must design an information processing system that allows the control process to function effectively.

The first element of this system is the formal and informal process that scans the environment that is being faced by a subunit. This scanning provides data that is used in formulating the goals, plans, and decisions. Then the organisation requires a planning process wherein goals, objectives, and performance measures are set.

The feed back for a responsibility centre comes from this environment scanning, while internally it comes in the form of performance measurement system. The performance measurement system is primarily developed from the internal accounting system. Of course the measurement system also includes non financial measures such as quality and customer satisfaction.

The decision making procedures may include standard operating procedures for meeting various recurring but not necessarily repetitive problems. It also includes cost-benefit procedure for comparing alternatives for their feasibility and acceptability. Procedures are also required to monitor the implementation of the decisions made at various points of time.

So it can be seen why it is important for all organisations to have a vibrant control system in place. Grissinger has given a blue print for designing such a control system. That can be used as a guideline. Many businesses have their own peculiarities and it is necessary that all those issues need to be taken into account while designing a control system.

The managers and the top management of the companies must review the effectiveness of their control systems to ensure that they are helping them for the purpose for which they are designed. If they are found to be ineffective then the necessary changes have to be made in them to make them effective.

Control systems are mainly designed for human beings and this focus must always be maintained. It is necessary that all employees of the organisations are well aware of all controls and they must have the freedom to express their views about their effectiveness or otherwise. Control systems are created to alter human behaviour whenever necessary.

1.5 Strategy and Strategic Management

As discussed earlier, today's business has become extremely competitive, indeed hyper competitive. The world/environment of business has never been so complex, dynamic and challenging ever before. As such, there is always an ongoing need to react to:

- Shifting market conditions
- New/emerging technologies
- Evolving customer preferences
- Political and regulatory changes
- New windows of opportunity
- Crisis situations.

The business organisations, therefore, have to endeavour finding answers to the following questions.

1. Where are we now?
2. Where do we want to go?
   - Business to be in and market positions to stake out?
   - Buyer/customer needs and groups to serve?
   - Outcomes to achieve?

Hence, today's business organisations have to work out a strategy ("what an organisation is today and what it ought to be tomorrow"), and work out in a proactive manner.

Strategy, today, is an absolute must, as, as stated by Joel Ross and Michael Kami, "without strategy, the organisation is like a ship without a rudder, going around in circles".

There is, therefore, need for strategy to achieve the goals and to make an organisation gain certain and sustain competitive advantage, and minimise competitive disadvantage, in today's competitive battlefield.

1.5.1 What is Strategy?

Putting it briefly and succinctly, strategy can be viewed as "what an organisation is today and what it ought to be tomorrow".

A strategy for/of a business organisation formulates a comprehensive master plan that states how the business organisation will achieve its mission and objectives.

Strategy, therefore, can be said to be *"the long-term directions and scope of the organisation that aims at gaining a competitive advantage for the business organisation's resources and constraints, in order to generate customer delight and to meet and exceed stakeholder expectations"*.

Strategy is also about deciding:
(a) WHERE TO COMPETE
    (i) Customer Segment
    (ii) Product Segment
    (iii) Channel Segment
    (iv) Vertical Integration
(b) HOW TO COMPETE
    (i) Value Proposition
    (ii) Competitive Advantage
    (iii) Partner Relationship
    (iv) Relationships with other Stakeholders

A business organisation typically, usually considers three types of strategy as illustrated below.

Corporate Strategy:
Overall Directions of Company and Management of its Business

Business Strategy:
Competitive and Co-operative Strategies

Functional Strategy:
Maximise Resource Productivity

Fig. 1.4: Levels of Strategy

1.5.2 Levels of Strategy

1. Corporate Strategy

Corporate strategy describes a corporate organisation's overall direction with reference to its general attitude towards growth and the management of its various business activities and product lines/mix. Corporate strategy is formulated by the Top Management.

Corporate strategies could be stability strategy, expansion strategy, entrenchment strategy, combination strategy, vertical strategy, integration strategy or horizontal strategy.

2. Business Strategy

Business (SBU) strategy is concerned with the interests and operations of a specific business unit or a specific line of business. It emphasises improvement of the competitive position of a business organisation's products or services in the specific industry or market segment served by that particular SBU. Business strategies could be either competitive or co-operative.

3. Functional Strategy

Functional strategy is chalked out by a functional specialist in order to further the SBU level strategy which helps in evolving operational plans. Such a strategy is in sync with the higher level strategies, mentioned earlier, and focuses on achieving corporate and business (SBU) strategy and objectives by maximising resource productivity.

Functional strategy facilitates developing and nurturing a distinctive competence to provide a company or business unit with a competitive advantage.

IT IS TO BE REMEMBERED THAT BUSINESS ORGANISATIONS USE ALL THREE TYPES OF STRATEGY SIMULTANEOUSLY.

1.5.3 Phases of Strategic Management

While Strategic Planning and Strategy would be able to come out with a set of procedures and pattern of actions for making decisions about the organisation's long term goals and strategies, Strategic Management is a set of managerial decisions and actions that would determine the long term performance of a business organisation. Strategic Management can also be viewed as a process that involves managers from all parts of the organisation in the formulation and implementation of strategic goals and strategies.

While we would shortly look at the Strategic Management Model, let us first note the four phases of Strategic Management, which are as follows:

PHASE 1: Basic Financial Planning
PHASE 2: Forecast-based Planning
PHASE 3: Externally-oriented Planning
PHASE 4: Strategic Management.

The four phases are briefly discussed as follows.

1. Basic Financial Planning

This generally tends to be indicative and at times focussed on the next year's budget. It is, therefore, more operational/short-term than strategic. It may, however, incorporate activities like proposing projects, funding capital projects that can make a contribution in future or shifting resources. Not much of environmental data is available and time horizons may tend to be a year.

2. **Forecast-based Planning**

Here, an attempt is made to increase the planning time span up to 3 to 5 years. Internally available company data and environmental data, which is gathered/collected on an *ad hoc* basis, are taken into account. This data is extrapolated with current trends for creating scenarios for the next 3 to 5 years. Assumptions and proposal evaluation might face an argumentative environment within organisations before some goals/plans are agreed upon.

3. **Externally-oriented Planning**

Here, Top Management takes command and initiates strategic planning. Typically, a Top-Down Approach is adopted as planning is taken out of the hands of lower-level managers and concentrated in a planning staff, which is assigned the task of developing strategic plans for the organisation. As such, five-year plans or strategy is formulated by the Top Management with the help from consultants/planning staff.

There are low/no inputs from the operational level but the strategy implementation is left to lower management level.

4. **Strategic Management**

It is realised that the Top-Down Approach does not help much. The strategic management phase involves inputs and commitments by functionaries at all levels and functions. The plans also detail the implementation, evaluation and control issues. Planning also evidently becomes interactive across all levels and function.

The focus is not only on long-term performance. The idea is to outperform others by becoming highly result and performance oriented.

1.5.4 Strategic Management Model

The Strategic Management Model consists of four basic elements viz.:
1. Environmental Scanning
2. Strategy Formulation
3. Strategy Implementation
4. Evaluation and Control

The Strategic Management Model is presented here.

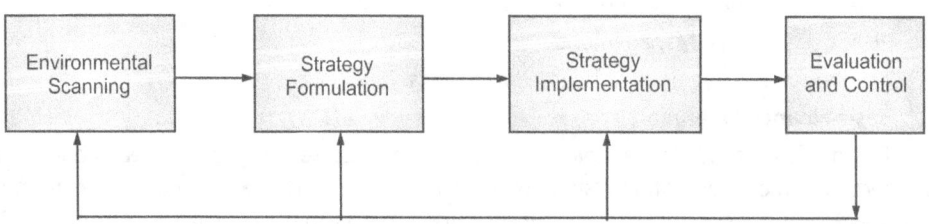

Fig. 1.5: Strategic Management Model

Let us now briefly discuss the four basic elements of the Strategic Management Model.

1. **Environmental Scanning**

   The environment is the sum-total or aggregate of all the factors, both internal as well as external, which profoundly affects the business operations, and, is, perhaps the most critical factor for the success or failure of the business/enterprise. Hence, business organisations must undertake environmental scanning which involves monitoring, evaluating and disseminating of information about internal and external environment to decision-makers in the organisations. External environment would encompass Governmental, Political, Social, Financial, Legal, Market, Technology, Quality, Customer and Competitive environments. The internal environment would include personal systems, procedures, control (delegation, technology and decision-making environment).

   Environmental scanning would enable undertaking SWOT, ETOP and PESTLE Analysis which can be leveraged while formulating strategy.

2. **Strategy Formulation**

   Strategy formulation encompasses the development of long range/term plans for the effective management of opportunities and threats, emerging from the internal and external business environment. These plans are evolved in the context of corporate strengths and weaknesses (SWOT) or ETOP or PESTLE Analysis. Strategy formulation would also include working out and specifying corporate mission/vision and spell out achievable objectives, developing strategies and establishing policy guidelines.

3. **Strategy Implementation**

   Strategy implementation is a process by which strategies and policies are put into action by developing programmes, budgets and procedures. The strategy implementation is usually carried out by Tactical/Middle-level Managers and involves the task of resource allocation. Strategy implementation is reviewed by the Top/Strategic Management.

4. **Evaluation and Control**

   Evaluation and Control is the process or mechanism, by/in which, corporate activities and performance results are monitored. The monitoring is undertaken to compare the actual performance with the desired performance and this data is used for initiating corrective action and resolving problem.

   Evaluation and control is the critical major element of strategic management and emphasises performance.

   Indeed, strategic management is adopted to ensure that organisations not only perform, but rather outperform their competitors.

1.5.5 Strategic, Tactical/Management and Operational Controls

As discussed earlier, the last phase of the Strategic Management Model is "Evaluation and Control", where the outcome is expected to be "Results" or "Performance".

However, 'Results' or 'Performance' does not happen just like that. Managers operating at various levels in an organisation have to get the things done the way they want it done, to ensure 'Results' and 'Performance'. The managers have to continuously monitor, get feedback, review and take appropriate corrective actions to ensure effective control.

1.5.5.1 What is Control?

'Control' is one of the critical functions of management in every organisation. The Control Function focuses on ensuring that the planning, organising, staffing and leading functions of the management lead to the accomplishment of organisational objectives/goals. Control, therefore, is an instrument or mechanism that helps organisations measure and compare their actual performance vis-à-vis their plan.

The Management Process, and the indeed 'Management' itself, would be futile and meaningless without the control function.

1.5.5.2 Control: Definition

Control is *"the system of ensuring that the actual state of affairs is in line with the desired state of affairs"*.

Control can also be defined as *"any process in which a person or group of persons or organisation of persons determines that is, intentionally affects, the behaviour of another person, group or organisation"*.

From the perspective of Performance Management, control can be said to be:

- Measurement of performance against pre-determined goals.
- Identification of deviations from these goals and the reasons for the deviations.
- Initiating appropriate course-corrective actions to rectify deviations to attain the pre-determined goals.

Control, therefore, has to be highly result and performance oriented.

1.5.5.3 Why Control?

Effective control has become a survival condition for contemporary business organisations in view of the extremely competitive business environment. The competitive environment is typically characterised by:

- 'Execute or Be Executed',
- 'Deliver or Be Delivered', and
- 'Perform or Perish'.

In view of this, the Control Function has become very critical as in the absence of effective control, the very survival of the business organisation is at stake.

The factors necessitating 'Control' can be summarised as follows:

➢ The dynamic, volatile and turbulent business environment.

➢ Need to cope with risk and uncertainty of the dynamic business environment (VUCA: Volatile, Uncertain, Complex and Ambiguous).

- Identifying, grabbing and exploiting opportunities.
- Growing complexity and need to handle complex situations.
- Emergence of 'Click', 'Virtual' and therefore flat/de-layered organisation.
- Controlling costs and becoming cost and price competitive.
- Prevent, detect and remove irregularities.
- High result/performance orientation and performance being a survival condition.

1.5.5.4 Levels of Control

An organisation is generally viewed from Strategic, Tactical and Operational perspective. Hence, there are different types/levels of control to facilitate effective and efficient execution of strategy/plans to ensure accomplishment of the plan/goals.

The controls could be:
- Strategic Control
- Tactical/Management Control
- Operational Control

Before we move further, let us take a quick look at the Levels of Management, Types of Planning and Types of Control.

Table 1.1 Levels of Control

Levels of Management	Type of Planning	Type of Control
Top Management • Organisation-wide perspective • Concerned with strategic issues • Long time frame	Strategic Planning	Strategic Control
Tactical/Middle Management • SBU/Department perspective • Concerned with departmental goals and objectives, programmes and budgets • Medium time frame	Tactical Planning	Tactical Control
Operational Management • Unit/Individual perspective • Concerned with schedules, budgets, rules, and specific individual output requirements • Short time frame	Operational Planning	Operational Control

1.5.5.5 Strategic Control

Strategic Control is the final component of the Strategic Management Process.

Strategic Control involves *monitoring critical environmental factors to ensure that strategic plans are executed and implemented as perceived/conceived, assessing the impact of strategic plans and adjusting such plans whenever and wherever so required.* Strategic Controls help Top Management in evaluating the organisation's performance and progress with its strategy, and when discrepancies arise/exist, in initiating corrective action.

Hence, strategic control would be exercised by the top managers who would usually view the events/happenings from an organisational perspective and would be concerned with strategic issues. They would also usually take a long-term view but would be able to respond quickly and decisively if the operating environment becomes volatile and turbulent.

While strategic control would be exercised by the top managers, they may, if so required, exercise-tactical and/or operational control to monitor the implementation of plans at the tactical/middle and/or operational/lower levels of management to ensure that the strategies get implemented and executed across the organisation.

However, as a norm, Strategic Control should be more focussed on creating and maintaining/sustaining competitiveness and long-term effectiveness.

Such controls must encompass performance indicators, information system and specific mechanism to detect deviations as well as monitor the results/performance.

1.5.5.6 Tactical/Management Control

Tactical/Management Control can be said to be *the control exercised by the management over the managers.* As such, it is a process that helps evaluate, monitor and control the various sub-units within the organisation to ensure efficient and effective procurement, allocation and utilisation of resources for accomplishing the pre-determined goals of an organisation.

Let us now note a few definitions.

1. *"It is a systematic effort by business management/managers to compare performance to pre-determined standards, plans or objectives in order to determine whether actual performance is in line with these standards and presumably in order to take any remedial action required to see that human and other corporate resources are being used in the most effective and efficient way possible in achieving corporate goals/objectives".*

2. *"Management control implies the measurement of accomplishments against the standards and the correction of deviations to assure attainment of objectives according to plans".*   **– Koontz and O'Donnel**

3. It is *"the handling of people - employees within the administration and clients, suppliers, Government officials, bankers, outside it - to get decisions made and carried out in ways that will achieve the firm's objectives.*   **– Arthur Mills**

Tactical/Management control is exercised by the middle/tactical managers. The tactical control focuses on ascertaining and ensuring the implementation of tactical plans at the functional or departmental levels. Tactical controls monitor periodic results as regards the functional area or department and help initiate corrective action whenever and wherever so required.

Tactical/Middle managers are responsible for departmental goals, objectives, programmes and budgets. Hence, the time frame is not long-term but medium-term and the cyclicality usually can be weekly, fortnightly or monthly.

Tactical managers take a clue/inputs from strategic control and give feedback to the top managers as regards strategic issues.

Tactical/Middle level managers exercise operational control by monitoring critical aspects of the implementation of operational plans.

Such controls also tend to encompass performance indicators, information system and specific mechanism to detect deviation as well as monitor the result/performance.

The organisational budget, covering a period of one year, is one of the most favourite Tactical Control Tool.

1.5.5.7 Operational Control

While strategy/strategic planning and top management provide vision/mission and intended pattern of action, the tactical planning/management provides the blue print of action and the implementable plans to convert strategy into reality. However, it is at the operational level and on the ground/shop floor that the grass-root result/performance actually happens.

Along with strategic controls and tactical controls, therefore, operational controls become critical for accomplishment of short-term and long-term organisational goals.

Operational controls are exercised by the front line/operational managers.

Operational controls involve ascertaining and ensuring the implementation/execution of operational plans at the grass-root level. Operational controls help facilitate tightly monitoring of day-to-day performance and results and initiating corrective action, whenever and wherever so required in real time. The operational managers look after ensuring the execution of shift-wise/schedule-wise/daily/weekly/monthly budgets, schedules, rules and activity/process-specific steps and outcomes.

Operational controls enable operational managers to assess ground-realities and provide feedback as regards the tasks being carried out on a shift/schedule/daily basis, basically involving very short-term periods and ensure/achieve short-term efficiency.

It must be remembered that attainment/accomplishment of operational goals, in turn, facilitates realisation of long-term, strategic goals of the organisation.

A quick comparison of Strategic Planning/Control, Tactical Control and Operational Controls could be presented as follows:

Area/Feature	Strategic Planning/Control	Tactical Control	Operational Control
• Level	Top Management / All levels	Tactical level	Supervisory
• Scope	Total / Wholistic	Overall	Operational
• Time Span	Long Range	1 to 3 years	Up to 1 year
• Decision Type	Unstructured	Semi-structured	Structured
• Environment	Internal and External (emphasis on external environment)	Internal and External	Mainly Internal
• Goals	Core	Specific / Tangible	Specific/Tangible
• Activity Period	Irregular	Regular	Routine
• Activity Type	Creative / Cognitive	Administrative	As directed (command / obey)
• Focal Point	Complete Organisation	All Activities / Departments / Functions	Operational level entities

1.5.6 Linkages among Strategic Planning, Management Control and Operational Control

We have earlier discussed that 'strategy' is basically all about 'what an organisation is today, and what it **OUGHT** to be tomorrow'.

For converting strategy into reality, organisations follow a process of Strategic Planning, Tactical Planning and Operational Planning and then, strategy implementation and execution, resulting in and leading to the desired performance. Strategy execution involves feedback, monitoring and initiating corrective action by means of strategic controls, tactical/ management control and operational control.

Strategic planning provides organisational vision/mission and illustrates the long-term commitment to a type of business and a distinctive place in the market. It describes the "scope of the firm and its dominant emphasis and values", based on the firm's history, present management preferences, resources, core competence and business environment. As such, strategic planning involves making decisions about an organisation's long-term goals and strategies.

Tactical planning helps provide Modus Operandi to translate/convert the overall strategic vision/mission/goals into implementation plans and time-bound specific goals, with respect to the SBU or a specific organisational function, like say, Finance, Production, Marketing etc. It describes the overall direction an organisation will follow within the given/expected business environment and would guide resource allocation. It also provides the logic that integrates the perspectives of functional departments and operating units and directs them all in the same direction to ensure goal congruence.

Operational planning emphasises identifying and working out a specific plan/procedure/ process required for implementing the tactical plans into actual results/output on the ground. The operational phases would be based on Standard Operating Procedure (SOPs) and hence, routine and repetitive. The operational plans would be for a very short term/period and would focus upon the result/output per machine/shift/day/week etc.

The Strategic, Tactical, and Operational Management / Planning must necessarily be accompanied by appropriate and corresponding Strategic, Tactical and Operational Management and Controls, so that strategy is converted into reality and the organisation actually 'becomes' what is 'aspired to be'.

Hence, there is an imperative need for linkages and fit, inter se, **between** "Strategic Planning, Tactical Planning and Operational Planning" and "Strategic Control, Tactical/ Management Control and Operational Control, on the other hand.

It must also be remembered that, historically and traditionally organisations used to follow a Top-Down Approach. Accordingly, the Top Management was assigned the task, initially, of setting 'Targets' and later, developing strategy, plans and goals for the organisation. Indeed, it was the prerogative and privilege of the top management to do so, and the tactical and operational managers used to be at the receiving end. There was, in essence, hierarchy-based command-and-obey structure.

Presently, however, thanks to the contemporary complex and competitive business environment, there is a critical need for innovation, flexibility and responsiveness. There is also an imperative need to "see the jungle and also the individual trees" as well as to "look at and aim for the stars, but keep your feet firmly on the ground".

Tactical and operational managers, who have their ears to the ground, are being increasingly involved in, and associated with, the Strategy Formulation Process in the organisation. It is also realised that Tactical and Operational Managers, more often than not, provide critical and valuable inputs and insights to organisation's strategic plan.

Today, in fact, we do not refer to Strategic Planning but talk of Strategic Management which involves managers from all parts of the organisation in the formulation and execution/implementation of strategy and strategic goals. It integrates strategic planning and management into a single process.

Strategic Planning has now become an ongoing and continuous activity in which all managers at all levels and functions are encouraged to think strategically and to focus on long-term externally oriented issues as well as medium-term tactical and short-term operational issues.

Without strategy, there would not be planning and goals, and without control, the plan cannot be implemented/executed and the organisational goals achieved/accomplished.

Hence, to conclude, it is an absolute must that the organisation's Strategic, Tactical and Operational plans and goals must be consistent and mutually supportive to ensure seamless integration of the perception, conception and execution to ensure synergistic performance.

The three levels of controls viz. strategic, tactical and operational - must be integrated, synchronised in an inter-related and inter-dependent manner so as to ensure efficiency and effectiveness, ultimately enabling the organisation to achieve the strategic goals and deliver performance and add value to/for the Stakeholders to gain, retain and sustain competitive advantage in today's globally and competitive battlefield.

1.6 Performance Evaluation Parameters: Financial

1.6.1 Responsibility Centres

Let us first establish that all enterprises are Investment and Profit Centres by themselves. For the investors who invest money in a company it becomes an Investment Centre, and they expect a return on this investment. All enterprises strive to make profits. Thus they are also Profit Centres. If a company is unable to generate profit then the investors cannot earn a return on their investment. The companies then create within themselves Profit Centres and Investment Centres as will be explained further. So an enterprise is always a profit centre but responsibility centres within a corporate need not be profit centres but all of them are investment centres! It is because a corporate has to make an investment in creating a responsibility centre. Thus all responsibility centres are Investment Centres for the Head Office. Some of these have profit responsibility and thus they become Profit Centres while others have no profit responsibility.

In the old days most organisations used to be under tight control of a single person or a group of persons and thus the decision making was concentrated. This has since been found untenable. As the business of the organisation increases, it is inevitable that some kind of decentralisation has to be adopted. Creating different types of responsibility centres is a way of doing this systematically. They are also called as Strategic Business Units (SBU) at times. However many times SBUs may be profit centres. But all responsibility centres are not profit centres. Different types of responsibility centres are thus created, which become independent units with specific tasks to be performed by them.

1.6.2 Definition

A responsibility centre is *an organisation unit that is headed by a manager who is responsible for its activities.* This is the way large companies are organised these days.

A decentralised company therefore becomes a collection of responsibility centres. The management decides the objective of each of these centres. The managers heading these are given requisite authority to run these centres and are expected to deliver the desired output, for which they are held responsible. Thus managers need to have authority to deliver the desired results. Thus authority and responsibility go hand in hand. It is an accepted principal of decentralisation that responsibility of goal achievement cannot be expected without empowering the manager with requisite authority to work towards achieving the goals. A manager can be held responsible for goals only if it has been granted the power that he has to have to get the work done so that the goals are achieved.

For the Board of Directors the entire company is a responsibility centre. As we go down the organisational hierarchy smaller responsibility centres are created, with requisite responsibility allocation and setting up of targets that they are required to achieve. The individual responsibility centres are thus many times dependent upon each other for achieving their targets. No responsibility centre normally is stand alone as the interdependence is inevitable. This fact itself makes them a good control system. If one centre does not perform the task allotted to it, it will surely, adversely affect the performance of other centres that are dependent on its performance. The job of the Controller is thus to make sure that different responsibility centre activities are coordinated and to see that they all work in perfect harmony in the larger interest of the company. It is important that the company's objectives always override the objectives of individual responsibility centres. Thus the Controller has to strive to achieve perfect Goal Congruence amongst all responsibility centres of the company. Perfect goal congruence achievement depends on the skills of the manager of the responsibility centre. Any manager who has the ambition to climb the corporate ladder quickly has to show his calibre here, so that he gets noticed by the top management by his work and results. Managers who are successful at this level may get fast tracked for promotions based on their individual achievements. Thus there is a great incentive for responsibility centre managers to do their best. This acts as a big motivating factor at this level and creates healthy competition among managers. If nurtured properly this can benefit the whole enterprise.

A responsibility centre may be expected to accomplish one or more goals, which are its objectives. The company has goals and the management team decides the way to accomplish these goals through different strategies. The objectives of a responsibility centre are to help implement these strategies successfully. However the responsibility managers have to create their own strategies at their level for the implementation of strategies that they are responsible for. The strategy is created at the corporate level but it is implemented at the level of the responsibility centres. An organisation is the sum of its different responsibility centres. If the corporate strategies are sound and if each responsibility centre can meet its objectives, then the organisation as a whole can achieve its goals. Thus it can be seen that responsibility centres are the units to make the strategy of an organisation successful.

1.6.3 Types of Responsibility Centres

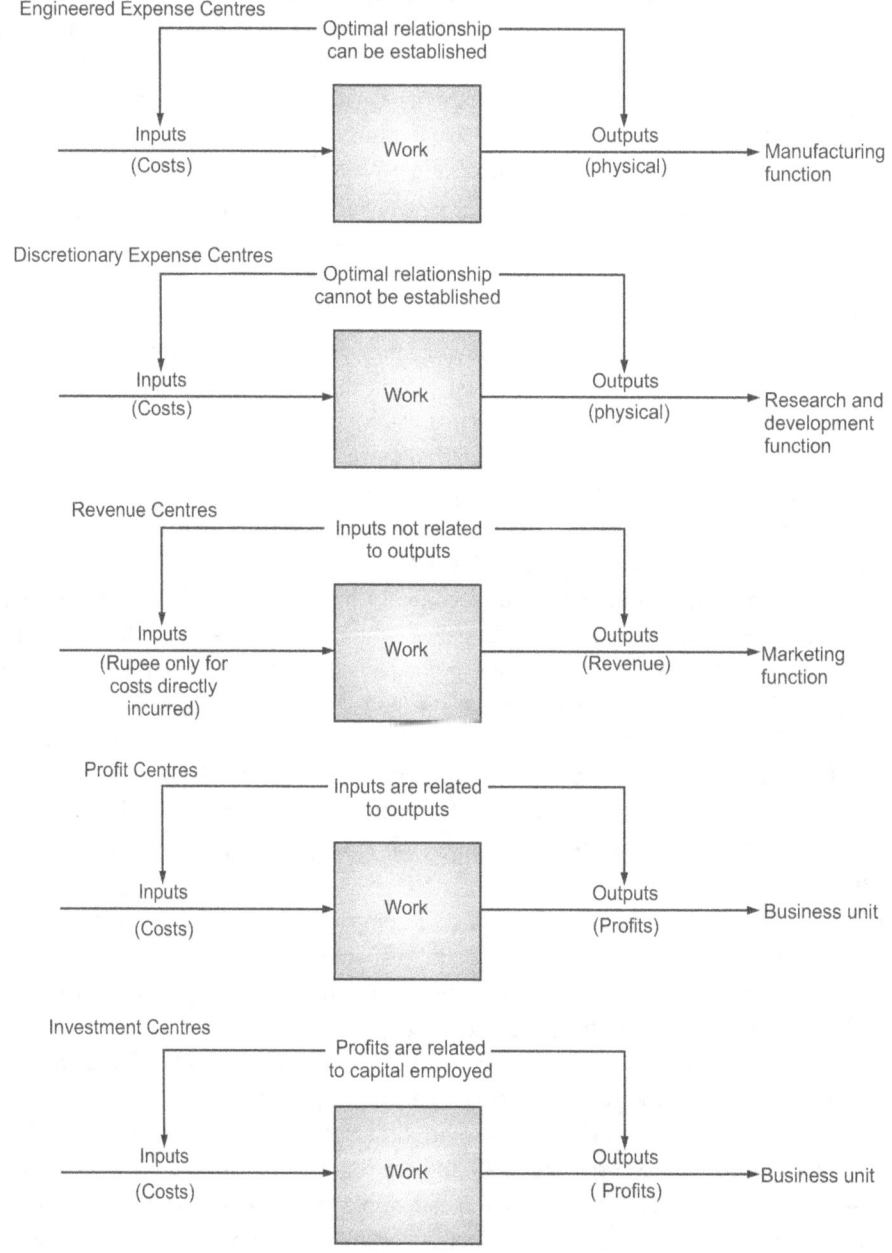

Fig. 1.6: Types of Responsibility Centres

The following are the four types of responsibility centres. They are:
1. Revenue centres.
2. Expense centres.
3. Profit centres, and
4. Investment centres

1.6.4 Revenue Centre

In a Revenue centre, outputs are measured in monetary terms, but no formal attempt is made to relate inputs to outputs because it is not possible to do so. This centre does not buy the products that it sells. Thus there is no monetary transaction involved between the two related responsibility centres. It essentially markets products that are manufactured by the Engineered Expense Centres. A revenue centre could be a marketing division of an organisation and does not have profit responsibility. This does not mean that they can ignore profitability. Marketing division generates the revenues for a company and it is an acceptable principal that all sales need to be profitable under normal circumstances.

It should be noted that each revenue centre is also an expense centre. The manager of this centre is accountable for the expenses incurred by his centre. The primary measurement of this type of centre is revenue generation. Such centres also do not pay for the goods that they sell. If a revenue centre pays for the goods that it sells, then such a revenue centre can become a Profit centre. In such a scenario the manager of the revenue centre will enjoy many more powers. However Revenue centres are normally not converted into Profit centres. This is so because as we shall later many conditions for creating a Profit centres are not fulfilled, by just charging for the goods sold by them.

The main responsibility of the marketing division is to generate more and more sales of the products of the company. The focus therefore is more on order booking than on generating profits. However it must be kept in mind that all sales have to be profitable for the company! The manager of a revenue centre does not have the knowledge that is needed to make cost / revenue trade-off required for optimum marketing decisions. He is not expected to do this either. These centres do not have the authority to set the selling prices of the products that they sell. The Head Office decides the pricing. The Manager has some flexibility that is allowed in terms of some discount that can be granted depending on the payment terms or on the volume of the order. He can also have some authority regarding delivery schedules.

The marketing department also is responsible for delivery of their goods either through the dealers or directly to the end user. Warehousing, distribution etc. in a marketing centre can be engineered expense centres. They may also be responsible for the logistics in their area of operations. So in a way they are also responsible for the supply chain management and logistics where input output can actually be established. Marketing personnel are also responsible for collection of the money. This is at times is neglected in some organisations. It has to be recognised that a sale is complete only once the payment from the buyer is collected. Since marketing departments are in continuous touch with the customers they also need to be responsible for collection of dues. It is important that buyers who have the habit of delaying payments need to be carefully watched and their outstandings do not exceed the set limits of credit that is based on their financial viability. This is especially true in sectors like FMCG, White Goods, Pharmaceuticals and Vehicles. There is a possibility of these creating conflicts between Revenue centres and the accounts department of a company. The accounts people block accounts of customers who have delayed payments, but the marketing department wishes not to have these locks as they fear they will lose business from these customers if they are not accommodated! These kind of situations need to be handled carefully by the Managers.

Many revenue centres are also responsible for sales promotion and advertising at their level.

Revenue centres are controlled through budgets. The managers of these centres are given expense budgets in line with their commitment to generate certain revenue. So the manager must control his expenses at the same time that he must try and surpass his revenue targets. A manager who spends his expenditure budget but fails to achieve his revenue targets will get in trouble. On the other hand a manager who keeps within his expenditure budget but over achieves his sales target will get rewarded.

1.6.5 Expense Centre

Expense Centres are responsibility centres for which inputs or expenses are measured in monetary terms, but for which outputs are not measured in monetary terms.

There are two types of expense centres (a) Engineered expense centres and (b) Discretionary expense centres.

In engineered cost centres the input costs can be measured with a great degree of certainty. In a production department the cost of inputs for a desired output can be calculated and the optimum relationship between the inputs and outputs can be established. This means that one can know the cost of production. In these centres input can be measured in monetary terms and output is measured in units manufactured.

Discretionary costs on the other hand are those costs for which no such engineered estimates are possible. The management based on their judgement incurs these costs. The example of these costs is the advertising expenditure or the expenditure incurred on R & D. In these types of centres the optimum relationship between the inputs and outputs cannot be established.

Engineered Expense Centres have the following characteristics:
(a) Their inputs can be measured in monetary terms.
(b) Their output can be measured in physical terms.
(c) The optimal amount of money of inputs required to produce one unit of output can be established.

In these centres, the output multiplied by the standard cost of each unit produced gives the cost of the finished product. By comparing this cost to actual costs, the difference between the two represents the efficiency of the organisation.

In these centres many other aspects are also the responsibility of the manager. Cost is one of the major considerations. The managers are responsible for the quality of the products and for the budgeted volumes of production as well. The top management sets the quality standards and the target volumes of production and sees to it that manufacturing costs are not minimised at the cost of quality. The managers also are responsible for activities such as training of the staff; however these expenses are not related to current costs of production. In many enterprises the wage agreements are based on the output per shift that is committed. Higher than targeted output brings incentives while shortage may lead to cut in pay. This is a fair system that punishes laggards while rewards the efficient.

It should be noted that in no responsibility centre all costs could be engineered. The term engineered expense centre refers to the responsibility centres in which engineered costs are predominant.

1.6.5.1 Committed, Discretionary, and Engineered Costs

An important issue when facing decisions over costs is the distinction between committed and discretionary costs. Some costs, like rent, are called **committed**. These costs are not easily changed and are often fixed. For example, once a company has decided to rent a place, the rent has to be paid regardless what happens. The cost of the rent remains as long as the company stays in the same location. If the company wants to lower this cost, they would have to relocate.

In contrast, **discretionary costs** are costs that can be adjusted relatively quickly. The costs of marketing, training, exploration of new ideas are typically discretionary costs because managers have the power to determine them. They are not variable costs because they do not change with volume, so are often treated as fixed.

Another concept associated with committed and discretionary costs is that of **engineered costs**. It is usually applied to variable costs and simply means that there are certain costs that "automatically" accompany a certain decision. For example, if a table manufacturer decides to sell an additional 100 tables, the material and labour costs will automatically increase. If this manufacturer decides not to sell the additional tables, then these variable costs do not apply. This is why they are relevant: they are engineered into the decision.

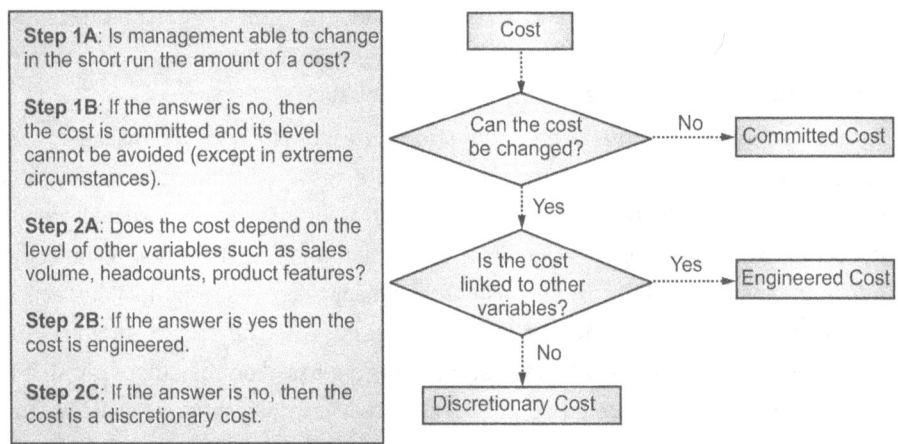

Fig. 1.7: Steps to Identify Different Types of Costs

1.6.6 Profit Centre

This is the most independent of all responsibility centres and many times has other responsibility centres as an integral part of it. The managers of such centres almost run a small company especially in bigger organisations like L & T, ITC, HUL, RIL or Tata Group of companies. This is where future CEOs make a name for themselves.

Profit centres are independent units within an organisation, whose performance is measured in terms of profit targets and the actual profits that are earned by them. This means that their performance is measured in terms of profit. Profit is a comprehensive tool of performance measurement, which includes many other performance criterions. It should be understood that profit is not just revenue – expenses. Many non-financial aspects also influence a unit's ability to make profits.

In decentralised organisations many SBUs are created. When the responsibility of generating profits is delegated to any of these SBUs they are called Profit centres. As we have already seen all responsibility centres cannot be profit centres for various reasons. In a profit centre the optimum relationship between inputs and outputs can be established. A company creates separate business units when it decides to delegate more authority to the managers in charge of these units.

1.6.6.1 Conditions for Delegation of Profit Responsibility

Certain conditions need to be fulfilled for the establishment of a profit centre. Many a times it is noticed that organisations have to commit more expenditure to generate additional revenues and consequently more profits. These decisions are often referred to as expense/revenue trade off. This is a major decision that has to be made by the management, because there is no guarantee that additional expenses will generate more sales volumes. If it does not then such additional expenditure may reduce the profits that are being generated at present. The examples of such expenditures could be advertising and sales promotion expenses or additional discounts to the customers, or something like "buy one get one free" kind of things which are very popular these days. Before the trade off decisions can be delegated the following two conditions must be fulfilled:

1. The manager should have the relevant information to make these trade offs. As said earlier these decisions are not easy to make. The manager can make them only after studying the environment and the other related facts required to be known for making these decisions. A good organisation makes every effort to provide all important information to its managers. However it is also true that many organisations do not have this mechanism.

2. There has to be some way to measure how effectively the manager is making these tradeoffs. It must be noted that decisions of tradeoffs can go wrong even after they have been made taking into consideration all relevant matters. The evaluation therefore must be based on whether the decision when made was wrong or did it go wrong due to the changes that occurred after it was made and on which the manager had no control. So it has to be seen under what circumstances was the decision made and did the variables change drastically to make the decision wrong later.

The concept of profit centres is comparatively new. We can today see many multinational companies who are organised as a cluster of various subsidiaries, which are independent profit centres. For example Hindustan Lever is an independent profit centre as far as Unilever is considered.

Many Indian corporates also operate on the basis of profit centres now. Hindustan Lever itself has many profit centres of its own within its organisation. Companies like Larsen & Toubro Ltd., Reliance Industries Ltd., TISCO, Tata Motors etc. to name just a few, also operate through profit centres. The branches of banks also are independent profit centres, in the sense that all branches are expected to make profits. In a hotel chain like Indian Hotels or EIH each hotel is a profit centre.

Companies across the world use financial performance as the major tool for strategy implementation. It is not as if they do not know that other non-financial tools are also required for this purpose and they do use many a non-financial tools for strategy evaluation.

1.6.6.2 Advantages of Profit Centres

- The speed of operating decisions can be increased, as many a decisions will now be made at the level of the responsibility centre without referring them to the corporate office. This actually is the essence of decentralisation. In today's competitive atmosphere quick decision making is a great asset.

- The quality of many decisions can be improved as the managers that are closest to the point of decision make them.

  This can be best illustrated by the example of the public sector in India. Since the board of these PSUs do not have complete autonomy regarding decision making and are dependent on their Ministries to clear many of the financial outlay proposals, many opportunities are lost as the time taken for final decision and the procedure for arriving at the decisions is cumbersome and torturous. As in the case of buying new aircrafts for Air India and Indian Airlines which is hanging for some years now, with no decision in sight. Such problems are also there in the private sector companies where managements are not willing to delegate authority and insist on being involved in all decisions.

  The General Manager of a plant had to wait for two days in Pune to get the clearance from the company's M.D. to renew the security contract of the factory!

- The management may be relieved of day to day business decisions and can therefore concentrate on broader issues.

- The corporate office of large companies has to be involved in strategic planning and implementation of strategies. They have no time to control the profit centres of the organisation on day to day business; neither should they be doing it. They must have in place, a good MIS system that will give them all the necessary information at regular intervals. With the revolution in communication technology, it is now possible to get reports on daily basis if required.

- In the profit centres the profit consciousness can be enhanced. As profits are the main criterion of performance measurement, managers will constantly try to improve the profitability. Since all managers will be doing this, it will benefit the organisation. It will also mean that managers will take all steps necessary to control costs. When cost control is done by the manager himself, it will prove more effective and the budgets will become more realistic.

- Profitability is a much broader measure of performance. If revenues or expenses are performance measurements in isolation of each other then such a measure is restrictive in nature. Profits as performance measurement can measure actions on both revenues and expenses.

- Since managers have lesser constraints in decision making and do not have to justify every action of theirs, they tend to be more imaginative and take more initiative. Also they are more responsible and cautious in decision-making.

- This also provides an excellent training ground for managers. Since the profit centres are almost like independent companies, the managers get trained in all aspects of the

management. The higher management can also judge the talent that is on display in the company for future promotions. It is also found that promising candidates are tested by making them in charge of the profit centres at an early age.
- When a company has a strategy of diversification this kind of structure allows organisations to appoint specialists and experts to manage different types of businesses.
- Profit centres provide top managements the information on the profitability of the components of the company. Many a times in profit making organisations, the top management is likely to ignore the performance of certain profit centres that could be lagging behind as this does not have profound effect on the overall profitability of the organisation. But when the time comes to review the profit performance the profit centre structure makes this task easy.
- Profit centres are always under pressure to improve their competitive performance.

1.6.6.3 Difficulties with Profit Centres

- As the decision-making is decentralised the top management is likely to loose some control. But this is the whole point in decentralisation. The top management has to rely more on reports received from these centres to effectively control them. Also the management must choose the right people to do this job.
- It is possible at the beginning of the decentralisation that competent people with requisite experience may not be available within the organisation. This problem can be tackled by training the managers before they are asked to head a profit centre. The other possibility is to recruit persons with requisite experience and continue to train people within the organisation.
- It is possible that organisational units would start competing amongst themselves disadvantageously.
- There can be increased friction in business units especially on the issue of transfer pricing mechanism. The friction can also arise in the area of sharing common costs, such as corporate office expenses.
- The managers of the profit centres are likely to focus on short-term profitability at the cost of long-term interest of the company. It is observed that managers to increase profitability may reduce expenditure on R & D, training and development or even maintenance. It is therefore the responsibility of the top management to make sure that they keep a watch on the sources where the cost cutting is taking place in a profit centre. This will help them to know if the manager is cutting costs where they should not be cut, in view of the long-term adverse effects on the organisation.
- There is no system that will guarantee that increase in profits of all profit centres will automatically increase the profits of the organisation as a whole. This will depend on how the profitability has been increased. If the increase in profits is due to cost cutting in areas discussed above, the company profitability in the long run may suffer.

- If the profit centre manager for some reason does not have all relevant information that may be available with headquarters, then quality of decisions made may suffer. This is where the Cybernetic comes in play. As seen in the cybernetic the Superior and Subordinate must have a very efficient communications network, so that the information flow will be maintained. The sensors at each level may report different information to the superior and the subordinate and they need to exchange this information, so that the manager of the profit centre has all the information that the headquarters will also have.
- Divisionalisation leads to additional costs. This is because some work duplication is inevitable. However the other positives of decentralisation outweigh such minor problems. The additional costs incurred are recovered because of better management and profit responsibility given to the managers.
- For realising the full potential of the profit centres it is imperative that the managers are as autonomous as the CEOs of the company. In practice so much autonomy is never possible. A company can never be completely divided in independent units and the powers that a CEO has cannot be given to the business unit managers. However delegating as many powers as possible has to be the goal.
- Another problem arises when business units have to deal with one another. Profit centres need to have control essentially on three things:
    1. The product decision- what products and services to make and sell.
    2. The procurement and sourcing decision.
    3. The marketing decision.

If a profit centre manager has control on the three there is no real problem. However the problem would start when other business units are involved. When the production, procurement and marketing decisions for a single product line are distributed among two or more units, separating the contribution of each unit becomes difficult.

There are also three constraints that are placed by the corporate management. These constraints result from strategic considerations, those resulting from the need for uniformity and those resulting from the economies of centralisation.

In most companies decisions such as investment decisions are in the purview of the corporate management only. Due to this business units have to compete amongst themselves for their share of new investments. Some managers are likely to feel aggrieved when their investment plans are not sanctioned.

All business units have to operate according to the constraints placed on them by the corporate office. This means that they have to operate within the limits of the targets and the freedom granted to them to achieve these targets.

These units are also constrained of corporate accounting standards and the management control systems put in place. This is particularly difficult for newly acquired units, which are used to a totally different regime.

In most organisations certain services are centralised for the use of all business units. One example of this could be H. R. function. Under this, this department will do the recruitment for all units and the business unit manager may have no authority to make any recruitment on his own. Other services that fall under this category are, internal audit, training, legal services, public relations etc.

Thus it is clear that the business unit managers have to live with these constraints. Any problems that may arise due to this must be resolved quickly through discussions and with transparency.

1.6.6.4 Profitability Measures to Measure Performance of Profit Centres

Let us now take a look at the types of profitability measures that are used to measure the performance of the profit centres.

1. **Contribution Margin:** It is assumed that fixed expenses are not controllable by the manager. He therefore, is expected to concentrate on maximising the spread between the revenue and variable expenses. However certain fixed expenses are controllable. This has been shown by many organisations when their margins are under pressure. Expenses like salaries cannot be changed in the short term, however by increasing the efficiency and productivity of the people a positive contribution can be achieved. Some of the expenses that are charged to this unit are depreciation, corporate overhead expenses and contribution to income tax.

2. **Direct Profit:** This shows the contribution of a profit centre to the general overheads and the profitability of the company.

3. **Income before Tax:** In this method all corporate overhead expenses are allocated to different profit centres. This allocation is done on the basis of relative amount of expenses that may have been incurred for a particular profit centre.

- There are some arguments put forth against this system. The first is that the costs incurred by the corporate office are not controllable by the profit centre manager. Therefore they cannot be held responsible for what they cannot control. The second problem is to find a system that will be acceptable to all as to how these expenses should be allotted.

- Corporate headquarters have a tendency of empire building. They are always looking to increase their power base. However they are not responsible for raising the money themselves for all this. The business units, who have to contribute this money from the profits that they make, can start feeling that the money that are earning is being spent on unnecessary things, and would start questioning such expenditure. This questioning in turn, it is said would keep such expenditure in check.

- It is argued that most companies commonly use this practice of dividing corporate office expenses among the business unit. If this method is followed it will give the realistic picture of profitability and will be comparable to other industries as well.

- By adopting this method a message is sent to the manager that his profit centre will actually not make profits unless it recovers all costs. This motivates managers to think long-term.
- When corporate expenses are debited they should be on the basis of actual costs incurred and not on the basis of budgeted expenses. This will ensure that these are not allocated in an arbitrary manner.
- In the net income approach the performance is measured in terms of post tax profits of a business unit. However this can be problematic as many decisions that affect the tax level are actually made at the level of the headquarters and profit centre managers may have no say in this. In case of MNCs the tax rates applicable in different countries are different.

Let us now see what one of the finest companies ITC says about this kind of an organisation structure and their philosophy about this as described in the company's annual report for the year ending March 2003.

"Transparency means explaining the company's policies and actions to those whom it has responsibilities. Externally this means maximum appropriate disclosures without jeopardising the company's strategic interests and internally, this mean openness in the company's relationship with its employees and the conduct of its business."

"Empowerment is a process of unleashing creativity and innovation throughout the organisation by truly vesting decision-making powers at the most appropriate levels and as close to the scene of action as feasible, thereby enabling actualisation of the potential of its employees. ITC believes that empowerment combined with accountability provides an impetus to performance and improves effectiveness, thereby enhancing shareholder value"

Control ensures that freedom of management is exercised within a framework of checks and balances and is designed to prevent misuse of power, facilitate timely management of change and ensure effective management of risks. ITC believes that control is necessary concomitant of its second core principal of governance that the freedom of management should be exercised within a framework of appropriate checks and balances."

ITC has evolved a three-tier structure:
1. Strategic supervision by the board of directors.
2. Strategic management by the corporate management committee.
3. Executive management by the divisional/SBU chief executives.

The philosophy in adopting this structure is as follows: This three-tier structure enables the board of directors to carry out the task of strategic supervision as trustees of shareholders, unencumbered by the task of strategic management, in a manner that imparts objectivity and secures sharpened accountability from the management. Similarly the corporate management committee can engage in the task of strategic management of the company as a whole, leaving the task of day-to-day executive management with the empowered divisional/SBU management committees focused around such business.

ITC has the following large profit centres and they also have profit centres within these subsidiaries of the company.

1. ITC Hotels Ltd.
2. Srinivasa Resorts Ltd.
3. Fortune Park Hotels Ltd.
4. Ray Islands Hotels Ltd.
5. ITC Infotech India Ltd.
6. ITC Infotech Ltd.
7. ITC Infotech (USA) Inc.
8. Russell Credit Ltd.
9. Greenacre Holdings Ltd.
10. Wills Corporation Ltd.
11. Gold Flake Corporation Ltd.
12. Landbase India Ltd.
13. BFIL Finance Ltd.

Let us now briefly look at what happened at Ranbaxy Laboratories Ltd. when the organisation became big and the management had to restructure it. This illustrates how companies find it difficult to rearrange the organisational structure and some of the problems that they may face in this task.

As the business grew new demands were placed on resources and capabilities. The geographically diverse operations made communications within the company more difficult. In response a regional reporting structure was created, this also helped in decentralised decision-making. In spite of this, the company's legacy of a hierarchical, top down management style was hard to change. Some managers found it hard to change and to delegate. On the other hand the employees felt that until they had truly been granted decision-making responsibility and were given adequate training, they would not be able to assume the responsibility demanded of them. However the moves by senior management delegation had been met with skepticism. Senior managers of the company found it hard to delegate responsibility and accountability till they had the confidence that those they delegated to had both the competence and the commitment to take the company forward. At the heart of this resistance was a profound loyalty to the company and a great deal of pride in how they had struggled to grow from a small pharmaceutical distributor into one of the most admired companies in India.

As the company became an international player, it was recognised that company's support systems like in-house legal and financial skills were inadequate to cater to new requirements.

1.6.7 Investment Centre

A subunit is designated an investment centre if it has control not only over sales revenues and operating costs but also over the assets employed in producing profits. In most companies the investment decisions for acquiring fixed assets are taken at the head office level and the responsibility centres generally have no power delegated to them. But the investment centres are different in this aspect. According to Kirby the manager of these centres must to some extent be able to influence the size of the investment base as well as profit variables. According to him the objective of any decentralised financial control system as it applies to investment in facilities is to provide an incentive for divisional management to purchase, retain or retire facilities in accordance with the best interests of the organisation.

Thus the investment centre is the broadest measure of economic performance for an entity as it incorporates all the elements of profits and investment. However there are many a practical difficulties in implementation of this.

Investment Centers are evaluated on the basis of Economic Value Addition (EVA) that they make. This is a recent technique comparatively but has been adopted by most top companies. Many Indian companies have also started calculating EVA and publishing it in their Annual Reports. The investors get a much better idea of a company's performance through this method.

1.6.7.1 Financial Measures in Investment Centres

As well as relying on detailed reports to communicate the financial performance of various responsibility centres, summary financial performance measures are commonly used to assess the performance of profit centres and investment centres. While some measure of profit is used to measure the performance of profit centres, for investment centres many firms employ measures that are based on profit and invested capital.

(A) Return on Investment (ROI) or Return on Assets (ROA)

Return on investment (ROI) is defined as follows:

$$\text{Return on Investment (ROI)} = \frac{\text{Profit}}{\text{Invested Capital}}$$

Invested capital is the assets that the investment centre has available to generate profit. Let's assume that in the previous year, the Alumina Refining and Smelting businesses generated profits of ₹ 32 million and ₹ 48 million on investments of ₹ 400 million and ₹ 800 million respectively. The return on investment for the Refining and Smelting businesses can be calculated as follows:

$$\text{Refining} = \frac{32}{400}$$
$$= 0.08 \text{ or } 8\%$$
$$\text{Smelting} = \frac{48}{800}$$
$$= 0.06 \text{ or } 6\%$$

ROI calculation for each investment centre takes into account both investment centre profit and the capital invested in that business unit. This is important. Suppose each business was evaluated only on the basis of its profit. Smelting reported a higher profit than Refining; however, this does not necessarily mean that Smelting had the better financial performance, as it used a much larger amount of invested capital to earn that profit. The Smelting business had double the assets of the Refining business.

The focus of ROI is not on how much profit each investment centre earned, but rather on how effectively each investment centre used its invested capital to earn a profit.

Advantages of ROI

ROI is used by many decentralised businesses to evaluate the performance of investment centres. It has some positive features:

1. It encourages managers to focus on both profits and the assets required to generate those profits. Thus, managers of investment centres must consider the relationships between revenues, costs and invested capital. It discourages excessive investment in assets, which may occur if performance is measured only on absolute profit.

2. ROI can be used to evaluate the relative performance of investment centres, even when those business units have different scales of operations. Thus, we can compare the ROI of a small business with that of a large business.

Limitations of ROI

Against these advantages, a significant emphasis on achieving ROI can encourage dysfunctional decisions:

1. It can encourage managers to focus on short-term financial performance, at the expense of the long term. Many ways of increasing ROI can result in reduced performance in the future. Excessive cost-cutting activities can improve short-term ROI, but weaken the business's future competitiveness. For example, research and development, or training expenditure, can be deferred. Reducing employee numbers can increase profit but may affect product quality or the level of customer service.

2. ROI can encourage managers to defer asset replacement. Asset replacement may be deferred (particularly when those old assets are fully written off), as any new assets would boost the size of the invested capital. Deferring the placement of assets may improve ROI in the short-term, but erode the competitiveness and profits of the business in later years. Disposing of productive assets can decrease the investment base, but also reduce the capacity of the business.

3. ROI may discourage managers from investing in projects that are acceptable from the total organisation's point of view. This will occur where the project decreases the investment centre's ROI.

(B) Economic Value addition (EVA)

There are various techniques that are used to evaluate the financial performance of an organisation. Some of the popular of these are Return on Investment or Return on Capital Employed (ROI, RECE), Profitability ratios, Return on Equity (ROE), Return on Net Worth (RONW) Earnings per Share, etc. The latest method that is gaining wide acceptance in the last few years is the method of Economic Value Added (EVA). This method was developed by **Stern** & **Stewart** in the 80s to evaluate the financial performance. Coca Cola and IBM were the first two companies to adopt this method. Since then many companies have adopted this method for their internal evaluation systems.

Many companies in India have also started reporting EVA in their balance sheets now. We can also see news reports issued by many companies' talk about when they expect to be EVA positive and the steps that are initiated by them to achieve these goals. Companies like Hero Honda, TISCO and Hindustan Lever are reporting EVA in their balance sheets for quite some time. The entire Godrej group is on this model. Even the compensation package and mainly the incentive package on the profit centre level is EVA compliant in Godrej.

EVA is a measure of corporate performance that differs from most others by including a charge against profit for the cost of all capital that a company employs.

The capital charge is described as the Opportunity Cost. It is a return that an investor could expect to get by putting his money in a portfolio of comparable risk.

For example, when shareholders expect a minimum return of say 12% on their investment, they do not begin to make money until profits rise above that.

Peter Drucker says, "What we call profits is usually not profit at all. Until a business returns a profit that is greater than the cost of capital, it operates at a loss. The enterprise will return less to the economy than it devours in resources—until then it does not create wealth, but it destroys it."

Conventional profits account for the interest charge on Debt, but have no provision at all for the cost of Equity capital. Conventionally it is argued that capital has no cost. This is based on the fact that capital has no fixed cost. The cost of capital is dividend, but dividend is to be paid by the company at its own discretion, i.e. in the years when the company wishes to make large investments, it may not pay dividend, or pay less dividend. Dividends are also linked to the company's profits. In most cases the company will not pay dividends if they have not made profits.

The theory of EVA is however based on the fact that the equity capital has a cost and it is not cost free. This cost of equity is taken into consideration while calculating the EVA of a company.

EVA is calculated by taking into consideration the after tax operating profit minus the appropriate capital charge for both debt and equity. What remains is the Rupee amount, by which the profits in any given period exceed or fall short of the cost of all capital used to produce these profits.

Many economists call this amount the Residual Income. It is also referred as Economic Profit by some.

EVA Calculation

EVA = Net operating profit after tax − C% (TC)

C% is the cost of capital. TC is the total capital.

It is a corporate performance measure tied directly to the creation of shareholders wealth. Managing higher EVA is by definition managing higher stock prices.

It is the only performance measure that always gives the right answer: that more EVA is always better for shareholders.

By charging for capital EVA discourages managers from making investments that return less than the cost of capital.

It measures the productivity of all factors of production. It shows us what we need to find out and whether we need to take remedial action.

Measures for increasing EVA

1. **Cut Costs:** Without adding capital i.e. operate more efficiently to earn a higher return on the capital already invested in the business. This will increase the profitability of the company, as it will produce more by efficiently using the assets that are already employed.

2. Undertake all investments in which increase in NOPAT will be greater than the increase in the capital charge plus NPV of the project. This will mean that if assets are purchased with a loan, then the cost of interest and the NPV together must be covered by the profits that will be earned, by making this investment, thereby making the project EVA positive.

3. To pull capital out of operations when the savings from the reduction in the capital charge exceeds any decrease in NOPAT. When a company disinvests form a profitable project, its overall profitability will decline. However if the savings that a company will achieve by such disinvestment, if is higher than the decline in profitability, the EVA of the company will improve.

4. Structure the finances of the company in a way that minimises the cost of capital. Many companies are these days restructuring their debt portfolio, by retiring their high cost debt by replacing it with low cost debt. This will naturally improve their profitability. Today this is possible because of the soft interest rate bias that is in evidence in the economy. However companies must constantly try and reduce their cost of capital. There are various ways available to accomplish this. For example, many companies are today borrowing working capital funds through the use of commercial paper rather than cash credit limits. This immediately reduces the cost. Companies when they need money for expansion can think in terms of raising funds by issuing equity at a premium thus reducing the requirement for borrowed funds.

Let us now take a look at the simplified version of EVA through a Balance sheet.

Current Assets		₹	Current Liabilities	₹
Cash		100	Accounts Payable	180
Receivables		300	Others	220
Inventory		400	Total C.L.	400
Total C.A.		800	Equity	1000
Fixed Assets				
Cost	1,200			
Depreciation	600			
Book Value		600		
		1,400		1,400

Income Statement

Revenues		2,000
Expenses	1,700	
Depreciation	100	(−) 1,800
Income Before Tax		200
Capital Charge (1000 * 10%)		100
Return on Investment 200/1000 = 20%		

(C) Market Value Added (MVA)

Market Value Added (MVA), is the difference between the current total market value of a company and the capital contributed by investors (including both shareholders and bondholders). This is known as Total Capital Employed in business. MVA is not a performance metric like EVA, but instead is a wealth metric, measuring the level of value a company has accumulated over time. As a company performs well over time, it will retain earnings. The simple fact is if a company generates EVA on a continuous basis it means its value is going up due to profits retained in business. This in turn would lead to its book value going up and also its market price going up thus creating MVA. In such situations investors expect that the company would maintain its financial performance and these expectations increase the demand for the shares of the company in the market thus this increased demand leads to increase in share prices of the company. As this occurs, the difference between the company's market value and the capital contributed by investors (its MVA) represents the excess price tag the market assigns to the company as a result of it past operating successes.

> MVA is calculated as MVA = Company's Market Value − Invested Capital

The MVA calculation offers a summary of how well the company has maximised shareholder value since its inception. It offers a judgement on the company's past, present and future use of investment capital. A higher number is better because it shows that shareholder value has increased over the life of the company. It is an aggregate figure because it provides information on the company as a whole. This is because figures such as market value and total investment apply to the entire firm. Thus it is considered to be a reliable figure.

For Managers it becomes then imperative that they invest only in those projects that will increase the EVA of the company. Higher EVA will automatically lead to higher MVA. This is the requirement of the investors in any company and if a company invests in such projects then it becomes a highly respected company.

(D) Du Pont Analysis

The DuPont analysis framework provides a means of integrating a number of separate financial ratios from the balance sheet and the income statement. Because it links critical ratios which influence company the DuPont Formula can diagnose the factors which influence performance of the business. If operations are successful (high Profit Margin) and management of assets is strong (high Total Assets Turnover) and management of the capital structure is tight (low Equity Margin), then for sound business reasons the ROI will be high. The business is then assesses as having a strong financial position.

The DuPont Analysis/System was developed in 1919 by a Finance Executive at E.I. DuPont de Nemours and Co as a way of visualising the information so that everyone can see it.

It is considered to be a good, simple and straightforward tool for getting people started in understanding how they can have an impact on results. It also helps assess the factors that influence a firm's financial performance and focus attention on Value Drivers.

Du Pont Analysis is the technique used for analysing the earnings power of an organisation. According to this technique, earning power indicates the overall profitability of the organisation and it has two elements –

(a) Profitability on sales which is indicated by net profit ratio

(b) Efficient use of the assets which is indicated by asserts turnover ratio

Hence, earning power of the organisation - Return on Total Assets (ROA) can be calculated as –

Net Profit Ratio × Total Assets Turnover Ratio

Measurement of earning power of the organisation can be further extended for the calculation of Return on Equity (ROE). ROE is the best possible indication of financial performance of the organisation from shareholders' point of view. Thus, ROE calculation is based upon three components.

(a) Profitability on sales which is indicated by net profit ratio.

(b) Efficient use of the assets which is indicated by assets turnover ratio.

(c) Amount of equity used to finance the assets.

Hence, earning power of the organisation from shareholders' point of view (i.e. Return on Equity – ROE) can be calculated as –

$$\frac{\text{Profit After Tax}}{\text{Sales}} \times \frac{\text{Sales}}{\text{Total Assets}} \times \frac{\text{Total Assets}}{\text{Equity}}$$

1.7 Performance Evaluation Parameters: Non-financial Performance Measures

1.7.1 Balanced Scorecard

Balanced Scorecard was developed by Kaplan and Norton. It is an improvement on Baldrige Model and takes the performance evaluation process several steps forward. Today many top 100 companies of the world use this for assessing the performance of their strategies. Many companies in India are also increasingly using this. Tata group has developed its own method which is known as Tata Business Excellence Model (TEBM).

Historically the measurement system for business has been financial. The financial aspect of business unit performance is highly developed. Many experts have questioned the extensive and at times exclusive use of financial measurements to analyse a business enterprise.

Financial performance actually depends upon a lot of things that are non-financial in nature. Financial performance is the result of all these non-financial aspects of the business. Success of a company highly depends upon its people and the skills that they possess and also on their performance. It also depends on the operational efficiency of the organisation. The operational cash flow decides the ultimate financial performance of a company. The effective and efficient utilisation of the factors of productions are crucial. The use of assets and financial resources can help a company fulfill its financial targets.

This point can be illustrated with the example of Xerox. Until mid 70s they enjoyed a virtual monopoly in this business. Xerox instead of selling these machines used to give them on lease to its customers. It thus earned revenues on every copy that was made. Sales and profits in this business were increasing continuously. But the customers were unhappy because of the high costs and the frequent breakdowns of the machines. Instead of redesigning the machines Xerox now started selling the machines outright to the customers and strengthened their maintenance work force. This activity was run through a separate profit centre. Since there was a great demand for these services the profit centre soon started contributing a substantial profit, to the company's overall profitability. Since the machine could not be used during the breakdowns the companies started buying more machines as stand by machines, so that their work did not get affected. Thus all the financial indicators like sales and profit growth, return on investment were showing a very successful strategy.

Customers however continued to be unhappy. They wanted low cost machines, which did not breakdown. The Japanese and American competitors of Xerox were eventually able to offer machines comparable in quality, that were cheaper and did not breakdown. The customers now had a choice that they did not have earlier and hence shifted to these machines.

Xerox, who dominated this market from 1955 to 1975, almost collapsed. However under a new CEO who was committed to quality and customer service the company made a turnaround in 1980.

This case amply demonstrates that just financial performance measures are an inadequate indicator especially in the long run.

1.7.1.1 Kapalan and Norton's Balance Scorecard

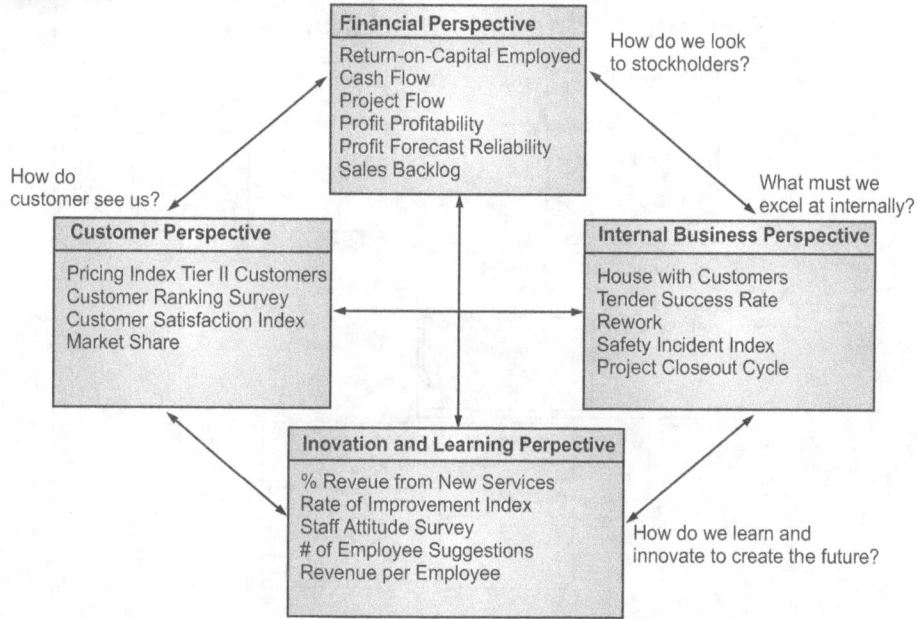

Fig. 1.8: Rockwater's Balanced Scorecard

The balance score card offers to the companies a framework that can translate a company's vision and strategy into a coherent set of performance measure. A balanced scorecard attempts to translate mission and strategy into objectives and measures, organised into four different perspectives. These perspectives are:

1. Financial
2. Customer
3. Internal business processes
4. Learning and growth.

These four perspectives of a balanced scorecard permit a balance between short and long-term objectives, between outcomes desired and the performance drivers of those outcomes, and between hard objective measures and softer, more subjective measures.

For a balanced scorecard approach to succeed it must have the full backing of the top management. This in turn will mean that the strategy has to be well crafted and the roadmap for implementation has to be in place. Strategy implementation requires resources, People and Money. Also since the strategy is long term the annual targets must be well defined.

All Managers at the SBUs must be trained in balanced scorecard approach. They must also be encouraged to create their own BSCs at their SUB level, which need to be derived from the Corporate Balanced Scorecard. Thus a drill down approach is normally adopted.

1.7.1.2 Roll out of BSC

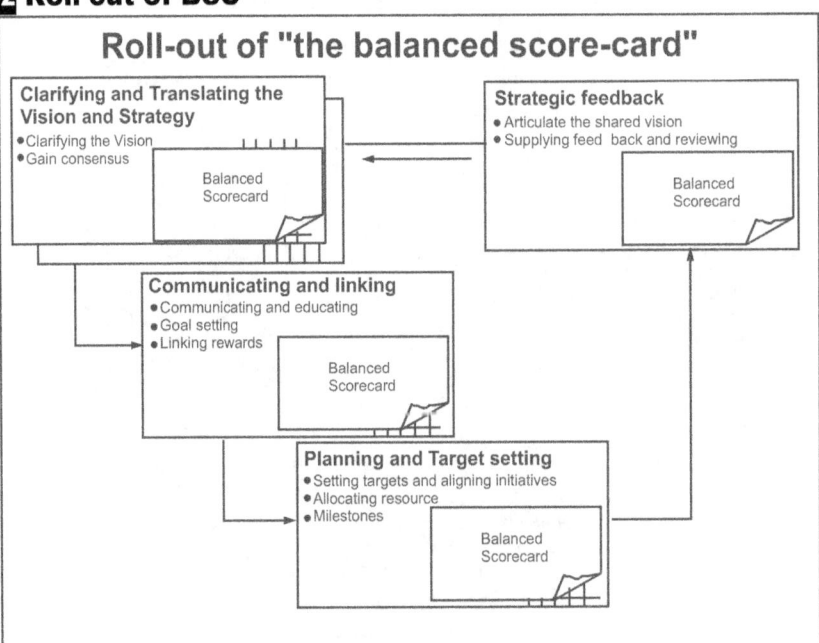

Fig. 1.9: Roll-out of "The Balanced Score-Card

The diagram above gives a road map for the roll out of a balanced scorecard. It starts with the vision and the strategy that is put in place in pursuance of the said vision. This is essentially done at the level of the top management. A consensus is built for this by the CEO in his top team and the approval of the Board of Directors is mandatory for this.

This is then communicated to the managers who are actually responsible for the implementation of the strategy. Short term goals are then set with their active participation in the planning process. Rewards for all concerned are linked to the achievement of these strategic goals.

The strategy implementation is an activity that may involve several SBUs. Thus their initiatives have to be aligned with each other and also with the corporate strategy. As mentioned above this requires resources and they have to be planned well in advance and allocated to each SBU. Acquiring these resources is normally done by the Head office. SBUs never acquire financial resources on their own. All the money required is raised by the HO. Once resources are allocated then milestones with time lines have to be set. The manager of a SBU is then required to deliver these milestones without tie and cost overruns!

1.7.1.3 Concept of BSC

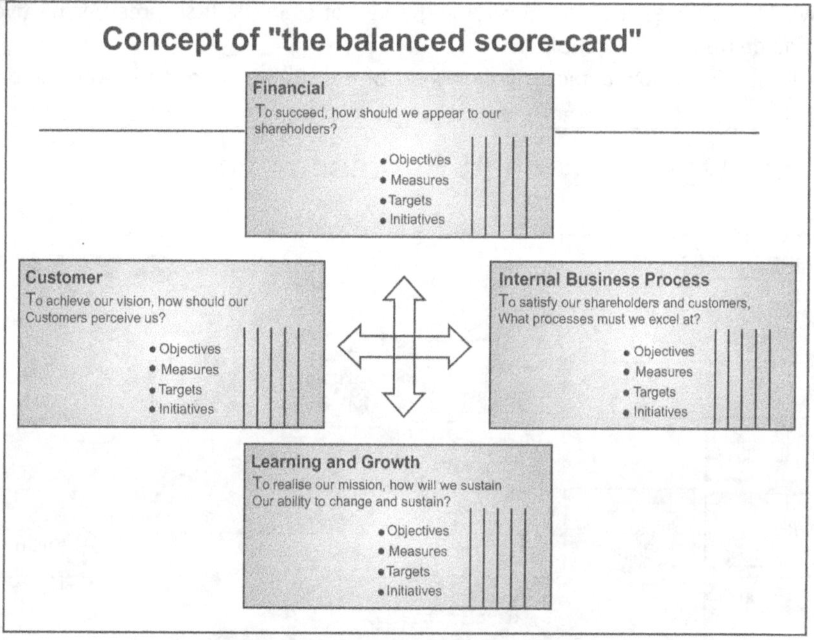

Concept of "the balanced score-card"

Financial
To succeed, how should we appear to our shareholders?
- Objectives
- Measures
- Targets
- Initiatives

Customer
To achieve our vision, how should our Customers perceive us?
- Objectives
- Measures
- Targets
- Initiatives

Internal Business Process
To satisfy our shareholders and customers, What processes must we excel at?
- Objectives
- Measures
- Targets
- Initiatives

Learning and Growth
To realise our mission, how will we sustain Our ability to change and sustain?
- Objectives
- Measures
- Targets
- Initiatives

Fig. 1.10: Concept of Balanced Scorecard

There are four questions that are posed to each perspective. The answer to these questions may lead you to what needs to be done.

In the Internal Business perspective the question asked is "What we must excel at?" The answer would be 'in everything that we do!" But that is easy to say than implement. This question will be answered on the basis of priorities. What happens in this perspective is likely to affect the customers and shareholders ultimately.

In Learning and Growth the question asked is, "How do we learn and innovate to create the future." The answer to this question is in the answer to the first question which says what we should excel at. Learning and innovation are the two pillars on which the excellence has to be built.

The Customer perspective asks the question" How do the customers see us." If we learn and innovate only then the customers are likely to get value for their money. Once they get value for money they are likely to buy more and are also likely to tell others their good experience. This will help the company twofold, one it will help it increase its market share and it will automatically start creating the Brand value for the company. Many fringe customers can then become loyal customers of the company and this increases the possibility of cross selling. Customers also want service to be part of the deal. The company will reap more benefits if this is given to the customers.

Finally in the Financial Perspective the question that needs to be answered is, "How do we look to the shareholders?" The shareholders want a consistent and growing return on their investment. If we have done everything asked of us in the first three perspectives then this can be delivered to shareholders.

The illustration below depicts the flowchart of the strategy integrated with the balanced scorecard.

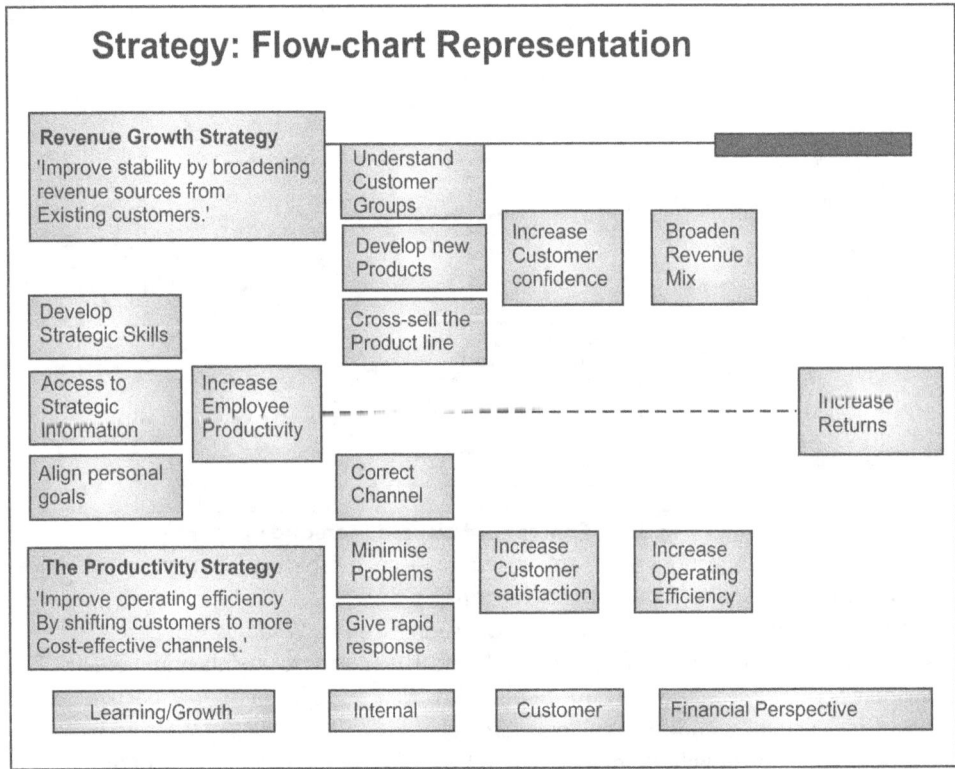

Fig. 1.11: Strategy: Flow Chart Representation

The chart below shows the relationship between Strategic Objective and Strategic Measurements. This is an example of cause and effect relationship. Grissinger says all objectives must be measurable wherever possible. Here that attempt is being made. The chart also shows the lagging and leading indicators of the balanced scorecard.

1.7.1.4 Four Perspectives of BSC

Table 1.2: The 'balanced' score-card

Strategic Objective		Strategic Measurements Lag (Outcomes)
F1	Improve Returns	R.O.I
F2	Broaden Revenue Mix	Revenue Growth
F3	Reduce Cost Structure	Deposit Service-Cost Change
C1	Increase Customer Satisfaction (with our people and products)	Share of segment
C2	Increase satisfaction after-sales	Customer retention
I1	Understand out Customers	
I2	Create innovative products	New Product revenue
I3	Cross-sell products	Cross-sell Ratio
I4	Shift customers to cost effective channels	Channel mix change
I5	Minimise operational problems	Service error count
I6	Responsive service	Fulfillment time
L1	Develop Strategic Skills	Employee Satisfaction
L2	Provide Strategic Information	
L3	Align Personal Goals	Revenue/Employee

1. Internal Business Process Perspective

In this the managers identify the processes that are most critical for achieving customer and shareholder objectives. Objectives and measures for this perspective are formed after formulating objectives and measures for financial and customer perspective.

All companies have to attempt to improve quality, reduce cycle times, increase yields, maximise throughput, and lower costs for their business process. Unless one can outperform competitors on all the above it may not be possible to be distinctive, with competitive advantage.

In this process following steps are crucial:
- Identify the market.
- Create the product/service.
- Build the product/service.
- Deliver the product/service.
- Service the customer.
  This will include two questions:
- What range of benefits will customers value in tomorrow's products?
- How might we, through innovation, preempt competitors in delivering those benefits to the market place?

Information on markets and customers provides the input for the actual product design and development. The R & D can then concentrate on following activities,

Perform basic research to develop radically new products and services for delivering value to customers.

- Perform applied research to exploit existing technology for the next generation of products.
- Make focused development efforts to bring new products to the markets.

In this perspective the companies have to use following measures:

- Percentage of sales from new products.
- Percentage of sales from proprietary products.
- New product introduction versus competitors.
- Time to develop next generation of products.

The other things that are observed are as given in the diagram of the BSC. It starts with Hours spent with the customers. A good company will always be in touch with the customers. The reason for this is twofold. One is to know the new requirements of the customers. The more pro-active companies will spend time with customers to inform them about the new developments that the company has undertaken. Many companies also try and improve their products continuously. They keep their customers informed about these things constantly.

Some companies seem to spend time with customers for some other reasons which are actually non-productive in nature. They spend time explaining delays in supplying the orders; others spend time apologising for inferior quality of products, other companies spend time with customers to get their payment released!

Out of this if a company spending time due to delay n supply and inferior quality standards then it is a clear signal to the company as to what is wrong internally and it must set these things right straight away or they will lose clientele and market share. Once this happens it is very difficult to recover.

If a customer always delays payment, then it may be a better idea to let go of such a customer even if that will mean a setback in the short run. Delayed payments means loss as the working capital gets blocked.

A company must also analyse the conversion rate of quotations to orders. Once the average conversion ratio is fixed, one can know how many inquiries need to be generated for achieving the sales targets. Normally a company loses an order for three main reasons; it cannot match the delivery schedule, its quality is not acceptable to the client, its price is not acceptable. When an order is lost it must be established why an order is lost. This will allow course correction for future orders.

Rework has to be avoided at all costs. When rework is required to be done it increases the cost and also leads to time overruns. Rework means that the company's manufacturing and testing processes are not perfect. A product is going to the market with some faults. This will lead to warranty and guarantee claims and thus will increase costs.

Project performance, project closure cycles need to be monitored strictly whenever a company is executing them.

Safety is to be constantly monitored and all safety measures have to be tested regularly. There can be no compromise about safety ever.

2. Learning and Growth perspective:

This perspective concentrates on development of objectives and measures, to drive organisational learning and growth. The earlier perspective identifies where the organisation must excel to achieve breakthrough performance. The objective here is to provide the infrastructure for achieving the objectives. The infrastructure includes people, systems and procedures. This perspective requires three categories for learning and growth viz.

(a) Employee capabilities

(b) Information system capabilities

(c) Motivation, empowerment, and alignment

The core employee measurement group would typically have three features,

(a) Employee satisfaction

(b) Employee retention

(c) Employee productivity.

Most companies are heard saying that they are unable to find good people. A company is as good as its employees. So employees are the most important asset of the company. Employee satisfaction objective recognises that employee morale and overall job satisfaction are now considered highly important by most companies. Employee morale is especially important for service industries as many a time, employees at the lowest end interact directly with the customers.

The major elements in the employee satisfaction survey should include:

- **Involvement with decisions:** Employees who are part of decision making may be more motivated. Listening to their point of view at all times is thus important. There has to be mechanism through which employees can express themselves to their managers their thoughts. Employees therefore need to be encouraged to make suggestions for improvement.
- **Recognition for doing a good job:** Human beings strive for appreciation. So it is necessary that good work is appreciated and it should be done publically. Recognition need not be financial at all times.
- **Access to sufficient information to do the job well:** If we want the employees to do a good job it is essential that they are given all the relevant information from time to time. This will improve their decision making greatly.
- **Active encouragement to be creative and use initiative:** Good companies encourage employees to take initiative. They also encourage risk taking. If creativity is encouraged then initiatives will come about. Creativity itself requires ability to take risks.

- **Overall satisfaction with company:** When employees are satisfied with their jobs and the general policies of the company they work for they become more productive and also pro-active.

In this perspective it is also seen that the companies' revenues from new products keep increasing as a percentage of the total sales. This is very important as old products over a time lose market share. The new products thus have to become successful.

Service industry also needs to watch revenue per employee and profit per employee. This will be helpful to find out the efficiency of the employees.

Some companies also conduct staff attitude surveys. This can tell the management what the employees feel about the company and the management. This if done diligently; will help them retain employees by making sure that any sore points can be dealt with before they become a large problem.

Employee retention captures an objective to retain those employees in whom the organisation has a long-term interest. Long term, loyal employees carry the values of the organisation, knowledge of organisational processes. Due to these factors companies need to retain such employees.

In employee productivity, it can be measured by calculating revenue or profit per employee. However there are some problems in this. At times the productivity per employee may increase but the profit per employee may fall as the result of non-recovery of the incremental costs incurred for higher revenue generation. When output is increased without adding to the number of employees it will result in better productivity ratio. Outsourcing of some services may also give the same result. These days outsourcing has become a norm in the industry as they have realised the potential of cost savings through this route. It is little wonder then many companies are coming to India to outsource services from here.

3. **Customer Perspective:**

In this managers identify the customer and market segments in which the business unit will compete. They also have to identify the measures of the business unit's performance in these targeted segments. The outcome measures include:

- **Customer Satisfaction:** All companies strive for achieving customer satisfaction. Satisfaction does not come only from lower prices than competitors. It comes from superior quality and performance of the product. It also comes from a great experience in service if required later. Prompt and high quality service will satisfy the customer. It is said that a satisfied customer will tell many others of his experience but an unsatisfied customer in these days is likely to use the social media very effectively to bring a bad name to the company.

- **Customer Retention:** It is obviously easy to retain a satisfied customer. A satisfied customer is also likely to buy other products of the company thus increasing the possibility of cross-sales.

- **New Customer Acquisition:** The marketing department's real responsibility would be to acquire new customers every year while retaining the earlier ones. The real effort is in acquiring new customers. A company that is able to do this is a good and successful company.
- **Customer Profitability:** It is important that the customers that a company deals with must generate a profit for the company. Delayed payments by customers destroy margins and thus it may be helpful to let go off such customers. This may impact the sales in the short run but it will help maintain profitability.
- **Market Share in Targeted Segments:** Market share of company has to rise every year at a rate that is higher than the segment growth rate. If this is not achieved then the company would be losing its market share progressively. Cash flows are directly related to market share growth and so are profits. Market share is also a matter of prestige and achievement and it is also a testimony for the quality of a company's products.

In this perspective the managers identify the critical internal processes in which the organisation must excel. This will enable the unit to achieve the following:

- Deliver the value propositions that will attract the retain customers in targeted market segments.
- Satisfy shareholder expectations of excellent financial returns.

The BSC usually identifies entirely new processes at which the organisation must excel to meet customer and financial objectives. It also incorporates innovation process, this is a departure from the traditional approach. The innovation process is a powerful driver of future financial performance. It also helps the organisation to identify the infrastructure that they must build to create long-term growth and improvement.

Once market share is achieved it becomes important for the companies to start working on retaining the existing customers. Many companies will also want to measure customer loyalty by the percentage growth of business with existing customers.

Companies while seeking growth need to increase their customer base in the targeted segments. The customer acquisition measure tracks the rate at which a business unit attracts new customers.

Meeting customers' needs drives customer retention and customer acquisitions. The importance of customer satisfaction need not be emphasised in today's world.

Even if a company succeeds in the all above measures, there is no guarantee that the company has profitable customers. One way of having satisfied customers is to sell your products at very low prices. But companies need not only satisfied customers but they need profitable customers. Not all customer demands can be satisfied in a way that is also profitable to the company.

4. Financial Perspective

These measures indicate whether a company's strategy, implementation and execution are contributing to the bottom-line improvement. The financial objectives that are normally measured can be growth in sales, increase in profit margins, return on investment and earning per share. One more important measure that is being used widely now, is Economic Value Addition.

While measuring financial performance following things need to be considered.

- **Sales Growth Rate by Percentage:** An increase in sales as stated earlier means greater cash flow and profits. It also reflects the acceptability of a company's products and their popularity.

- **Percentage Revenue form New Products, Services and Customers:** When new products are launched they are many times expected to replace the cash flows that the company will lose in future due to the withdrawal if older products that may have become outdated. Therefore a company needs to introduce newer products periodically. This is exactly what the BCG Matrix talks about.

- **Share of Targeted Customers and Accounts:** A company naturally concentrates on certain prospective targeted customers, because it believes their potential. This share has to be increasing at all times.

- **Cross-selling:** Cross selling is selling more products to the existing customers. For example if one buys a TV set of Samsung and if the customer is satisfied with the product, then there is an opportunity to sale more Samsung products to such a customer. A satisfied customer is likely to buy more products from a company with whom he has a good experience. Maruti Suzuki has used this very successfully in India

- **Percentage of Unprofitable Customers:** As discussed above the percentage of non-profitable customers has to be brought down year on year as far as possible. This has to be done as a well thought out strategy.

- **Revenue/Employees Ratio:** Revenue per employee and Profit per employee are tools to measure the efficiency of employees and are very useful especially in service organisation. It also tells the company whether it is over or under staffed in various areas.

- **Cost Reduction Rates and Research and Development:** Cost reduction has to be a committed strategy that is in the force at all times. Targets for reducing costs must be set and closely monitored. However it is easier said than done. Cost reduction requires total commitment to research and development and total commitment of employees and top management. Only innovative companies can achieve this on a regular basis.

- **Working Capital Ratio:** This ratio will tell the efficiency of working capital utilisation. Higher the ratio better it would be. However the requirement of working capital will change from business to business and there cannot be common yardstick for this. Suffice to say a close monitoring will help all companies to improve this ratio.
- **Asset Utilisation Ratio:** Companies need to invest large sums of money in fixed assets. These assets have to be utilised to the maximum. Idle assets mean no cash flow and profits.
- **Return on Capital Employed or Return on Investment:** This is a very important aspect of business for the investors who invest money in the capital of a company. Investors are happy only when ROI keeps increasing. But this can happen if assets are properly used, market share is increased consistently, and the company is innovative and is able to reduce costs regularly. It will also depend upon how efficiently the management uses the capital at its disposal productively.
- **Payback of Investments:** Shorter the payback period better it will be for the company.
- **Economic Value Added (EVA):** We have already discussed this measure in a earlier chapter and its superiority over ROI.

Let us now briefly discuss how to link the balance score card to the strategy of the organisation:

The objective of any performance measurement system is to motivate all managers and employees to implement successfully the strategy of the organisation. For this to happen it is necessary that objectives and targets be communicated.

The importance of communication of the strategy while building a BSC is:
- The scorecard describes the organisation's vision for the future to the entire organisation. This helps create shared understanding.
- This allows all employees to contribute to the success of the entire organisation. This is important because otherwise employees and departments will try to optimise their performance without contributing to the achievement of strategic objectives.
- The scorecard helps in changing the level of efforts in favour of the organisational goals.

Cause and Effect Relationship

A strategy is the set of hypotheses about cause and effect. This relationship is expressed by a sequence of if-then statements. A BSC tells the story of the business unit's strategy through the sequence of the cause result relationship.

Every measure selected for a balanced scorecard should be an element of a chain of cause-and effect relationships that communicates the meaning of the business unit's strategy to the organisation.

1.7.1.5 Cause and Effect Relationship in BSC

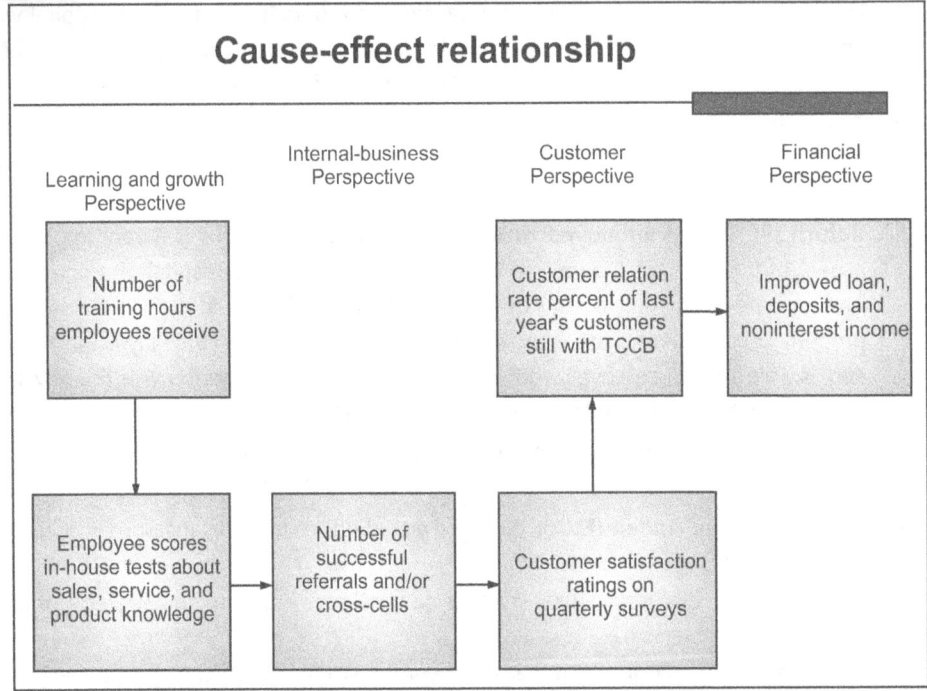

Fig. 1.12: Cause and Effect Relationship in BSC

Reminder: What a Score Card must do

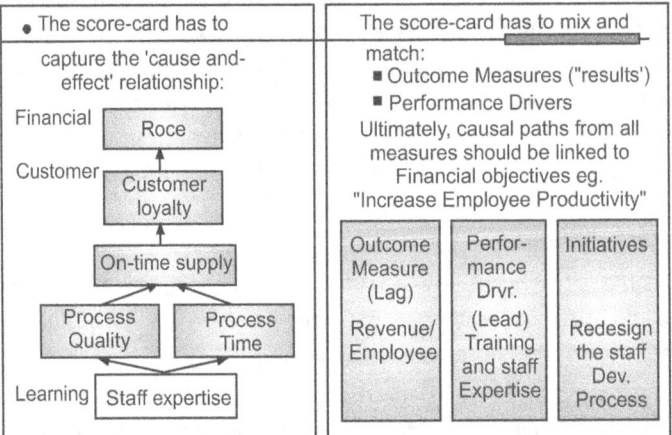

Fig. 1.13: Reminder: What a Scorecard Must Do

Outcome and Performance Drivers

All balanced Scorecards use certain generic measures. They are the core outcome measures and include things like, market share, profitability, customer satisfaction and retention and employee skills.

On the other hand there are performance drivers or the lead indicators that are unique to a particular business. They therefore reflect the uniqueness of the business unit's strategy.

A good balanced scorecard needs to have a mix of outcome measures and performance drivers that are customised to the business unit's strategy. Outcome measures without the performance drivers do not communicate how the outcomes are to be achieved.

1.7.1.6 Review of BSC

Once the balance score card is built and implemented the top management must consistently review it. The review should look for the following:

- How do the outcome measures say the organisation is doing?
- How do the driver measures say the organisation is doing?
- How has the organisation's strategy changed since the last review?
- How have the scorecard measures changed?

This review is likely to reveal some of the following things:

- Whether the strategy is being implemented correctly and how successfully the strategy is working?
- Is the management serious about the importance of these measures?
- Are the measures aligned to the ever-changing strategies?

There are some pitfalls that are identified in the creation and the implementation of the balanced scorecard. Let us now take a look at these pitfalls.

- **Poor Co-relation between Non-financial Measures and Results:** This means that if an organisation achieves targets that are non-financial in nature, there is no guarantee that this will lead to increased profitability.
- **Fixation on Financial Results:** The board of Directors and shareholders are primarily concerned about the financial performance of the companies. The senior level executives are also well versed in this performance measurement. All this can result in more emphasis being given to only one perspective of the scorecard. This needs to be avoided.
- **No Mechanism for Improvement:** Achieving what are known as stretch goals, requires a mechanism for improvement. Achieving such goals may require complete shift in the way the business is being presently done. Many companies may lack the mechanism for putting this in practice. This may also require a change in the culture of the company. These changes do not respond automatically to a new stretch target.
- **Measures are not Updated:** Companies lack the mechanism of updating the measures with the changes and shifts in the strategy. It is found that measures often build up inertia when people get comfortable with them.

- **Measurement Overload:** The measurements required must be limited in number, so that the manager can monitor them.
- **Difficulty in Making Trade-offs:** Some companies combine financial and non-financial measures in one single report by giving weightage to the individual measures. This can make the trade-off between the two measures very difficult.

1.7.1.7 Balanced Scorecard and Knowledge Management

In recent years there has been a renewed interest in "human resources" and "collaboration" under the term "knowledge management". In another white paper, the meaning of knowledge management is explored in more detail. Here, the focus is on the relationship between the balanced scorecard and knowledge management.

In their book The Balanced Scorecard, Kaplan and Norton set forth a hypothesis about the chain of cause and effect that leads to strategic success. This cause-and-effect hypothesis is fundamental to understanding the metrics that the balanced scorecard prescribes. There are four stages to this chain of cause and effect, outlined as follows:

1. The foundation or fundamental cause for strategic success has to do with people. Decades ago Peter Drucker recognised that innovation from creative people provides the only assured source of long-term success and competitiveness, because every other aspect of an organisation can be duplicated by others. The right people must be hired, properly trained and mentored, and the learning process should become continuous and endless. Peter Senge, in his very influential book The Learning Organisation, described a healthy organisation as one in which a learning culture prevails, fostered both by formal and informal learning and by abundant internal communication in all media.

2. In learning and growing organisation, where the culture encourages people to make suggestions and question the status quo, a steady flow of new ideas arises from the rank-and-file employees. These ideas are vital to the future of the organisation, because they come from the experts -- the people who are involved with the business processes on a daily basis. This insight about employees traces back to Deming, who saw the vital need for managers and shop-floor supervisors to listen to workers' complaints and empower them to make suggestions and improvements. Conversely, an organisation that stifles or ignores new ideas from its employees is probably doomed. The balanced scorecard, using efforts such as employee surveys and analysis of training data, is able to measure the degree of learning and growth, allowing leaders to assess the potential for long-term success.

3. Improved business processes lead to improved products and services. For example, if an improved process saves time, this results directly in a shorter delivery time to the customer, something that any customer will appreciate. In the government context,

cost reduction is also always of importance to the customer, because the customer is the sponsor of the whole organisation's budget – direct and overhead. The balanced scorecard measures customer satisfaction, but improving processes produces it.

4. Finally, improved customer satisfaction leads to loyal customers and increased market share, which directly affect the bottom line – whether that line equals profit, ROI (return on investment) or ROCE (return on capital employed) in the private sector, or NOR (net operating result) or IOH (overhead) in the public sector.

Note that the four steps in the causal chain are also the four perspectives of the balanced scorecard in its original formulation. This shows the basic reason why the perspectives (and their underlying metrics) are defined as they are. Any modifications to the metrics should take into account the hypothesis that is being proposed as the cause of long-term strategic success.

This causal chain is illustrated in the figure below.

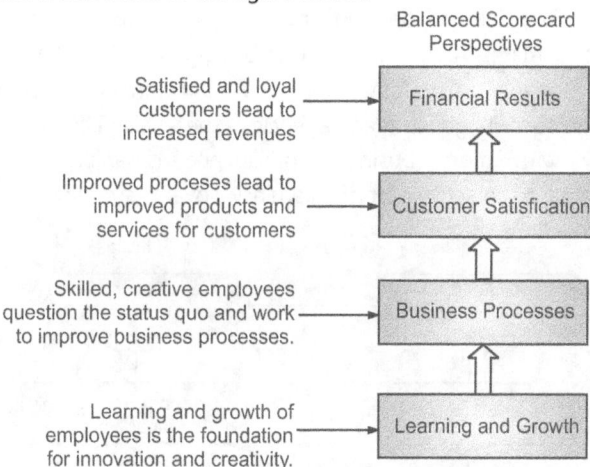

Fig. 1.14: Cause and Effect Hypothesis

Corresponding to the steps in the causal chain are four general areas of strategic management activities, as follows:

1. Learning and growth is fostered by knowledge management activities and initiatives. These include strategic recruiting, hiring, training (both formal and informal), team development, document management, collaborative communication systems, knowledge and skills audits of employees, knowledge base developments, and fostering of communities of interest within the organisation.

2. Business process improvements may range from moderate and localised changes to wide-scale changes in business processes, the elimination of paperwork and steps in

processes, and the introduction of automation and improved technology. Deployment of the balanced scorecard measurement system itself is one of these processes.

3. Customer loyalty cannot any longer be taken for granted within the government, nor is it sufficient to manage it in an ad hoc or anecdotal way. Rather, customer relationships are becoming increasingly structured and measured. Not only must the agency work closely with customers on a personal level, it must also gain documented and continuous feedback on customer perceptions and loyalty. These efforts come under the general heading of customer relationship management (CRM).

4. Financial management - in the passive sense of "bean counting" -is giving way to proactive initiatives in Activity-Based Costing (ABC), Functional Economic Analysis (FEA), Earned-Value Management (EVM) and other practices by which managers can learn more from financial data, in order to track projects more closely and make better cost estimates. Also, innovations in budgeting -- including the GPRA's goal of linking performance to budgets -- are replacing Zero-Based Budgeting and other earlier techniques in government agencies. The availability of improved database technology with more business intelligence capability is turning financial management into an active part of an agency's overall strategy for success.

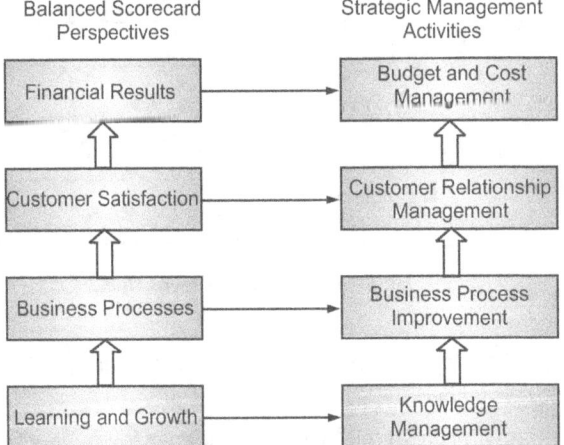

Fig. 1.15: Linkage between Causes and Strategic Activities

In conclusion, management experts agree that learning and growth are the key to strategic success, the foundation for the future. A learning and growing organisation is one in which knowledge management activities are deployed and expanding in order to leverage the creativity of all the people in the organisation.

1.7.2 Malcolm Baldrige Framework

As we are all aware, in today's competitive corporate world, every organisation has to be always on it toes, or it would have to be flat on its face. Today's world is a rather cruel manifestation of the dictum –"Perform or Perish", "Execute or Be Executed" and "Deliver or Be Delivered". Further, the competition is not only local but global and no country or corporate could afford to rest on its laurels.

Post-World War II, the U.S.A. emerged as the military, economic, political and technological Super Power. Its currency - THE US DOLLAR - effectively replaced the Gold Standard and, till 1971, one ounce equal to U.S. $ 35, was the global parity. However, 1960s onwards, Europe, West Germany in particular, and Japan, slowly started moving up and by 1980s the US Supremacy was being challenged. The Japanese, in particular, rose from ashes like the proverbial Phoenix and emerged as a major trade and economic competitor globally. Indeed, the Japanese Business organisations challenged the U.S. corporations, not only across the globe, but in the U.S.A. itself and started capturing markets aggressively - be it automobiles, electronics or entertainment.

The Japanese corporations used a very simple strategy of the Total Quality Management to gain, retain and sustain competitive advantage over others as regards cost, price, quality, technology and innovation. The U.S. corporations were not much of a match in these areas.

In the early and mid-1980s, therefore, many U.S. Industry and Government leaders realised that a renewed emphasis on quality and performance was an absolute necessity for doing business in the ever-expanding and ruthlessly and relentlessly competitive global market place.

However, quite a few U.S. business organisations either did not really believe quality mattered for them or did not know where to begin! (This, notwithstanding the fact that Dr. Dening, who is credited to have taught quality to the Japanese was an American!).

It was in this background and with this perspective that the Baldridge Award was envisioned as a standard of excellence that would help the U.S. Business organisations achieve world-class competitive quality and emerge winners.

In 1987, President Ronald Reagan established a bipartisan programme to develop world class management criteria that would help revitalise U.S. Economy and the U.S. Industry. The programme is one that overseas U.S.A's only Presidential Award for Performance Excellence. The Quality Focussed Programme was developed through the actions of the National Productivity Advisory Committee, which facilitated the Malcolm Baldrige Quality Improvement Act of 1987, signed into law on 20th August, 1987.

The National Institute of Standard and Technology (NIST) developed an award implementation framework in the same year.

The Malcolm Baldrige National Quality Award (MBNQA) is awarded for recognising American Business for excellence in applying the principles of Total Quality Management as embodied in the Baldrige criteria for Performance Excellence.

The Award is given in memory and honour of Late Howard Malcolm 'Mac' Baldrige (2nd October, 1922 - 25th July, 1987) who was the U.S. Secretary of Commerce from 10th January, 1981 to 25th July, 1987). Baldrige was a STRONG proponent of Quality Management as a key to U.S.A. and long term growth.

The Baldrige Award now covers the following sectors:

- Education
- Health Care
- Manufacturing
- Service
- Small Business

The Baldrige Award is awarded on the basis of certain criteria. The criteria are basically:

- A set of expectations or requirements.
- A structured approach to Performance Improvement.
- A Framework for a systems view of Performance Management.

The Baldrige Criteria Framework, from the systems perspective, could be presented as follows:

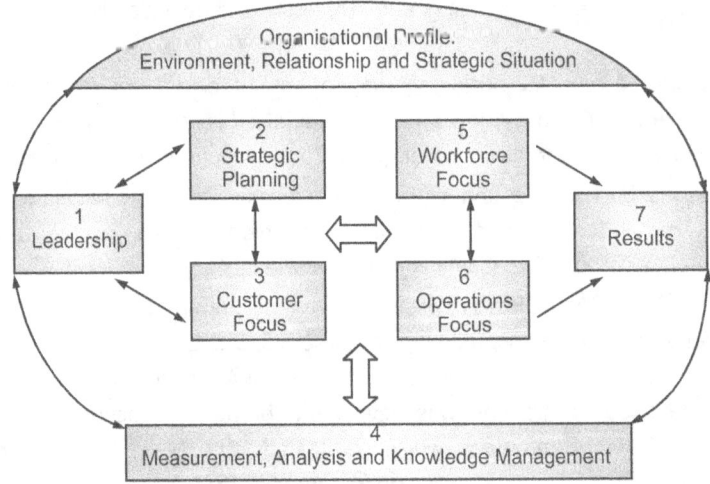

Fig. 1.16: Baldrige Criteria Framework: A System Perspective

The basic goals of the criteria are:
- To help organisations enhance their performance by focusing on processes and results.
- To deliver ever-improving value to customer and stakeholders, contributing to organisational sustainability.
- To improve overall organisational effectiveness and capabilities.
- To ensure/promote organisational and personal learning.

1.7.2.1 Baldrige Criteria: Key Characteristics

Before we discuss the criteria of the Baldrige Framework in detail, let us note the Key Characteristics of the criteria which can be summarized as follows:
1. There is a distinct focus on Results/Performance.
2. They are non-prescriptive and adaptable.
3. They support a Systems Perspective.
4. They support goal-based diagnosis.

The Baldrige Criteria

The Baldrige Criteria includes the following categories/items:
1. Leadership
2. Strategic Planning
3. Customer Focus
4. Measurement, Analysis and Knowledge Management
5. Workforce Focus
6. Operations Focus
7. Results

Let us now note the key excellence indicator of each of these criteria.

Leadership

Senior leaders
- Communicate and demonstrate clear direction and values.
- Inspire the highest standards of legal and ethical behaviour.
- Model and encourage learning, innovation, excellence and a focus on the future.
- Drive strategies for performance excellence and sustainability.
- The Governance body is informed, transparent and accountable and takes responsibility for ethics, actions and performance.
- The organisation surpasses legal and regulatory compliances, stresses ethical behaviour and strengthens environmental, social and economic systems.

Strategic Planning

Strategic Planning and Strategic Development should:

- Aim at sustained leadership.
- Balance short and long-term factors.
- Anticipate future environment.
- Incorporate innovation, stakeholders' needs, challenges and advantages.
- Align work systems and learning with strategic directions.
- Develop aligned, consistent action plans.
- Deploy action plans to the workforce, key suppliers and partners.
- Track the accomplishment of action plans.
- Use performance projections and comparisons.

Customer Focus

Customer focus should:

- Proactively capture the voice of the customer.
- Gather information on customer decision and marketplace potential.
- Listen to current, former and potential customer.
- Collect actionable information on engagement, satisfaction and dissatisfaction.
- Innovate product offerings and services to not only meet, but exceed, expectations.
- Further define and innovate support and communication.
- Build confidence, trust and loyalty.
- Resolve complaints promptly and eliminate the (root) causes.

Measurement, Analysis and Knowledge Management

Measurement, Analysis and Knowledge Management should:

- Create a balanced composite of measures in sync with needs, goals and strategy.
- Collect and use data to determine trends, projections and cause and effect.
- Use performance analysis in decision-making and for bringing about improvement and innovation.
- Maintain and safeguard information systems.
- Share and transfer critical knowledge.
- Provide/make available the requisite knowledge required/needed for work, improvement and innovation.
- Leverage knowledge for workforce, customers, suppliers, collaborators and partners.
- Capture and share knowledge to provide further impetus to innovation.

Workforce Focus

The Workforce Focus should:

- Optimise capability and capacity.
- Organise and manage the workforce to serve customers and achieve strategy.
- Design proactive processes and policies to ensure safety and security.
- Offer practices and policies tailored to workforce the needs of the workforce.
- Engage the workforce through meaningful work, clear direction and accountability.
- Ensure a trusting, effective and co-operative work environment.
- Support, recognise and reward high performance.
- Optimise workforce.
- Develop leadership/leaders.

Operations Focus

The Operations Focus should:

- Design and innovate work systems to capitalise on core competencies.
- Design agile work systems.
- Optimise work systems to deliver value to/for customers.
- Establish a comprehensive emergency preparedness system/programme, in a proactive manner.
- Design and innovate work processes to meet requirements.
- Design work processes for agility, excellence, efficiency and effectiveness.
- Manage, measure and improve work processes.
- Manage the supply chain to improve suppliers' and partners' performance.

Results

The 'Results' criteria should ensure that:

- Performance levels are excellent in areas which are important in accomplishing the organisational mission.
- Reflect offerings with superior value as viewed by the customers and the market place.
- Reflect superior performance as regards operational, workforce, legal, ethical, societal and financial indicators.
- Serve as measures of progress for evaluating and improving performance in alignment with strategy.

1.7.2.2 Performance Evaluation

The performance of an organisation, using the Baldrige Framework/Criteria, is assessed as per the points/values assigned to the seven criteria, as illustrated hereafter:

Categories and Items			Points	Values
1.	Leadership			120
	1.1	Senior Leadership	70	
	1.2	Governance and Societal Responsibilities	50	
2.	Strategic Planning			85
	2.1	Strategic Development	45	
	2.2	Strategy Implementation	40	
3.	Customer Focus			85
	3.1	Voice of the Customer	40	
	3.2	Customer Engagement	45	
4.	Measurement, Analysis, and Knowledge Management			90
	4.1	Measurement, Analysis and Improvement of Organisational Performance	45	
	4.2	Knowledge Management, Information and Information Technology	45	
5.	Workforce Focus			85
	5.1	Workforce Environment	40	
	5.2	Workforce Engagement	45	
6.	Operations Focus			85
	6.1	Work Processes	45	
	6.2	Operational Effectiveness	40	
7.	Results			450
	7.1	Product and Process Results	120	
	7.2	Customer-Focused Results	85	
	7.3	Workforce-Focused Results	85	
	7.4	Leadership and Governance Results	80	
	7.5	Financial and Market Results	80	
Total				**1,000**

1.7.2.3 The Performance Management and Managerial Contribution of the Baldrige Award Criteria

The Performance Management and Managerial Contribution of the Baldrige Award criteria could be summarised as follows:

1. Aims at an integrated, holistic and systems approach in viewing an organisation's performance management system across seven categories.
2. Lays emphasis on feedback and a fact-based, knowledge-driven system for improving performance and competitiveness.
3. Help organisations assess their improvement/innovation efforts by facilitating personal and organisational learning.
4. Diagnose the overall organisational performance management system and identify strengths and opportunities for further improvements.
5. Provide role model by coming out with world class product and service outcome.
6. Improve organisational performance practices, effectiveness, capabilities and results.
7. Facilitate communication and sharing of information as regards best practices and thereby help raise the bar of performance standards.
8. Serve as an instrument for understanding and managing performance and for guiding strategic planning / management and exploring learning opportunities.
9. Help organisations in delivering ever-improving value to customers and other stakeholders, thereby contributing to organisational sustainability.
10. Help in improving customer and workforce satisfaction, engagement and loyalty.
11. Improved revenues and market share and the resultant improved financial and competitive performance.

Before we conclude, let us remember what Ken Shille, 2010 Baldrige Award Winner, had said: "Baldrige criteria are the key to winning results and world class excellence".

1.7.2.4 Baldrige in India

In India, the Tata Group of Industries took keen interest in the Baldrige Criteria and Framework and made pioneering efforts in introducing the Baldrige Criteria and Framework within the Tata Group Companies to make them competitive, both locally and globally.

The Tata Group of Industries have modified and internalised the Baldrige Criteria and is known as the "Tata Business Excellence Model (TBEM)".

1.8 Measuring SBU Level Performance

As we are aware, management is broadly defined as "a process of planning, organising, leading/directing and controlling the resources of an organisation in the efficient and effective manner for attaining the specified, pre-determined goals".

While the 'Planning' function would come out with strategy - "what an organisation is today, and what it ought to be tomorrow" - spelling out goals and objectives, these goals and objectives need to be achieved and converted into reality. One of the important factors impacting the achievement is the structure of the organisation. The organisational structure, in a way, acts as a vehicle in achieving the strategic goals and objectives efficiently and effectively.

Organising, therefore, is an important managerial function. While 'Planning' comes out with 'what to do', 'organising' specifies 'how to do it'.

'Organising' can be said to be the process of identifying and clubbing together, the tasks to be carried out, defining and deciding responsibility, authority and accountability and establishing the reporting and reviewing relationship structure to enable people to work together to accomplish the pre-determined goal, effectively, effectively and with synergy.

The organisational structures have evolved over the years. The major types of organisational structures could be stated as follows:

1. Hierarchy-based structure.
2. Functional structure.
3. Divisional structure.
4. Product-based structure.
5. Territorial/Geographical structure.
6. Customer Support-based structure.
7. Hybrid structure.
8. Matrix structure.

During the 1970s and 1980s, the Divisional Structures started evolving into SBUs to better reflect the product-market considerations. The SBU, hence, is considered to be a modification of the divisional structure. The idea was to decentralise on the basis of strategic elements and not on the basis of size, product characteristics or span of control. It also helped create horizontal linkages among units kept separate earlier.

SBUs enable Corporate Head Quarters to co-ordinate the activities of its SBUs (operating divisions) through performance - as well as result-oriented control and reporting systems and by laying emphasis on corporate planning techniques.

SBUs, which are separate business set-up as units within a large company, are more recent form of organisational structure adopted by several corporates. The SBUs are tightly controlled but are held responsible for their own performance and results. It is, however, imperative that for the SBUs to be effective, the Corporate has to have a decentralised decision-process.

1.8.1 Definition of Strategic Business Unit (SBU)

Having discussed the evolution of SBU as an organisational structure, let us now take a look at the SBU definitions.

1. "The SBU is a distinct business entity, which can be managed independently with respect to other business within an organisation".
2. The SBUs are divisions or groups of divisions composed of independent product-market-segments that are given primary responsibility and authority for the management of their own functional areas".
3. "The SBU is a subsidiary, division or unit of an organisation that markets a set of related offerings to a clearly defined group of customers".
4. "SBU is an autonomous division or organisation unit, small enough to be flexible and large enough to exercise control over most of the factors affecting long-term performance".
5. "An SBU is a profit centre which focuses on product offering and market situations".
6. "A SBU is a part of an organisation for which there is a distinct external market for goods or services that is different from another SBU".

1.8.2 Characteristics/Attributes of Strategic Business Unit (SBU)

Keeping in view the various definitions of SBUs, discussed earlier, let us now summarise their attributes/characteristics.

1. The SBUs are the natural 'grouping' of part of an corporation.
2. The SBU has a range of related products/services which has similar technologies and production process.
3. The SBUs typically have a discrete marketing plan, analysis of competition and marketing campaign, though they may be part of a larger business entity.
4. The SBUs allow the corporates to respond quickly to changing economic or market situations, as they enjoy reasonable autonomy.
5. The SBU should have a clearly drawn distinct strategy/vision/mission of its own which is unique and different from other SBUs.
6. It should have its own set of a specific, well-distinct, identifiable set of competitors and be a basic competitive unit of the company.
7. It should have an external market focus and a specific target market.
8. Each SBU in a particular organisation should be able to operate independently of any other SBU and should have control of its own business functions.
9. It should be neither too small or too large, but have an appropriate size and scale so as to manage its resources optimally.
10. The SBU should be managed largely as an independent unit.
11. The SBU should possess distinct differential advantage.

1.8.3 Linkages of SBU with Enterprise Performance Management

From the viewpoint of strategic management, the corporations are collections of different "product-market-consumer-resource packages". These "packages" are also referred to as the SBUs.

The SBU level is the level in a corporation where managers set a more specific strategic direction for their business to exploit value creating opportunities, capture markets and acquire customers. The SBUs have autonomy and are managed as separate business entity within the larger context of the parent body corporate. SBUs are, therefore expected to deliver results and perform as they can impact/affect most factors which influence their performance and profitability.

Performance, as discussed earlier, is the end-result of activity undertaken by an entity. As resources are deployed for the SBU, it is expected to execute, deliver and perform.

Hence, the performance of the SBU need to be monitored and assessed.

The measures to assess the performance, however, would need to be selected based on the objectives set out to be achieved.

The objectives set out earlier in the strategy formulation part of the strategic management process could be used to measure performance of the SBU, once the strategic are implemented.

Companies use a variety of techniques to measure, evaluate and control performance in divisions, SBUs and functional areas. Most of the corporations, comprising of SBUs on divisions, would use (many of) the same parameters/performance measures that they would use to assess overall corporate performance.

Performance has to be measured as "what cannot be measured, needs to be controlled". The SBU performance, therefore, needs to be measured to enable the management to:

(a) Monitor and control business operations.
(b) Drive improvement of process efficiency.
(c) Maximise the effectiveness of the improvement effort.
(d) Achieve organisational goals and objectives.

The SBU performance measures, like the corporate performance measures, would address:

- Financial performance measures.
- Non-financial performance measures.

Let us note some of these measures: These measures have been specifically added to as there cannot be Performance Management without Performance Measures.

1.8.4 Various Performance Measures

(A) Financial Performance Measures
- Return on Investment (RoI)
- Earnings Per Share (EPS)/Stock Price
- Return on Equity (RoE)/Market Capital
- Free Cash Flow
- Return on Assets (RoA)
- Return on Capital Employed (ROCE)
- Liquidity and Profitability Ratios

(B) Non-financial Performance Measures

The non-financial performance measures could be divided into the following categories:
1. Customers
2. Product
3. Service
4. Marketing
5. Production and Operations/Maintenance
6. Human Resources
7. Public/Society/Environment
8. Shareholder value.

(C) Customer-Related Performance Measures
- Customer - Sales Revenue and Volume.
- Customer satisfaction.
- Customer growth and retention.
- New customer.
- Customer loyalty/Repeat customer.

(D) Product Related Performance Measures
- Product Life Cycle.
- New Product Development.
- Product Features - Innovations.
- Product Quality.

(E) Service Related Performance Measures
- Service quality.
- Response time.

(F) Marketing Related Performance Measures
- Total market and market share.
- Market growth rate - Incremental and absolute
- Competitive position in terms of brand equity, brand image, brand recall, differentiation.
- Innovative marketing initiatives.

(G) Production/Operations/Maintenance Performance Measures
- Capacity utilisation.
- Product quality (rejection/rework).
- Down time/Up time/Idle time.
- Product innovation.
- Quality system/Standard adherence.
- Lead time.
- Inventory turnover.
- Cycle time.

(H) Human Resources Performance Measures
- Employee satisfaction/Engagement.
- Attrition.
- Retention/Turnover.
- Preferred employer.
- Productivity.
- Grievance handling incidents.
- Worker safety.
- Training Core Competency.
- Number of suggestions.
- Employee compensation (benefits).
- Employee morale.

(I) Public/Society/Environment Performance Measures
- Employment creation.
- Reduced pollution.
- Support to community services.
- Corporate social responsibility.
- Contribution by way of taxes paid.
- Regulatory compliances.

(J) Shareholder Value Performance Measures:
- Economic Value Added (EVA).
- Market Value Added (MVA).

1.9 Transfer Pricing

1.9.1 Meaning

Transfer price is the price one sub-unit charges for a product or service supplied to another subunit of the same organisation. Intermediate products are the products transferred between subunits of an organisation. Transfer pricing should help achieve a company's Strategies and Goals. They must fit the organisation's structure. It must promote Goal Congruence. It should help promote a sustained high level of management effort.

In a decentralised organisation there are various profit centres. This profit centres many times have to deal with each other. One of the most difficult things in such organisations is the setting up transfer prices among the profit centres. Unless this is established the profitability of the profit centres cannot be calculated.

It is quite possible that in a company two or more profit centres are jointly responsible for product development, manufacturing and marketing in such a case each one of them has to get a share in the profit generated when the product is sold. The Transfer Price is the mechanism for distributing these profits among all the centres involved. Transfer price is not only an accounting tool, but it can be used as a behavioural tool, that will help motivate the manager to make right decisions.

The transfer price system has to be simple to understand and should be easy to administer. The managers should not evolve a complicated transfer pricing mechanism, which will require a lot of time to implement and operate.

Designing a good transfer pricing system is a big challenge that is faced by most organisations.

Transfer price is defined in two ways. It is defined as the amount used in accounting for any transfer of goods and services between responsibility centres. Anthony and Govindrajan use a narrower definition. They limit the term transfer price to the value placed on a transfer of goods or services in transactions in which at least one of the two parties involved is a profit centre. Transfer price should include an element of profit, the logic being that no company will transfer goods or services to another company at cost. The independent profit centres are therefore required to make a profit even while transferring the goods or services to another business unit of their own company. This is so because they have to generate a return on investments made by them and that return has to be greater than the cost of such investment.

The fundamental principle of transfer pricing mechanism is that the transfer price should be similar or equal to the price that would be charged if the product were sold to outside customers or purchased from outside vendors. This principle is not very easy to apply in the actual practice. Some people believe that there should be no element of profit in the transfer price, and the transfer price should be set on marginal costs. However in the corporate world transfer price includes an element of profit. Unless the transfer price includes profit it will be impossible to find out the profitability of a profit centre.

1.9.2 Objectives of Transfer Pricing

1. It should provide each segment with the relevant information required to determine the optimum trade-off between company costs and revenues. This means that the manager must know what cost he would incur if he were to make the product or at what price could he source it from outside vendors.

2. It should induce goal congruent decisions that mean that the system should be so designed that decisions that improve business unit profits will also improve company profits. What it means is that a transfer price decision would be correct only if it helps increase the overall profitability of the company and not only that of the profit centre. This is one of the most important factors that need to be considered. At times it may be necessary to sacrifice the profitability of a profit centre if that is going to increase the profit of the organisation. Organisational interest has been protected at all times.

3. It should help measure the economic performance of the individual profit centres. The cost of a product actually depends on the efficiency with which it is produced. Thus wastages need to be avoided and efficiencies have to be improved to achieve good economic performance. Cost would also depend on the technology used.

1.9.3 Transfer Pricing Decisions

When profit centres of a company buy and sell from and to each other, they are required to make two decisions with regard to the product made by one and sold to the other unit.

1. The first decision is known as the Sourcing Decision. The decision is also known as Make or Buy decision. The company has to decide if it should produce the product by itself or buy it from outside. This decision will depend on the cost comparison of the two options.

2. The second decision is the transfer pricing decision. The decision to be made is if the product is to be produced inside then at what price should it be transferred between the profit centres? This is the most crucial and difficult decision. This will also involve the decision regarding the method of transfer pricing that should be adopted. A company will naturally wish to have a uniform method of transfer pricing for all its profit centres.

Enterprise Performance Management

Performance Management

1.9.4 Transfer Pricing and Goal Congruence

Transfer prices should help achieve a company' strategies and goals and fit its organisation structure. In particular, they should promote goal congruence and a sustained high level of management effort. Subunits selling a product or service should be motivated to hold down their costs; subunits buying the product or service should be motivated to acquire and use inputs efficiently.

The ideal situation that should necessarily exist in a company for the transfer price to be goal congruent are:

1. The first is that the people who are going to make the transfer pricing decisions should be competent, in the sense that they must understand the short-term and long-term performance of the responsibility centre. They also have to be good in the art of negotiation. All these decisions must be in the long term interests of an organisation.

2. The managers must understand their responsibility towards profitability as an important goal and the means of measurement of their performance. They should perceive transfer price as just. The manager therefore has to think about larger perspective of the entire organisation; while making sure that his profit centre makes adequate profits.

1.9.5 Example of Transfer Price

Let us see this with an example:

Division A of a company sells 1,00,000 units of a product to Division B annually. Division A has no outside market. The selling price (transfer price) is ₹ 10000 per unit.

Divisions A's costs are: Variable cost ₹ 8000 per unit.

The Fixed Costs are ₹ 30,00,000 per year.

Division A now wants to increase the transfer price to ₹ 11,000 per unit.

Division B says if the price is increased then they will source the product from the outside market @ ₹ 10000 per unit.

If A does not sale to B then its facilities will lie idle as it has no market outside.

Now you have to decide:

(a) Should A be allowed to increase the price? What will be the impact of your decision on the company?

(b) Should B be allowed to procure from the market? What will be the impact on the company?

Discussion

As things stand today Division A is already making profit of 10,000 (SP) – (8000 (VC) + 30 (FC) = Profit per unit ₹ 1970. So its total profit for the year is 1790 × 1,00,000 = 17,90,00,000.

A has not given any reason to increase the price to ₹ 11,000, so it would seem that the Manager of Division A is only trying to increase his own profit. He is probably confident that the top management would force Division B to pay him this price.

Manager of B thinks that if he were to pay the new price his profit will decrease or to compensate he will have to increase the price of the final product in the market; therefore he wants to buy the product from outside. His other argument is that the transfer price should be equal to market price and since he can procure from the market at ₹ 10000, why should he pay ₹ 11,000 to division A? He also argues that if the price of his final product is increased; the company may lose its market share and they would be detrimental to the company.

The situation is thus leading to major conflict between the two managers as A seems to be firm on increasing the price.

Now if B does not buy from A, A's facilities will remain idle and the company will have to bear the fixed cost of the division. Thus the amount B will pay to outsider will be ₹ 10000 per unit plus ₹ 30 per unit which is the overhead of division A will have to be borne by the company. In this situation the profit made by A will go out of the company and company's profitability will suffer. This is not advisable.

If A is allowed to increase the price it is true that B's profitability will suffer and A's profits will increase. In companies where variable salaries are linked to profit performance Division B will suffer unnecessarily while A will be rewarded for no reason at all.

However if the price is increased as demanded by A, the overall profitability of the company will remain same. Company's profits are sum total of profits of all Profit Centers and as such it would not matter where the profit is booked.

As a matter of fact think what should be done if division B argues that A is making a lot of profit even with the present price. B therefore says that the transfer price should actually be cut by ₹ 1000 per unit and if this is done, B says it will be able to sale additional 10,000 units per annum. What should be done in this situation? Calculate the profit for both the divisions and the company and arrive at a decision.

1.9.6 Pre-requisites of Transfer Pricing

The ideal transfer price should be equal to the market price of the identical product that is being transferred between units. This market price should reflect the same conditions regarding the quality of the product, delivery time, etc. However in practice the transfer price would have to be scaled downwards due to the savings that will accrue from making the product inside the company. The transfer price does not have to be factored with sales promotion expenses, advertising expenses or risk premium for bad debts. All the three factors are not present when goods or services are transferred between profit centres of the same company. The transfer price will be bereft of excise duties and sales tax as well. If the products are bought from another unit of the same company under different name then the taxes may be applicable. As long as Reliance Industries and Reliance Petroleum were different companies, Reliance Industries for its purchases from Reliance Petroleum had to pay the taxes. However after the merger of these two companies, the tax liability ceased to exist. In any case in India excise duty on most products is covered under the CENTVAT and is therefore refundable. Also whenever VAT will be introduced, the problem of sales tax will get solved.

Market based transfer prices in a perfectly competitive market, a company can achieve the following:

- Goal Congruence
- Management effort
- Sub-unit performance evaluation
- Subunit autonomy

As regards freedom to source a profit centre manager should be free to sell his products outside the company, while the manager of the buying division should be free to buy from an outside source. This has to be so because the managers are responsible for the profit performance of the profit centre. If such a situation really exists, then the market would determine the transfer price. The transfer price quoted by the selling division will be compared against the quotes received from the outside suppliers. This will involve negotiations between the buying and selling division. If the selling division is unable to match or improve upon the price of the outside supplier, then the buying division manager will be free to source his requirements from the outside market. This can however be done only if the decision is in the overall interest of the company. It is pertinent to note that when a product is outsourced the profit element goes out of the company.

The market price is the opportunity cost to the seller, because if he could not sell it inside the company, he has a ready market outside. Market price works well when the selling unit is not dependent only on the inside buyer and when the buying division has the option to procure from the outside market. From the company's point of view the market price is relevant cost of the product, because that will be the amount of cash that will be foregone by selling inside.

The managers before deciding the transfer price must have full information available, on the possible alternatives and the costs thereof.

A smooth mechanism for negotiation between the buying and selling unit must exist for this method of transfer pricing to work effectively safeguarding the interests of both the units and the company as a whole.

Let us now take a look at the possible constraints that may exist in the way of the smooth functioning of this method of transfer pricing mechanism.

The first is whether the buying unit manager will have the real freedom in the field of Sourcing? This freedom in reality may either not be feasible or may be constrained by the corporate policy of the company.

One constraint that is possible is that selling or buying from outside may not be possible due to limited markets. If a company is normally sourcing internally, then outside capacity may not even exist. This will put limitations on outsourcing such components. Even if some capacity is available it may not be possible to source from there if the demand is not regular.

Secondly if the company is the sole producer of a differentiated product, no outside capacity may exist.

If a company has made investments in facilities to produce the components required, then it will not buy from outside, even if the capacity exists. However if the market price is close to the company's variable cost then the company can be interested, though this kind of a situation will be difficult to find.

The next point that needs to be looked at is how to find out the competitive prices especially when the company is neither selling nor buying from outside.

One way is that if published price list of the products is available then that can be used. The price will have to found out for bulk quantity, as many times the published price could be the price for a single unit. The price that a supplier will quote will depend on the quantity likely to be ordered, delivery period and payment terms, etc.

In case published prices are not available then they have to found out through the bidding process. This means that the company should float the inquiry for the product and ask the interested vendors to quote their prices. However serious bidding will take place only if the vendors are confident that the company will actually give them orders for the supply of these components.

If the units of the company are selling part of their production outside, or buying part of their requirements from outside then the market price will be known.

When the selling profit centre cannot utilise its full capacity, it affects the profitability of the company. In such a case it will make no sense if the buying unit is partially buying its requirements from the outside market. On the other hand if the buying profit centre is unable to buy from outside, while selling profit centre is selling part of its production to outside market, the company will not be able to optimise its profitability.

When intra-company buying or selling is small or temporary, then the matter will be left entirely to the buying and selling profit centres. In most companies there is a mechanism in the form of intervention from the top management in cases where there is a dispute between the buying and selling profit centre. For example if the selling profit centre has excess capacity and the buying profit centre still buys from outside, the selling profit centre will appeal to the higher management to intervene and force the buying profit centre to procure its requirements from them. In the same the buying profit centre can appeal if selling profit centre sells outside when buying centres requirements are not fully met. There can also be disputes related to the pricing.

1.9.7 Methods of Setting Transfer Prices

There are three methods for determining transfer prices:

1. Market-based Transfer Prices: Top management may choose to use the price of a similar product or service publicly listed in, say, a trade association Web site. Also, top management may select, for the internal price, the external price that a subunit charges to outside customers.

The market-price method sets the transfer price as the current price of the product in the external market. Its key advantage is objectivity; it best satisfies the arm's-length criterion desired for both management and tax purposes. A key disadvantage is that the market price, especially for intermediate products, is often not available.

Transferring products or services at market prices generally leads to optimal decisions when three conditions are satisfied:

(1) The market for the intermediate product is perfectly competitive,
(2) Interdependencies of subunits are minimal, and
(3) There are no additional costs or benefits to the company as a whole from buying or selling in the external market instead of transacting internally.

A perfectly competitive market exists when there is a homogeneous product with buying prices equal to selling prices and no individual buyers or sellers can affect those prices by their own actions.

By using market-base transfer prices in perfectly competitive markets, a company can achieve (1) goal congruence, (2) management effort, (3) subunit performance evaluation, and (4) subunit autonomy

In perfectly competitive markets, the minimum price the selling division is willing to accept from the buying division is the market price, because the selling division can always sell its output in the external market at that price. The maximum price the buying division is willing to pay to the selling division is the market price, because the buying division can always buy its input in the external market at that price.

2. Cost Based Transfer Price

These transfer prices are difficult and complex to set. But if market prices are not available then this method has to be used. In this type two crucial decisions have to be made (a) How to define costs? And (b) what should be the profit mark-up?

The usual basis used for setting these prices is Standard Costs. Standard costs are the total of Variable cost + Fixed costs attributable to the product.

The buying division will have to accept this cost. But the most crucial decision would be how much profit margin is to be added to this cost. There has to be some basis for doing this. Because of these complexities this method can become a little cumbersome.

Under both the systems market based and cost based pricing the companies eliminate advertising, financing and any other expenses that the selling division will not incur if the sale is within the company.

3. Negotiated Transfer Prices

In some cases, the subunits of a company are free to negotiate the transfer price between themselves and then to decide whether to buy and sell internally or deal with outside parties. Subunits may use information about costs and market prices in these negotiations, but there is no requirement that the chosen transfer price bear any specific relationship to either cost or market-price data.

Negotiated transfer prices are often employed when market prices are volatile and change occurs constantly. The negotiated transfer price is the outcome of a bargaining process between the selling and buying subunits.

The negotiated-price method involves a negotiation process and sometimes arbitration between units to determine the transfer price. This method is desirable when the units have a history of significant conflict and negotiation can result in an agreed-upon price. The primary limitation is that the method can reduce the desired autonomy of the units. Further, this method may be costly and time-consuming to implement.

1.9.8 Applicability of Transfer Pricing

Illustration 1

MNC Ltd. has two divisions X and Y, X sells one third of its output in the open market and transfers the rest to Div Y. Costs and revenue during the year are as follows:

	X	Y	Total
			₹
Sales	16,000	48,000	64,000
Cost of production			
In the division	24,000	20,000	44,000
Profit during the period			20,000

There is no opening or closing stocks. You are required to find out profit of each division and the profit of the company using transfer price:

(a) At cost

(b) At cost plus a margin of 25%

(c) At cost plus 25%, but there is over spending in Div X by ₹ 3000.
(d) At standard cost of ₹ 16000 plus 25% and state its advantage over (B).
(e) At market price.

Solution

Transfer Price At Cost

Particulars	X	Y	Total
Sales	32,000	48,000	80,000
Cost of Production	24,000	36,000	60,000
Profit	8,000	12,000	20,000

Transfer Price At Cost + 25%

Particulars	X	Y	Total
Sales	36,000	48,000	84,000
Cost of Production	24,000	40,000	64,000
Profit	12,000	8,000	20,000

Transfer Price At Cost + 25% and overspending of ₹ 3,000

Particulars	X	Y	Total
Sales	33,500	48,000	81,500
Cost of Production	21,000	37,500	58,500
Profit	12,500	10,500	23,000

Transfer Price At Standard Cost

Particulars	X	Y	Total
Sales	36,000	48,000	84,000
Cost of Production	24,000	40,000	64,000
Profit	12,000	8,000	20,000

Transfer Price Market Price

Particulars	X	Y	Total
Sales	48,000	48,000	96,000
Cost of Production	24,000	52,000	76,000
Profit	24,000	(-)4,000	20,000

Enterprise Performance Management — Performance Management

Illustration 2:

A company usually produces 10000 units of product "A" p.a. Present selling price of the product is ₹ 60 per unit. The cost per unit for the next year at current output level is:

	₹
Direct material	23
Direct labour	10
Variable overheads	11
Fixed overheads	10
Total	**54**

The management is not happy with the present profitability of 10% of sales. In a corporate meeting suggestions were invited to improve profitability.

Following three suggestions we made.

Proposal 1: Increase volume by 30% which will force the selling price to be reduced by 5%. It is ascertained that capacity is available to accommodate increased volume.

Proposal 2: Increase selling price by 10% as a result of which volume will reduce to 75% of the present volume.

Proposal 3: Spend ₹ 1,20,000 additionally on advertisement. These expenses can be amortized over 4 years. Such additional advertisement cost is likely to increase the volume by 25% without reducing the price.

Considering the management's view of profitability, which of the above 3 suggestions would you accept? Explain with detailed calculations of profitability. Are there any other considerations that the management should take into account other than their view of profitability? Discuss in detail.

Solution

Proposal I

Particulars	₹
Sales – 13,000 units @ ₹ 57 per unit	7,41,000
Less – Variable Cost per unit	5,72,000
Contribution	1,69,000
Less – Fixed Cost	1,00,000
Profit	69,000

Proposal II

Particulars	₹
Sales – 7,500 units @ ₹ 66 per unit	4,95,000
Less – Variable Cost per unit	3,30,000
Contribution	1,65,000
Less – Fixed Cost	1,00,000
Profit	65,000

Proposal III

Particulars	₹
Sales – 12,500 units @ ₹ 60 per unit	7,50,000
Less – Variable Cost per unit	5,50,000
Contribution	2,00,000
Less – Fixed Cost	1,30,000
Profit	70,000

Conclusion: Considering Management's intentions to increase the profitability, Proposal No. III should be accepted. However, in case of Proposal No. II, there will be the released production capacity. If the company can make the profitable use of this released production capacity, the calculations may be different.

Points to Remember

- Performance Management is a Business Process intended to ensure alignment of group and individual efforts for achievement of continuous business improvement.
- Enterprise Performance Management consists of "a set of management and analytic process, supported by technology, that enable business to define strategic goals and then measure and manage performance against these goals".
- Performance indicator is a measurable or tangible sign that something has been done or achieved.
- Strategy can be said to be "the long-term directions and scope of the organisation that aims at gaining a competitive advantage for the business organisation's resources and constraints, in order to generate customer delight and to meet and exceed stakeholder expectations".
- Phases of Strategic Management
  Phase 1: Basic Financial Planning
  Phase 2: Forecast-based Planning
  Phase 3: Externally-oriented Planning
  Phase 4: Strategic Management.
- The Strategic Management Model consists of four basic elements viz.:
  1. Environmental Scanning
  2. Strategy Formulation
  3. Strategy Implementation
  4. Evaluation and Control
- Strategic Control involves monitoring critical environmental factors to ensure that strategic plans are executed and implemented as perceived/conceived, assessing the impact of strategic plans and adjusting such plans whenever and wherever so required.
- Management control implies the measurement of accomplishments against the standards and the correction of deviations to assure attainment of objectives according to plans.

- Operational controls involve ascertaining and ensuring the implementation/execution of operational plans at the grass-root level.
- A responsibility centre is an organisation unit that is headed by a manager who is responsible for its activities. This is the way large companies are organised these days.
- The following given are the four types of responsibility centres. They are:
    1. Revenue centres
    2. Expense centres
    3. Profit centres and
    4. Investment centres.
- In a Revenue centre, outputs are measured in monetary terms, but no formal attempt is made to relate inputs to outputs because it is not possible to do so.
- Expense Centers are responsibility centres for which inputs or expenses are measured in monetary terms, but for which outputs are not measured in monetary terms.
- Profit centres are independent units within an organisation, whose performance is measured in terms of profit targets and the actual profits that are earned by them.
- A subunit is designated an investment centre if it has control not only over sales revenues and operating costs but also over the assets employed in producing profits.
- The balance score card offers to the companies a framework that can translate a company's vision and strategy into a coherent set of performance measure. A balanced scorecard attempts to translate mission and strategy into objectives and measures, organised into four different perspectives. These perspectives are:
    1. Financial
    2. Customer
    3. Internal business processes
    4. Learning and growth.
- The Baldrige Criteria includes the following categories/items:
    1. Leadership
    2. Strategic Planning
    3. Customer Focus
    4. Measurement, Analysis and Knowledge Management
    5. Workforce Focus
    6. Operations Focus
    7. Results
- Transfer price is defined as the amount used in accounting for any transfer of goods and services between responsibility centres.

Questions for Discussion

1. Explain the need and desirability of creating Responsibility Centres.
2. Discuss the working of Revenue Centres.
3. Explain the concept of engineered and discretionary Expense.
4. Why are Profit Centres so important?
5. Discuss the advantages and disadvantages of profit centres.
6. Discuss the concept of EVA and MVA.
7. How can an enterprise increase its EVA?
8. Compare EVA and ROI, and comment on which is one of these better performance evaluation tool.
9. Explain with the help of a diagram the concept of BSC.
10. Explain why financial performance alone should not be considered?
11. What is the relationship between the BSC and Grissinger's design of control system?
12. Explain Malcolm Baldrige Framework.
13. Explain the key characteristics of Baldrige Criteria.
14. Write note: Performance Evaluation using the Baldrige Framework.
15. Explain: Measuring SBU Level Performance.
16. State the various Performance Measures.
17. Discuss the essential pre- requisites for setting transfer prices.
18. What are the different types of methods for setting transfer prices?

Project Questions

1. Select a company like Tata Motors, TISCO or HUL and see how it has been structured on the lines of SBUs or Responsibility Centres.
2. Find out any one company that creates its own BSC.
3. Try and build a BSC for any one of the following industries
   (a) Airline,
   (b) Hotel,
   (c) Your college.
4. Visit a company that has many profit centres who deal with each other and find out how transfer prices are set in this company.

Chapter 2...

Capital Expenditure Control

Contents ...

- 2.1 Cost of Capital
  - 2.1.1 Concepts of Cost of Capital
  - 2.1.2 Importance of Cost of Capital
  - 2.1.3 Measurement of Cost of Capital
  - 2.1.4 Composite Cost of Capital
- 2.2 Capital Expenditure Decisions / Capital Budgeting Decisions
  - 2.2.1 Introduction
  - 2.2.2 Importance of Capital Budgeting
  - 2.2.3 The Process of Capital Budgeting
  - 2.2.4 Evaluation of the Projects
  - 2.2.5 Limitations of Capital Budgeting
  - 2.2.6 Planning, Organisation and Control of Capital Expenditure
- 2.3 Types of Capital Expenditure Decisions: Pre Sanction, Operational and Post Sanction Control of Capital Expenditure
  - 2.3.1 Pre-sanction Control of Capital Expenditure
  - 2.3.2 Operational Control of Capital Expenditure
  - 2.3.3 Post-sanction Control of Capital Expenditure
- 2.4 Tools and Techniques of Capital Expenditure Control
  - 2.4.1 Performance Index
  - 2.4.2 Technical Performance Measurement
  - 2.4.3 Post Completion Audit (PCA)
- Points to Remember
- Questions for Discussion

Learning Objectives ...

- To understand the concept of Cost of Capital
- To understand the concept of Capital Budgeting Decisions
- To know about the Types of Capital Expenditure Control
- To know about the various Tools and Techniques of Capital Expenditure Control

2.1 Cost of Capital

Each of the sources of funds involves some cost. The cost of capital can be defined as *"the rate of return which an organisation must pay to the suppliers of capital for the use of their funds"*.

In economic terms, the cost of capital is viewed from two different angles:

1. The cost of raising funds to finance a project. This cost may be in the form of the interest which the company may be required to pay to the suppliers of funds. This may be the explicit cost attached with the various sources of capital.

2. The cost of capital may be in the form of opportunity cost of the funds of company i.e. rate of return which the company would have earned if the funds are not invested. E.g. Suppose that a company has an amount of ₹ 100,000 which may either be utilised for purchasing a machine or may be invested with a bank as fixed deposit carrying the interest 10% p.a. If the company decides to use the interest for purchasing the machine, obviously it will have to forgo the interest which it would have earned by investing the same in fixed deposit with the bank. Thus, the cost of capital of this capital of ₹ 1,00,000 is 10%.

2.1.1 Concepts of Cost of Capital

Besides the general concept of cost of capital, the following concepts are also used frequently.

1. Component Cost and Composite Cost

Component cost refers to the cost of individual components of capital viz. equity shares, preference shares, debentures and so on. Composite cost of capital refers to the combined or weighted average cost of capital of the various individual components. For capital budgeting decisions, it is the composite cost of capital which is considered.

2. Average Cost and Marginal Cost

The average cost refers to the weighted average cost of capital. Marginal cost refers to the incremental cost attached with new funds raised by the company.

3. Explicit Cost and Implicit Cost

Explicit cost is the one which is attached with the source of capital explicitly or apparently. Implicit cost is the hidden cost which is not incurred directly. E.g. In case of the debt capital, the interest which the company is required to pay on the same is explicit cost of capital. However, if the company introduces more and more doses of debt capital in the overall capital structure, it makes the investment in the company a risky proposition. As such, the expectations of the investors in terms of return on their investment may increase and share prices of the company may decrease. These increased expectations of the investors or the decreased share prices may be considered to be implicit cost of debt capital.

2.1.2 Importance of Cost of Capital

The term cost of capital is important for a company basically for following purposes:

1. The concept of cost of capital is used as a tool for screening the investment proposals. E.g. In case of the net present value method, the cost of capital is used as the discounting rate for discounting the future inflow of funds. Any project resulting into positive net present value only will be accepted. All other projects will be rejected. Similarly, in case of Internal Rate of Return Method (IRR), the resultant IRR is compared with the cost of capital. It is expected, that if a project is to be accepted, IRR resulting from the same should be more than cost of capital. If project generates IRR which is less than cost of capital, the project will be rejected.

2. The cost of capital is used as the capitalisation rate to decide the amount of capitalisation in case of a new concern.

3. The concept of cost of capital provides useful guidelines for determining the optimal capital structure. Optimal capital structure is the one where overall cost of capital is minimum and the overall valuation of the firm is maximum.

2.1.3 Measurement of Cost of Capital

1. Cost of Debt: The debts may be either short-term debts or long term debts. Very naturally, the cost of capital in the form of debt is the interest which the company has to pay. But this is not the real cost attached with debt capital. The real cost is something less than the rate of interest which the company has to pay. This is due to the fact that the interest on debt is a tax deductible expenditure. If the amount of interest is considered as a part of expenses, the tax liability of the company reduces proportionately. As such, while computing the cost of debt, adjustments are required to be made for its tax impact. E.g. Suppose a company issues the debentures having the face value of ₹ 100 and bearing the rate of interest of 10% p.a. If the tax rate applicable to the company is 50%, the cost of debentures is net 10% which is the rate of interest, but it is to be duly reduced by the tax benefit available for this interest. The tax benefit is 50% of 10%, hence the cost of debentures is only 5%.

Further, the interest payable on the debentures has to be viewed from the angle of the amount actually received on their issue. E.g. A company issues 1000 debentures of ₹ 100 each bearing interest @8% p.a. Company incurs the expenses in connection with the issue of debentures to the extent of ₹ 10,000. (These expenses may be in the form of discount allowed, underwriting commission, advertisement etc.) Thus, the company will have to pay the annual interest of ₹ 8,000 on the net amount received to the extent of only ₹ 90,000 (i.e. ₹ 1,00,000 minus ₹ 10,000). Cost of debenture in this case works out to around 8.89% and assuming that the tax rate applicable is 50%, the tax benefit makes the cost of debentures equal to 4.45%. However, the debt capital has a hidden cost also. If the debt content in the capital structure of a company exceeds the optimum level, the investors start considering company as too risky and their expectations from equity shares increase. This is the hidden cost of debt.

2. Cost of Preference Shares: The cost of capital preference shares is the dividend rate payable on them. As in case of debentures, the cost capital is adjusted for the amount excess or less received on the issue of preference shares. E.g. Suppose, a company issues 1,000 preference shares of ₹ 100 each at the value of ₹ 105 each. Rate of dividend is 10% and the expenses involved with the issue of preference shares amount to ₹ 10,000. Thus the net amount received works out to ₹ 95,000 whereas the amount of the dividend is ₹ 10,000. Here, the cost of capital works out to:

$$\frac{₹ 10,000}{₹ 95,000} \times 100 = 10.52\%$$

As the amount of dividend payable on preference shares is not tax deductible expenditure, there is no question of further adjustment for the tax benefit.

3. Cost of Equity Shares: Computation of cost of equity shares is the most complex procedure. It is due to the fact that unlike preference shares or debentures, equity shares do not have either the interest or dividend to be paid at a fixed rate. The cost of equity shares basically depends upon the expectations of the equity shareholders. There are following approaches to compute the cost of equity shares.

(a) D/P Approach: According to this approach, before an investor pays certain price for purchasing equity shares of the company, he expects certain return on the investment which is in the form of the dividend. The expected rate of dividend is the cost of equity shares. This means, that the investor calculates the market price of the shares by capitalising the present dividend rate which is expected to be same for all times to come at a given level. E.g. If the market price of Equity shares of a company (Face value ₹ 10) is ₹ 15 and if the company at present is paying the dividend @ 20% which is expected to be continued in future also, the cost of Equity Shares will be:

$$\frac{20\% \times ₹ 10}{₹ 15} = 13.33\%$$

However, it can also be argued that the cost of equity shares may be 20%, because on the expectation of rate of dividend at 20%, market price of the shares is ₹ 15.

This approach is objected on certain grounds. Firstly, this presupposes that an investor looks forward only to receive dividend on equity shares. This may not always be correct. He may also look forward to capital appreciation in the value of his shares. Secondly, this approach assumes that the company will not earn on its retained earnings and that the retained earnings will not result in either appreciation of the market price or increase in dividends. This assumption can be a wrong assumption which may lead to wrong conclusions.

(b) E/P Approach: According to this approach, the cost of equity shares is based upon the stream of unchanged earnings earned by a company. This approach holds that each investor expects a certain amount of earnings whether distributed by way of dividend or not, from the company in whose shares he invests.

Thus, if an investor expects that the company in which he is investing should have at least 20% rate of earnings, cost of equity shares will be calculated on that basis. If a company is expected to earn 30%, he will be prepared to pay ₹ 150 for one share of ₹ 100 each.

This approach can be objected on the following grounds. Firstly, it wrongly assumes that the earnings per share will remain constant in future. Secondly, the market prices of the shares will not remain constant as the shareholders will expect capital gains as a result of reinvestment of retained earnings. Thirdly, all the earnings may not be distributed among the shareholders by way of dividend.

(c) D/P + G Approach: According to this approach, the investor is prepared to pay the market price of the shares as he expects not only the payment of the dividend but also expects a growth in the dividend rate at a uniform rate perpetually.

Thus, the cost of equity shares can be calculated as

D/P + G where

D = Expected dividend per share

P = Market price per share

G = Growth in expected dividends.

E.g. If the dividend per share is ₹ 1 per share with the expected growth of 6% per year perpetually, the cost of equity shares, with the assumed market price of the share of ₹ 25, will be

$$\frac{₹1}{₹25} + 0.06$$

$$= 0.04 + 0.06$$

$$= 10\%$$

This approach involves the difficulty of determining the growth rate.

(d) Realised Yield Approach: According to this approach, the cost of equity shares may be decided on the basis of yields actually realised over the period of past few years which may be expected to be continued in future also. This approach basically considers D/P + G approach, but instead of considering the future expectations of dividends and growth factor, the actual yields in past are considered.

(e) Cost of Retained Earnings: Many a times, it is argued that the retained earnings do not cost anything to the company. This is argued like this as there is no obligation, either formal or implied, to pay return on retained earnings even though they constitute one of the major sources of funds for the company. In case of debt, the company has fixed obligation to pay interest on it. Almost similar obligation exists in case of preference share also. In case of equity shares, though there is no legal obligation, the expectations of the shareholders at least provides a starting point for computing the cost of equity shares. The retained earnings do not involved any of such obligations, either, formal or implied. As such, it may be felt that retained earnings involve no cost as they are not raised from outside source. But this contention is not correct. Retained earnings involve cost and this cost is in the form of the opportunity cost in terms of dividend foregone by or withheld from the equity shareholders.

E.g. Assuming that the profits earned by the company are not retained but are distributed among shareholders by way of dividend. These amounts of dividends which would have been received by the shareholders, after due adjustments for tax deducted at source, could have been invested by the shareholders elsewhere to earn some return. The company, by retaining the profits, prohibits the shareholder from earnings these returns. As such, the company is required to earn on the retained earnings atleast equal to the rate which would have been earned by the shareholders if they were distributed to them. This is the cost of retained earnings.

2.1.4 Composite Cost of Capital

After ascertaining the cost of each source of the capital constituting the capital structure, the next step is to compute the composite cost of capital which is defined as the weighted average of the cost of each specific type of capital. The reason behind considering weighted average and not the simple average is to give consideration to the proportion of various sources of funds in the capital structure of the company. Thus, the process of computing the composite cost of capital is carried on by following the steps stated below.

(1) Assign weights to various sources of funds. It may be stated here that the weights may be in the form of book value of funds or market value of funds.

(2) Multiply the cost of each source of funds by the weights assigned.

(3) Calculate the composite cost by dividing total weighted cost by the total weights.

The above process can be explained with the help of following illustrations.

Illustration 1:

The capital structure of a company and the cost of specific sources of funds is as below:

Sources of funds	Book Value (weights) ₹	Specific Cost	Weighted Cost ₹
	1	2	3 (1 × 2)
Debentures	1,50,000	5%	7,500
Preference shares	50,000	9%	4,500
Equity shares	2,00,000	15%	30,000
Retained earnings	1,00,000	8%	8,000
	5,00,000		50,000

$$\text{Composite cost of capital} = \frac{\text{Total weighted costs} \times 100}{\text{Total weights}}$$

$$= \frac{50,000 \times 100}{5,00,000}$$

$$= 10\%$$

Illustration 2:

From the information given below, calculate the weighted average cost of capital for Z Ltd.

₹ in Lakhs

1. Shareholders' funds

Share Capital	– Equity	500
	– Preference	100
Retained Earnings		300

Enterprise Performance Management — Capital Expenditure Control

2. Loan Funds

Secured Loans	800
Unsecured Loans (Incl. intercorporate deposit)	700
	2,400

(a) Normal yield on Equity shareholders' fund anticipated at 15%.
(b) Dividend rate on preference shares - 12%.
(c) Tax rate for Z Ltd. - 60%.
(d) Interest on secured loans - 16.25%.
(e) Interest on unsecured loans - 20%.

Solution:

Computation of after tax cost of capital –

Sources	Book Value (weights)	Tax Adjusted Cost	Weighted Cost
1	2	3	4 i.e. 2 × 3
Equity shares	500	15%	75
Preference shares	100	12%	12
Retained Earnings	300	15%	45
Secured Loans	800	6.50% i.e. 40% of 16.25%	52
Unsecured loans	700	8% i.e. 40% of 20%	56
	2400		240

Weighted Average Cost

$$\text{After tax} = \frac{\text{Weighted cost} \times 100}{\text{Total weights}}$$

$$= \frac{240}{2,400} \times 100$$

$$= 10\%$$

Computation of before tax cost of capital:

$$= \frac{\text{After tax cost of capital}}{(100\% - \text{Tax rate})}$$

$$= \frac{10\%}{(100\% - 60\%)}$$

$$= \frac{10\%}{40\%}$$

$$= 25\%$$

2.2 Capital Expenditure Decisions / Capital Budgeting Decisions

2.2.1 Introduction

Capital Expenditure Decisions are the decisions relating to the investment in Fixed Assets, and in financial terms these decision are technically referred to as 'Capital Budgeting Decisions'. Fixed Assets are the assets which do not give the returns over a shorter span of time. These returns are available over a longer span of time depending upon the life of fixed assets. Thus, the capital budgeting decisions are decisions as to whether or not money should be invested in fixed assets or long-term projects. It includes analysis of various proposals regarding capital expenditure to evaluate their impact on the financial situation of the organisation and to choose the best out of the various alternatives. The function of finance in this area is to enable the management to take a proper capital budgeting decision.

2.2.2 Importance of Capital Budgeting

Capital budgeting decisions are the most crucial and critical decisions for a business to take. This is the fact due to the various reasons:

(1) Capital budgeting decisions have long term implications on the operations of the business. A wrong decision may affect the long-term survival of the organisation. The investment in fixed assets which is more than required may increase the operating costs of the organisation. The inadequate investment in fixed assets may make it difficult for the organisation to compete in the market and may affect its market share.

(2) Capital budgeting decisions involve large amount of the funds. As such, it is necessary to take the decision very very carefully and to make the arrangement of the funds for the procurement of these assets.

(3) The capital budgeting decisions are irreversible due to the fact that it is difficult to find the market for such capital goods. The only alternative is to scrap these assets which involves huge losses.

(4) Capital budgeting decisions are difficult to make because it involves the assessment of future events which are difficult to ascertain. The investments are required to be made immediately but the returns are expected over a number of years.

2.2.3 The Process of Capital Budgeting

The process of capital budgeting involves generally the following steps.

(1) **Project Generation:** The generation of the proposals may fall under any of the following categories.

(a) Additions to the present product line.

(b) Expand the capacity of the existing product line.

(c) Proposals to reduce costs of the existing product line without affecting the scale of operations.

The generation of the projects may take place at the levels of top management or at the level of workers also. E.g. Proposal to replace an old machine or to improve the production techniques may originate at the worker's level also.

(2) **Project Evaluation:** As in case of any types of decision makings, the capital budgeting decisions also have two faces. Firstly, estimation of the benefits and costs measured in terms of cash flows and Secondly, selection of an appropriate criteria to judge the desirability of the projects. It is necessary that the evaluation of the projects is done by impartial group and experts in the field. Care must be taken to choose the criteria to judge the desirability of the projects and it should be consistent with the organisation's basic objective to maximise the wealth.

(3) **Project Selection:** There is no fixed and laid down procedure to select the final criteria among the various available alternatives. Generally, the selection of the final project is done by the top management though it may be scrutinised at various levels. In many cases, top management may delegate the authority to approve certain projects to lower management also.

(4) **Project Execution:** After the final selection of the project is made, the funds are appropriated and the execution of the project is carried on. However, there has to be a proper system to check that the execution of the project is being made as per the predecided plans and schedules.

2.2.4 Evaluation of the Projects

The process of evaluation of the projects necessarily involves the cost benefit analysis. This cost benefit analysis will generally be made in financial terms, though in some cases non-financial considerations may also come into play. E.g. Some times a project may be undertaken to get established in the market or to satisfy certain legal requirements or for some social welfare benefits or just for some emotional reasons. However in majority of the cases, financial cost benefit analysis will be the basic evaluation criteria.

For the purpose of Project Evaluation, rather than the profitability what is more significant is the Cash Flows i.e. Cash Inflows and Cash Outflows.

There are many techniques and tools to evaluate the various investment proposals. But before going into the details of these various techniques, one most important aspect of the evaluation has to be studied and that is 'how to compute the cash flows?'

How to Compute the Cash Flows?

As the estimation of cash flows – both outflows as well as inflows – is the crux for evaluating the projects, this estimation should be made as carefully as possible. The following stages should be considered for this purpose.

(1) Following items constitute the cash outflow.

    (i) Landed cost of new fixed asset. The landed cost will consist of the basic cost as well as all the applicable taxes (like excise duty / import duty, VAT etc.) and other allied expenses (like transportation charges, packing charges, transit insurance etc.)

    (ii) Cost for demolition of old fixed asset (similarly, if there is some scrap value receivable from the disposal of the old asset, the outflow on account of the new asset should be suitably adjusted.)

    (iii) Cost of preparing site and installation charges incurred with respect to the new fixed asset.

Following factors should also be taken into consideration:

    (i) If the cost of the new fixed asset is not to be incurred in one single installment, but is to be paid over a period of years, it will involve the cash outflow not only in the first year but in the subsequent years also. Similarly, if the cost of the asset/project is met by raising the term borrowing, the cash outflow will come into consideration as and when the installment of term borrowings and interest on the same are paid.

    (ii) If the new asset/project brings certain scrap value after the useful life is over, the amount realised as scrap value will constitute the cash inflow, but in relation to the year in which the amount is actually received.

    (iii) In some cases, implementation of the project may involve investment in the form of additional working capital due to increased inventory, increased debtors etc. This additional investment in working capital constitutes cash outflow. Similarly, after the useful life of the project is over, this investment in the working capital is released and hence should be considered as inflow but only with respect to the year in which it is so released. Further, if the company resorts to some outside source of funds for financing working capital requirements, the cash outflow on account of investment in working capital will be the amount invested by the company itself. The amount received from the outside source of working capital finance constitute the cash inflow.

    (iv) If a new asset is intended to be purchased in order to replace an existing asset, the sale proceeds of the old asset should be considered as the cash inflow and the cash outflow required to purchase new asset should be adjusted accordingly.

(2) Following factors should be considered while **computing cash inflows**.
   (i) Computation of cash inflows highly depends upon correct estimation of production and sales. On the basis of the additional production units which can be sold and the price at which they can be sold, the gross revenue from the project can be worked out. However, while doing so, the possibility of reduction in selling price, introduction of a cheaper product by competitors, etc. should also be considered.
   (ii) Second stage in deciding the cash inflows is to estimate the costs attached to the project. These costs may be in the form of fixed costs or variable costs or depreciation.
   (iii) The difference between the gross revenue and the costs give the result of the net revenue which should be adjusted for taxation factor for computation of cash inflows as the amount of taxes involves the actual payment of cash. However, the amount of depreciation, if it is already included in the cost to consider the taxation factor should be added back while computing the cash inflow as depreciation does not involve the cash outflow. In simple words, the cash inflows should be computed in the following stages.

   Sales Revenue
   Less: Costs (including depreciation)
   Net Revenue
   Less: Tax Liability
   Revenue after taxes.
   Add: Depreciation
   Net cash inflow

   (iv) Care should be taken not to include the cost of interest and dividends while considering the costs attached to the project. This is due to the fact that for evaluating the proposals if weighted average cost of capital is considered as the discounting factor (as discussed in details later), the amounts of interest and dividend are already given due consideration while computing the cost of capital.
   (v) Sometimes the cash inflows may be considered in terms of net savings in costs rather than in terms of excess of sales over the additional cost. Thus, for computing the cash inflows these savings in costs will be the starting point which will have to be adjusted further for taxation and depreciation factor. The cash inflows will be computed as below.

   Saving in costs
   (Other than Depreciation)
   Less: Depreciation
   Net Savings in costs.

Less: Tax liability

Savings after tax

Add: Depreciation

Net cash inflows.

Time Value of Money:

As discussed earlier, the evaluation of capital expenditure proposals involves the comparison between cash outflows and cash inflows. The peculiarity of evaluation of capital expenditure proposals is that it involves the decisions to be taken today whereas the flow of funds, either outflow or inflow, may be spread over a number of years. It goes without saying that for a meaningful comparison between the cash outflows and cash inflows, both the variables should be on comparable basis. As such, the question which arises is that "is the value of flows arising in future the same in terms of today?" E.g. If a proposal involves the cash inflow of ₹ 10,000 after one year, is the value of this cash inflow really ₹ 10,000 as on today when the capital expenditure proposal is to be evaluated? The ideal reply to this question is 'no'. The value of ₹ 10,000 received after one year is less than ₹ 10,000 if received today. The reasons for this can be stated as below:

(1) There is always an element of uncertainty attached with the future cash flows.

(2) The purchasing power of cash inflows received after the year may be less than that of equivalent sum if received today.

(3) There may be investment opportunities available if the amount is received today which cannot be exploited if the equivalent sum is received after one year.

E.g. If Mr. X is given the option that he can receive an amount of ₹ 10,000 either on today or after one year, he will most obviously select the first option. Why? Because, if he receives ₹ 10,000 today he can always invest the same say in the fixed deposits with a bank carrying the interest of say 10% p.a. As such, if the choice is given to him, he will like to receive ₹ 10,000 today or ₹ 11,000 (i.e. ₹ 10,000 plus interest @ 10% p.a. on ₹ 10,000) after one year. If he has to receive ₹ 10,000 only after one year, the real value of the same in terms of today is not ₹ 10,000 but something less than that. This concept is called **time value of money.**

In the capital budgeting decisions, if there has to be a meaningful comparison between the cash outflows and cash inflows which may arise in future at different points of time whereas the evaluation is required to be done as on today, both the future cash outflows and cash inflows are required to be expressed in terms of today.

There are two techniques available for this.

(a) Compounding

(b) Discounting

Enterprise Performance Management   **Capital Expenditure Control**

(a) Compounding:

In this technique, the interest is compounded and becomes a part of initial principal at the end of compounding period.

E.g. If Mr. X invests ₹ 10,000 in fixed deposit carrying interest @ 10% p.a. compounded annually, at the end of first year, ₹ 10,000 will be worth ₹ 11,000 (i.e. ₹ 10,000 + interest on ₹ 10,000 @ 10% p.a.). If ₹ 11,000 are reinvested in the same fixed deposit, at the end of second year ₹ 11,000 will be worth ₹ 12,100 (i.e. ₹ 11,000 + interest on ₹ 11,000 @ 10% p.a.) In other words, the value of today's ₹ 10,000 if received after two years becomes ₹ 12,100.

The compounding of interest can be calculated with the help of following equation.

$A = P(1+i)^n$ where

A = Amount at the end of the period.

P = Amount of principal at the beginning of the period.

i = Rate of interest

n = Number of years

E.g. In the above example, after two years, the value of today's ₹ 10,000 if invested in the investment carrying the interest of 10% p.a. can be computed as:

$$A = 10,000 \times (1 + 0.10)^2$$
$$= 10,000 \times 1.21$$
$$= ₹ 12,100$$

(b) Discounting:

This technique involves the process which is exactly opposite to that involved in the technique of compounding. This technique tries to find out the present value of ₹ 1 if received or spent after n years, provided that the interest rate of i can be earned on investment. The present value is calculated with the help of following equation:

$$P = \frac{A}{(1+i)^n}$$

where

P = Present value of sum received or spent

A = Sum received or spent in future

i = Rate of interest

n = Number of years.

E.g. If Mr. X is given the opportunity to receive ₹ 10,000 after two years, when he can earn interest of 10% p.a. on his investment, what should be the amount which he should invest today so that he may be able to receive ₹ 10,000 after two years.

It can be computed as:

$$P = \frac{A}{(1+i)^n}$$

$$= \frac{10,000}{(1+0.10)^2}$$

In other words, if Mr. X invests ₹ 8,264.46 today in the investment carrying interest rate of 10% p.a. he may be able to receive ₹ 10,000 after two years or the present value or ₹ 10,000 if received after two years is only ₹ 8,264.46 as on today if investment opportunities are available to earn the interest of 10% p.a.

The question arises that in the process of compounding or discounting, what should be the value of "I"? The value of "I" may be in either of the following forms –

(a) Weighted Average Cost of Capital
(b) If the fixed asset / project is financed by the borrowed funds, the rate of interest payable on these borrowed funds
(c) Return on Investment (ROI) of the organisation.

Present Value Tables:

To simplify the computation of present value, use can be made of the Interest and Discount Rate Tables which give the present value of rupee one for the various interest rates (i) and years (n) for computing the present value of a future lump sum, the said sum can be multiplied by choosing the interest factor/discounting factor/present value factor for the relevant combination of i and n.

E.g. To find out the present value of ₹ 4,000 received after 7 years, assuming interest rate to be 15%, we ascertain the present value factor to be 0.513. We ascertain the present value to be

= ₹ 4000 x 0.513
= ₹ 2,052.

Present Value of Series of Cashflows

In capital budgeting decisions, the cashflows, either cash outflow or cash inflow, may occur at various points of time. For finding out the present value of this series of cashflows, it is necessary to find out the present value of each future cashflow and then aggregate them.

Illustration 1

A project involves cash inflows as below.

Year Cash	Inflows
1	10,000
2	12,000
3	15,000
4	20,000

Assuming interest rate to be 15%, find out the present value of cash inflows.

Solution: Calculation of present value of cash inflows.

Year	Cash inflows ₹	Present Value Factor 15%	Total Present Value ₹
1	10,000	0.870	8,700
2	12,000	0.756	9,072
3	15,000	0.658	9,870
4	20,000	0.572	11,440
			39,082

Illustration 2:

A machine costing ₹ 1,00,000 is to be purchased as below:

₹ 20,000 – Down payment out of own contribution.

₹ 80,000 – Borrowing by way of term loan. To be paid in 4 equal annual installment along with the interest @ 15% p.a. The interest being computed on opening outstanding balance.

Calculate present value of the cash outflow.

Solution: Calculation of present value of cash outflows.

Year	Principal Sum/Own Contribution ₹	Interest ₹	Total outflow ₹	PV. Factor 15%	Total PV ₹
0	20,000	-	20,000	1.000	20,000
1	20,000	12,000	32,000	0.870	27,840
2	20,000	9,000	29,000	0.756	21,924
3	20,000	6,000	26,000	0.658	17,108
4	20,000	3,000	23,000	0.572	13,156
					1,00,028

If a project involves uniform cashflows, the present value of the cashflows can be calculated by a short cut method. Instead of calculating present value for each cashflow and then summing up the present values, the discounting factors (interest factor or present value factors) themselves can be summed up to find out the Accumulated Discounting Factor for the various interest rates (i) and years (n) and the multiplication of Accumulated Discounting Factor and cashflow will give present value of cashflow. Table B given in the Appendix gives the Accumulated Discounting Factors for the various interest rates (i) and years (n).

Illustration 3

A project involves the cash inflow of ₹ 20,000 per year for 4 years. Assuming interest rate of 15%, find out the present value of cash inflows.

Solution: Accumulated Discounting factor at 15% for 4 years is 2.855.

Present value of cash inflows ₹ 20,000 × 2.855

= ₹ 57,100.

Relevance in Capital Budgeting Decisions:

As discussed earlier, to make the value of cash outflows and cash inflows comparable, it is necessary to reduce future cash outflows or cash inflows to their present value by discounting them by proper discounting factor or interest factor or present value factor. Usually, weighted average cost of capital or the rate of interest payable on the amount of funds borrowed is considered as the discounting factor in capital budgeting decisions.

2.2.5 Limitations of Capital Budgeting

The basic limitation of the capital budgeting process lies in this fact that it involves various estimations. These estimations are specifically in respect of -

(a) Cash outflow.

(b) Revenues / Savings and costs attached with projects.

(c) Life of the projects.

Whereas the cash outflows can be estimated with a reasonable accuracy, the cash inflows and life of the projects can not be estimated accurately. Further, the changes in fiscal and taxation policies of the Government also have the impact on determination of cash inflows. If the techniques use the discounted flows to evaluate the projects, the weighted average cost of capital is generally used as discounting rate. Difficulties in deciding the cost of capital prove to be the limitation of capital budgeting process.

2.2.6 Planning, Organisation and Control of Capital Expenditure

It has already been discussed that the various proposals for incurring capital expenditure may be generated either at top management level or even at lower management level though latter is the rare possibility. The various proposals generated are evaluated with the help of various techniques as discussed above. The ultimate selection for proposals depends upon the evaluation made by these techniques, however the factors like urgency or availability of funds may also play important role.

The ultimate power to reject or accept various capital expenditure proposals rests with the top management which may be in the form of Board of Directors or Executive Committee or Management Committee. In some cases, the power may rest with the Chairman or Managing Director. The proposals involving the outlay to a certain extent may fall within the powers of chief executive also and the proposals involving the outlay beyond that extent will have to be referred to top management as described above. If the actual implementation of the selected proposals involve the arrangement of funds from the financial institutions or require certain Government approvals, it is the responsibility of middle management to arrange for the same.

If it is intended to exercise proper control on the capital budgeting process, an organisation may be required to take the following steps.

(1) Planning: The capital expenditure has to be planned properly taking into consideration the present and future needs of the business. It should be planned in such a way as to ensure the balanced development of all the sections of the organisation individually as well as of the organisation as a whole. Usually, the plans in respect of capital expenditure are prepared in the form of capital expenditure budget. Care should be taken to select the period for which capital expenditure budget should be prepared. Too long a period may not be useful.

(2) Evaluation: Utmost care should be taken while evaluating the capital expenditure proposals. As the capital expenditure proposals involve long term and irreversible decisions, a wrong decision may disturb the entire financial structure of the organisation. The evaluation of various proposals should be done as rationally as possible. Proper weightage should be given to the elements of risk and uncertainly.

(3) Control Over Progress: Usually, the implementation of capital expenditure proposals are spread over more than one year. As such proper control is required to be exercised over issue of work orders/purchase orders, acquisition of material, labour force and other assets, supply of funds etc.

(4) Periodic and Post Completion Audit: These are required to be conducted in order to confirm whether the proposal has been implemented as per the original plan or not. If some faults are pointed out regarding planning process, they may be corrected while considering future projects. If some faults are pointed out during mid-term review of the projects, corrective actions may be taken during the remaining period of implementation.

(5) Forms and Procedures: In order to ensure proper control over capital expenditure, certain forms and procedures may be prescribed. Care should be taken that the said forms are used and procedures are followed at each and every stage of implementation of the capital expenditure proposals.

2.3 Types of Capital Expenditure Decisions: Pre Sanction, Operational and Post Sanction Control of Capital Expenditure

Various techniques are available for evaluation of capital expenditure proposals. They can be broadly categorised under three heads.

2.3.1 Pre-sanction Control of Capital Expenditure

(1) Pay Back Period:

Pay back period indicates the period within which the cost of the project will be completely recovered. In other words, it indicates the period within which the total cash inflows equal to the total cash outflows. Thus,

$$\text{Pay back period} = \frac{\text{Cash outlay}}{\text{Annual cash inflow}}$$

Illustration 1:

A project requires an outlay of ₹ 5,00,000 and earns, an annual cash inflow of ₹ 1,00,000 for 8 years. Calculate pay back period.

Solution: Pay back period for the project is

$$\frac{5,00,000}{₹\ 1,00,000} = 5 \text{ years}$$

If the project involves unequal cash inflows, the payback period can be computed by adding up the cash inflow till the total is equal to cash outlay.

Illustration 2

A project requires an outlay of ₹ 1,00,000 and earns, the annual cash inflow or ₹ 25,000, ₹ 30,000, ₹ 20,000 and ₹ 50,000. Calculate pay back period.

Solution: If we add up cash inflows, we find that in the first 3 years, an amount of ₹ 75,000 of the cash outlay is recovered. Fourth year generates the cash inflow of ₹ 50,000, whereas the amount of ₹ 25,000 only remains to be recovered. Assuming that the cash inflows occur evenly during the year, the time which will be required to recover ₹ 25,000 will be

$$\frac{₹\ 25,000}{₹\ 50,000} \times 12 \text{ months} = 6 \text{ months}$$

Thus, the pay back period is 3 years and 6 months.

Acceptance Rule

Payback period method can be used as an accept or reject criteria or as a method of ranking the project. If the payback period computed for a project is more than maximum pay back period estimated by the management it would be rejected or vice versa. As a ranking method, the projects having shortest pay back period will be ranked highest.

Advantages:

(1) It is quite simple to calculate and easy to understand. It makes it quite clear that there are no profits on a project unless pay back period is over.

(2) It costs less.

(3) It may be a suitable technique where risk of obsolescence is high. In such cases, projects with shorter pay back period may be preferred as the changes in technology may make other projects obsolete before their costs are recovered.

Disadvantages:

(1) It does not consider the returns from a project after its pay back period is over. Thus, one project A may have a pay back period of 5 years while another project B may have a pay back period of 3 years, thus making project B more preferable. But it is quite possible that project A may generate good cash inflows after 5 years till the end of 10 years, while project B may stop generating cash inflows after 3 years only. In such cases, project A may prove to be more advantageous. As a result, the projects having longer gestation period are likely to suffer under this criteria.

(2) It may not be a suitable method to evaluate the projects if they involve uneven cash inflows.

(3) It ignores time value of money.

(4) To decide the acceptable payback period is a difficult task. There is no rational basis for deciding the maximum payback period. It is a subjective decision.

(2) Discounted Pay Back Period:

This is an improvement over the payback period method in the sense that it considers time value of money. Thus, discounted payback period indicates that period within which the discounted cash inflows equal to the discounted cash outflows involved in a project.

Illustration:

A project requires an outlay of ₹ 1,00,000 and earns the annual cash inflows of ₹ 35,000, ₹ 40,000, ₹ 30,000 and ₹ 50,000. Calculate discounted pay back assuming the discounting rate of 15%.

Solution:

Years	Cash inflows	Discounting Factor @ 15%	Discounted Cash Inflow ₹	Cumulative Discounted Cash inflows ₹
1	35,000	0.870	30,450	30,450
2	40,000	0.756	30,240	60,690
3	30,000	0.658	19,740	80,430
4	50,000	0.572	28,600	1,09,030

Thus, pay back periods after 3 years but before 4 years. Assuming that cash inflows accrue evenly during year. Pay Back Period will be 3 years 8 months (Approx.).

Acceptance rule, advantages and disadvantages

They are the same as in case of pay back period method except the fact that it considers time value of money

(3) Net Present Value:

Net present Value (NPV) is a method of calculating present value of cash inflows and cash outflows in an investment project, by using cost of capital as the discounting rate, and finding out net present value by subtracting present value of cash outflows from present value of cash inflows. Thus,

NPV = {Total Discounted cash Inflows} Less {Total × Discounted Cash Outflows}

Illustration:

Calculate net present value of a project involving initial cash outflow ₹ 1,00,000 and generating annual cash inflows of ₹ 35,000, ₹ 40,000 ₹ 30,000 and ₹ 50,000 Discounting rate is 15%.

Solution:

Years	Cash inflows ₹	Discounting factor 15%	Present Value of cash inflows ₹
1	35,000	0.870	30,450
2	40,000	0.756	30,240
3	30,000	0.658	19,740
4	50,000	0.572	28,600
			1,09,030
Less: Investment outlay			1,00,000
Net Present Value (NPV)			9,030

Acceptance Rule:

As accept or reject criteria, all the projects which involve positive NPV i.e. NPV > 0 will be accepted and vice versa.

As a ranking method, the projects having maximum positive NPV will be ranked highest.

Advantages:

(1) It considers time value of money.

(2) It considers cash inflows from the project throughout its life.

Disadvantages:

(1) It is difficult to use, calculate and understand.

(2) It presupposes that the discounting rate, i.e. cost of capital is known. But cost of capital is difficult to measure in practice.

(3) It may give dissatisfactory results if the alternative projects involve varying investment outlay. A project involving maximum positive NPV may not be desirable if it involves huge investment.

(4) It presupposes that the cash inflows can be reinvested immediately to yield the return equivalent to the discounting rate, which may not be possible always.

(4) Internal Rate of Return:

Internal Rate of Return (IRR) is that rate at which the discounted cash inflows match with discounted cash outflows. The indication given by IRR is that this is the maximum rate at which the organisation will be able to pay towards the interest on amounts borrowed for investing in the projects, without losing anything. Thus, IRR may be called as the "break even rate" of borrowing for the organisation.

In simple words, IRR indicates that discounting rate at which NPV is zero. If by applying 10% as the discounting rate, the resultant NPV is positive, while by applying 12% discounting rate, the resultant NPV is negative, it means that IRR, i.e. the discounting rate at which NPV is zero, falls between 10% and 12%. Thus, by applying the trial and error method, one can find out the discounting rate at which NPV is zero. The process to compute IRR will be to select any discounting rate and compute NPV. If NPV is negative, a lower discounting rate should be tried and the process should be repeated till the NPV becomes zero. Following illustration explains the process to calculate IRR.

Illustration:

A project cost ₹ 1,00,000 and generates annual cash flows of ₹ 35,000, ₹ 40,000, ₹ 30,000 and ₹ 50,000 over its life of 4 years. Calculate the Internal Rate of Return.

Solution: Using 15% as discounting rate, the present value of cash inflows can be calculated as below:

Year	Cash inflows ₹	PV factor 15%	Total PV ₹
1	35,000	0.870	30,450
2	40,000	0.756	30,240
3	30,000	0.658	19,740
4	50,000	0.572	28,600
			1,09,030

Using 18% as discounting rate, the present value of cash inflows can be calculated as below:

Year	Cash inflows ₹	PV factor 18%	Total PV ₹
1	35,000	0.847	29,645
2	40,000	0.718	28,720
3	30,000	0.609	18,270
4	50,000	0.516	25,800
			1,02,435

Using 20% as discounting rate, the present value of cash inflows can be calculated as below:

Year	Cash inflows ₹	PV factor 20%	Total PV ₹
1	35,000	0.833	29,155
2	40,000	0.694	27,760
3	30,000	0.579	17,370
4	50,000	0.482	24,100
			98,385

Thus, at 18% discounting rate, NPV, is ₹ 2,435 and at 20% discounting rate, NPV is (–) ₹ 1615. Hence, IRR is between 18% and 20%, i.e. more than 18% but less than 20%. Difference between PV at 18% and 20% is ₹ 4050 (i.e. ₹ 1,02,435 – ₹ 98,385) and the negative NPV of ₹ 1615 has to be covered by this amount to arrive as IRR.

$$\text{Thus IRR will be} = 20\% - \frac{1615 \times 2}{4050}$$

$$= 19.2\% \text{ (Appr.)}$$

Acceptance Rule:

The computed IRR will be compared with the cost of capital. If the IRR is more than or at least equal to the cost of capital the project may be accepted (IRR > Cost of Capital – Accept). If the IRR is less than cost of capital, the project may be rejected. (IRR < Cost of Capital – Reject)

Advantages:

(1) It considers time value of money.

(2) It considers cash inflows from the project throughout its life.

(3) It can be computed even in the absence of the knowledge about the firm's cost of capital. But in order to draw the final conclusion, the comparison with the cost of capital is a must.

Disadvantages:

(1) It is difficult to use, calculate and understand.

(2) It presupposes that the cash inflows can be reinvested immediately to yield the return equivalent to the IRR. NPV method, on the other hand, presupposes that the cash inflows can be reinvested to yield the return equivalent to the cost of capital, which is more realistic.

2.3.2 Operational Control of Capital Expenditure

Accounting Rate of Return:

Accounting rate of return (ARR) computes the average annual yield on the net investment in the project. ARR is computed by dividing the average profits after depreciation and taxes by net investments in the project. Thus ARR can be computed as.

$$\frac{\text{Total Profits}}{\text{Net investment in project} \times \text{Number of years of profits}} \times 100$$

Illustration:

A project involves the investment of ₹ 5,00,000 which yields profits after depreciation and tax as stated below.

Years	Profits after depreciation and tax
1	₹ 25,000
2	₹ 37,500
3	₹ 62,500
4	₹ 65,000
5	₹ 40,000
	₹ 2,30,000

At the end of 5 years, the machineries in the project can be sold for ₹ 40,000. Find the ARR.

Solution: The total profits after depreciation and taxes are ₹ 2,30,000.

The net investment in the project will be Original cost Less salvage value i.e.

₹ 5,00,000 – ₹ 40,000 = ₹ 4,60,000

ARR will be

$$\frac{₹ 2,30,000}{₹ 4,60,000 \times 5 \text{ years}} \times 100 = 10\%$$

Acceptance Rule:

As pay back period method, ARR also can be used as accept or reject criteria or as a method for ranking the projects. As accept or reject criteria, the projects having the ARR more than minimum rate prescribed by the management will be accepted and vice versa. As a ranking method, the projects having maximum ARR will be ranked highest.

Advantages:

(i) It is simple to calculate and easy to understand.

(ii) It considers the profits from the project throughout its life.

(iii) It can be calculated from the accounting data.

Disadvantages:

(i) It uses profits after depreciation and taxes and not the cash inflows for evaluating the projects.

(ii) It ignores time value of money.

2.3.3 Post-sanction Control of Capital Expenditure

Profitability Index (PI)/Benefit Cost Ratio (B/C Ratio)

It is the ratio between total discounted cash inflows and total discounted cash outflows. Thus the Profitability Index can be computed as:

$$PI = \frac{\text{Total Discounted cash inflows}}{\text{Total} \div \text{Discounted cash outflows}}$$

PI can be computed as gross one as stated above or as net one which means gross minus one.

Illustration:

A project requires an outlay of ₹ 1,00,000 and earns the annual cash inflows of ₹ 35,000, ₹ 40,000, ₹ 30,000 and ₹ 50,000. Calculate, Profitability Index assuming the discounting rate of 15%.

Year	Cash flows ₹	Discounting factor @ 15%	Discounted Cash Inflows ₹
1	35,000	0.870	30,450
2	40,000	0.756	30,420
3	30,000	0.658	19,740
4	50,000	0.572	28,600
			1,09,210

Solution: Profitability Index can be calculated as:

$$= \frac{\text{Total Discounted cash inflows}}{\text{Total Discounted cash outflows}}$$

Thus, PI (Gross) $= \dfrac{₹\,1,09,030}{₹\,1,00,000} = 1.09$

PI (Net) 1.09 − 1.00 = 0.9

Acceptance Rule:

As accept or reject criteria, the projects having the Profitability Index of more than one will be accepted and vice versa. As a ranking method, the projects having highest profitability index will be ranked highest.

Final Choice of Evaluation Method:

Between the basic two types of techniques as described above, the techniques considering time value of money are generally preferred for the obvious reasons. However, the choice of the evaluation technique depends upon the objective of the management in the investment decisions. The objective is naturally in the form of maximization of wealth of the shareholders. As such, only those projects will be in the interest of the shareholders which can earn more rate of return than other alternative investment opportunities.

2.4 Tools and Techniques of Capital Expenditure Control

2.4.1 Performance Index

This measure of risk incorporates both the expected returns and the risk. It serves as a complete measure of the feasibility of an investment subject to risk constraint. The risk constraint means the investor's decision is constrained by choosing the less risky investment. Mathematically, the performance index is given as,

$$I = \frac{EMV}{s} = \frac{\text{Expected Monetary Value}}{\text{Standard Deviation}}$$

Since the objective of any investment is to maximise the economic returns at the lowest risk, maximizing the value of the performance index achieves this objective. Typically, an investor sets a minimum performance index value as a threshold for screening investments. This minimum is based on the investors' risk aversion and investment's objective. Once this minimum desirable performance index threshold is set, then projects with performance index value greater than this, minimum desirable value would he considered as economically feasible.

For example, the performance indexes for the three investment alternatives are: (a) 0.539 for the drill option, (b) 1,371 for the farmout option, and (c) 0.772 for the back-in option. The higher the performance index, the lesser is the associated risk. The performance index clearly ranks the riskiness of each alternative. For example, the farmout option carries minimum risk (therefore highest I of 1.371), followed by the back-in option (with I = 0.772), and then the drill option (with I = 0.539),

However, maximizing the EMV criteria does not account for the risk preference of the investor, meaning it assumes the investor is risk neutral (indifferent to risk).

2.4.2 Technical Performance Measurement

Measuring technical performance is as important as measuring schedule and cost performance. Although technical performance is often assumed, the opposite can be true. The ramifications of poor technical performance frequently are more profound—something works or it doesn't if technical specifications, are not adhered to.

Assessing technical performance of a system, facility. or product is often accomplished by examining the documents found in the scope statement and/or work package documentation. These documents should specify criteria and tolerance limits against which performance can be measured. For example, the technical performance of a software project suffered because the feature of "drag and drop" was deleted in the final product. Conversely, the prototype of an experimental car exceeded the miles per gallon technical specification and, thus, its technical performance. Frequently tests are conducted on different performance dimensions. These tests become an integral part of the project schedule,

It is very difficult to specify how to measure technical performance because it depends on the nature of the project. Suffice it to say, measuring technical performance must he done. Technical performance is frequently where quality control processes arc needed and used. Project managers must be creative in finding ways to control this very important area.

2.4.3 Post Completion Audit (PCA)

"Things look very easy and fascinating in retrospect" is an old saying. But we can always learn from our past experiences so that we can do better in the future. Though the project planning is done after a lot of estimates and projections for the future yet not all things would go as planned. For being competitive in today's fast changing world, companies need to analyse the results of their capital projects after these projects have been implemented, instead of turning blind eyes towards error. A post completion audit may serve as a major vehicle for project analysis and also to help reinforce the learning curve for the organisation.

'Audit' is generally defined as 'an examination of documents and results to find out whether they are in the desired order'. Thus the PCA is an attempt at assessing the actual profile of the given project in terms of results vis-a-vis the intended profile besides focussing on whatever matters the senior management desires.

Many authors have defined post completion audit in different ways. Some definitions and meanings are given below:

Murdick and Deming: *"It is a check on whether the planned benefits are being realised after the project has been operating for some period of time."*

Kohler: *"It is an audit at some point after the occurrence of a transaction or a group of transactions."*

Points to Remember

- The cost of capital can be defined as "the rate of return which an organisation must pay to the suppliers of capital for the use of their funds".
- Capital Expenditure Decisions are the decisions relating to the investment in Fixed Assets. And in financial terms these decision are technically referred to as 'Capital Budgeting Decisions'.

Questions for Discussion

1. What is Cost of Capital? State its importance.
2. What is Capital Budgeting? State its importance.
3. Explain the Process of Capital Budgeting
4. Write short notes on:
    (a) Time Value of Money
    (b) Accounting Rate of Return
    (c) Net Present Value
    (d) Limitations of Capital Budgeting
    (e) Performance Index
    (f) Technical Performance Measurement
    (g) Types of Capital Expenditure Decisions.

✱✱✱

Chapter 3...

Performance Evaluation Parameters for Banks and Retail

Contents ...

- 3.1 Performance Evaluation of Banks
    - 3.1.1 Control Points for a Bank
    - 3.1.2 Performance Evaluation Parameters for Banks
    - 3.1.3 Use of Risk Management Indicators by Banks
    - 3.1.4 Some More Parameters for Evaluating Bank Performance
- 3.2 Performance Evaluation Parameters for Retail
    - 3.2.1 ABC Analysis
    - 3.2.2 Sell Through Analysis
    - 3.2.3 Multiple Attribute Method
    - 3.2.4 Gross Margin Return on Investment (GMROI)
- Points to Remember
- Questions for Discussion
- Project Question

Learning Objectives ...

- Different regulatory and statutory controls on a bank
- Learn the four perspectives of Balanced Scorecard applicable to a bank
- Understand risks faced by a bank
- Understand the concepts of ABC Analysis, Sell Through Analysis, Multiple Attribute Method, GMRoI

3.1 Performance Evaluation of Banks

Banks are one of the most controlled entities in India. The control system of a bank is complicated as banks are subject to their own internal controls as well as controls imposed by the central bank i.e. Reserve Bank of India in case of Indian banks. They also are indirectly controlled by the Basel accords that are being revised from time to time. Basel accord is an international agreement about the control system to be imposed on the banks across the world. Though Basel accord is not mandatory for countries to follow it is seen that most central banks adhere to these recommendations keeping in mind the special conditions in their own countries. So it can be seen that Banks are tightly controlled entities, but in spite of this they still enjoy a lot of operational freedom as long as they adhere to the overall control system. This is an example where in spite of control, the entity has freedom to do its business within the boundaries drawn by the regulators and the law. The banks thus have to create their own control systems that have been to be drawn from the regulatory environment.

Some of the laws under which a bank is expected to work are Banking Regulation Act, Negotiable instrument Act, SARFESAI Act, Contract Act etc. These acts themselves act as control systems for the banks.

3.1.1 Control Points for a Bank

Following are the control points for a bank. Some of these controls are regulatory in kind and some others are in the form of internal control system.

1. **Capital Adequacy Ratio (CAR):** Banks are required to have capital in proportion to its assets. Banks assets can be divided in three categories. One are its own assets like buildings, office equipments like computers, furniture etc. The second class of assets is its investments. Banks are required to maintain 23% Statutory Liquidity Ratio (SLR) of its total deposits, plus they have to maintain a Cash Reserve Ratio (CRR) of 6%. They also make other investments. This class is relatively less risky. The biggest assets that a bank has are the loans that it gives. This is the riskiest asset class on its balance sheet. The Capital Adequacy Ratio is calculated by assigning a risk weight to all assets. This risk weight is decided by RBI in India. In developed countries banks are free to fix risk weight as per their perception of the risk. The CAR requirement in India is 12% at present and is likely to go up in future. Internationally banks have to maintain a CAR of 8%.

2. **Asset Liability Management (ALM):** Banks have liabilities that have a certain maturity period. Its assets also have a maturity period. Repayment of loan by borrowers should ideally match the maturing deposits. However, in reality, the average maturity of deposits in a bank is between 2 to 3 years; while assets mature between 3 and 5 years. Thus theoretically a bank may not have enough money to

repay its deposits is maturity mismatch becomes a reality. Banks are therefore required to make sure that such a situation does not arise. Banks therefore are required to have Asset Liability Management Committee (ALCO). This committee works at the banks head office.

Banks divide their liabilities and assets in different time buckets like 7 days, 15 days, 30 days so on. This analysis tells them in which bucket they are likely to have a mismatch. Once this is done the banks decide what action they need to take to bridge this gap.

Managing the ALM properly is an important control system. The RBI has given detailed guidelines for the banks for this. If banks were to mis-manage this aspect then they can get in serious trouble as they will find that they may not have sufficient funds to honour their liabilities.

Banks therefore need proper controls to track their borrowers and follow up with them for the timely payment of interest and installments of their loans. If the banks can manage this properly they are likely to have better control on their ALM.

When banks are faced with large defaults by their borrowers, their problems will accentuate.

3. **Priority Sector lending:** All banks in India have to adhere to the guidelines of RBI towards priority sector lending. They have to make sure that out of their loan assets 40% loans are given to this sector. Banks falling short of these stipulations can be fined by the RBI or even their license can be revoked by the RBI. The Priority Sector caters to Agriculture, Exports, SSI Units and small and cottage industries. There have been suggestions from various quarters including the Narsimhan Committee that was formed in early 90s, that this sector needs to be redesigned. They have suggested that the overall Priority Sector lending should be brought down to 10% of outstanding loans. They have also suggested that Agriculture and Export and SSI sectors should be dropped from the Priority Sector as both these sectors have now achieved maturity. They believe that only the small and cottage industry should be in priority sector. These suggestions and recommendations have not yet been accepted by the government. So banks have to make sure that they must adhere to these guidelines.

Home loans up to ₹ 20 lakhs are also part of priority sector lending.

Banks have to make sure through their internal controls that they are in line with the RBI guidelines with priority sector lending. Falling short of the target can invite penalties from the RBI.

4. **Statutory Liquidity Ratio (SLR):** Statutory liquidity ratio (SLR) refers to the amount that the commercial banks require to maintain in the form of gold or govt. approved

securities before providing credit to the customers. Banks are required to maintain the SLR as stipulated by the RBI. SLR is calculated on the total Demand and Time liabilities of the bank. Total Demand and Time liabilities are the total deposits in the bank. At present this ratio is 23%. Banks have to invest this amount in what are known as SLR securities. These are mainly securities that are issued by the Government of India or state governments. These securities are guaranteed by the government and thus there is no risk of default. These securities carry a fixed interest rate. Banks thus earn some return on these securities. These securities are to be held at all times by a bank. This investment is also for the benefit of the depositors of the bank. In case something were to go wrong with the bank, then these securities can be used to protect the depositors money.

Banks can also use these securities for REPO (Ready Purchase Operations) transactions. REPO is a transaction normally between a bank and the RBI. In this transaction, the bank sells its government securities to the RBI to tide over their short term liquidity problems. This is done for a definite period of time. At the end of the period the bank buys back these securities from RBI. The RBI, when it wishes to decrease liquidity in the market, it does what is known as Reverse REPO transaction. In this kind of transaction the RBI sells securities to the banks and buys them back at the end of the period.

Banks hold their security portfolio in two categories. One is known as Held to Maturity (HTL). These securities are held till maturity by a bank. Thus the banks will not trade on these.

The second category of the securities are known as Held for Trading (HT). The banks buy and sale securities held in this category and try and book profits. However such securities have to be marked to market by the banks. This means that any loss that even though notional in nature will have to accounted for in the P/L account of the bank. For example if banks buy a security at a price of ₹ 109 and on the day of the balance sheet if it is quoting @ ₹ 106, then bank has to book the notional loss is ₹ 3. This loss has to be accounted for. Banks Treasury departments have to be very careful about this category. The loss on account of Mark to Market (MTM) can ruin a bank's profitability.

Treasury operations in a bank are a risky operation at all times. The exposure limits have to be set up to monitor these

5. **Cash Reserve Ratio (CRR):** Every commercial bank has to keep certain minimum cash reserves with the RBI. Cash reserve Ratio is stipulated by the RBI from time to time. At present it is at 4.5% of the total deposits of the bank. This money is to be kept by the banks with RBI and they do not earn any interest on these deposits. Thus

the banks lose out in this transaction. RBI uses CRR to manage the level of liquidity in the system. Since excess liquidity leads to higher inflation, the RBI would increase CRR in times of inflationary pressures and reduce it when inflation level is low. Thus it is an instrument that is extremely important for the RBI in its fight against inflation.

6. **Bank Rate:** Bank rate is the rate at which RBI lends or refinances a bank. This is also known as benchmark rate. A bank's lending rates are related to this rate and a bank does not lend below the bank rate. Some loans are made below the bank rate if the government so directs the banks. In such cases the government has to pay the difference to the banks. Agriculture loans are sometimes given below the bank rate.

7. **Cost of Funds:** The banks are free to decide the rates at which they will accept deposits from the public. The RBI only stipulates the savings account interest rates. The existing rate on these deposits is stipulated to be 4 %. Some banks are actually offering 6% rate on these deposits but they insist on minimum balance requirement of ₹ 1 lakh. For all other deposits banks are free to offer rates that they deem fit. The rate of interest on deposits tracks the REPO rate as well as Inter Bank Call Money Market rates. Also banks from their Asset- Liability profile know when they may be short of funds and for that period they may offer a higher rate of interest on deposits.

Banks' deposits are normally classified in two parts. One is known as Current Account and Savings Account deposits (CASA). These are also known as Demand deposits. These are the cheapest source of funds for a bank. The money in Current Accounts do not gain any interest at all. As we have seen above, the money in savings accounts is paid Interest @ 4%. As a part of cost management banks would naturally try and increase the proportion of these deposits. However these deposits can be volatile. The money in these two accounts can be withdrawn at any time by the depositor. If large amounts are suddenly withdrawn the bank can get into trouble. So banks try to have judicious mix of Demand and Time deposits. Banks use its past experience to know how much money will be available on an average in their Demand deposit accounts. This helps them in planning their ALM structure.

The second kind of deposit is known as Time Deposits. These are the ones we commonly know as Fixed Deposits and Recurring Deposits. These are placed with the bank by its customer for a fixed time at a fixed interest rate. These deposits have more cost for bank than the Demand Deposits. The deposits have a maturity period of as less as seven days and maximum of ten years. The rate normally is higher for the long term deposits. Thus the rates at present are ranged between 5% to 9 %. This would translate into a higher interest outgo for banks. The experience shows that the average maturity of deposits in a bank is around two to three years. Thus the cost of these deposits these days would average about 7%.

When the combined cost of Demand and Time deposits is calculated, it would work out to around 6% on an average.

The minimum rate at which a bank can lend money would depend on the cost of deposits + overhead costs + profit margin. If we consider that most banks would have overheads of 2% and the profit requirement of 2% then the Base interest rate of a bank would work out to be 10%. This is also known as prime Lending Rate (PLR) of the bank.

The RBI allows a bank to charge interest rate on loan in the band of bank's PLR + maximum 4% premium on PLR. Thus most loans of a bank would be priced between 10 and 14%.

The rate of interest charged by a bank on loan would depend on the risk that the bank perceives it is taking in making on that loan. Higher the perceived risk, higher would be the rate charged and lower the perception of risk, lower will be the interest charged.

Banks internally undertake the credit rating of every borrower. This allows the banks to assess the risk. Based on the ratings interest rates are set. Thus good companies like say L andT will be rated AAA and thus will get the loan at the best possible rate of interest.

Thus a complex control system will have to be evolved by all banks. With the use of IT solutions in banks the necessary record keeping and calculations have become easy. IT solutions have helped the banks greatly in setting robust process that can red flag deviations through the system itself.

8. **Non-Performing Assets:** Non-Performing Assets are loans that are not repaid in time or interest on loans is not paid regularly. An asset becomes non- performing if the interest of principal repayment is not done by the borrower within 90 days of the due dates. Banks have to monitor all the outstanding loans on this criterion.

9. **Creation of Charge:** This is a very important control mechanism. A bank normally lends money after obtaining some security. Very few loans are given adequate security.

   Especially in cases of loans that are granted to Limited companies a mechanism of creation of charge is available. There are different types of charges that a bank can create in company's books with the "Registrar of Companies" office where the concerned company is registered.

   Charges are of following types:

   (a) Mortgage: These are of two types a) Registered Mortgage and b) Equitable Mortgage. Mortgages are created mainly on land and building. In a registered mortgage the underlying asset is transferred in the name of the bank. This is thus expensive. Banks resort to this type of mortgage in very rare cases where they have serious doubt about the borrower's ability to repay the money borrowed. Thus if a bank thinks it's risk is very high it will insist on Registered Mortgage.

In most other cases the bank will create Equitable Mortgage. In this case the original title deeds are deposited with the bank. Thus the borrower cannot enter into any transactions with relation with the said property. Housing loans are secured by equitable mortgage.

(b) **Hypothecation:** In this kind of charge the underlying securities can be Fixed Assets like Plant and Machinery or it can be Current Assets like inventory and Book Debts.

(c) **Pledge:** In this type of charge the borrower has to give possession of inventory to the bank and the assets pledged under the lock and key of the bank on the premises of the borrower.

Importance of Charge: Essentially charge is registered to protect the interest of the bank in the event of a default occurring. In case of default, the bank is legally empowered to take control of the assets and sell them off to recover its money. Under the SARFESAI act that allows bank easier way of recovery of defaulted loans it is necessary that the bank has to prove that it has a charge on the assets of the company. Its claim can be entertained only if the charge is registered.

The charge has to be registered within 30 days from disbursement of the loan by filing all necessary papers with the Registrar of Companies (ROC). This is the responsibility of the borrower. However since it is in the interest of bankers to register the charge many banks file the documents with ROC before they allow the companies to draw down the sanctioned loans.

There are other types of charges like Parri Passue in which a consortium of banks register charge equal to their exposure to a company.

There is also a provision on second charge. In this case, banks can create second charge on assets that are already charged to another bank provided the bank holding first charge gives a No Objection Letter (NOC).

10. **Fee Based Income:** A bank's main income comes from interest earned on loans and on investments. But banks are now increasingly looking at generating income from other sources as well. The income earned by providing various services is known as Fee based income. This income increases a bank's profitability without increasing its risk. When a bank gives a loan it is taking a risk of default by the borrower.

There are some major sources of fee based income for a bank. The banks issue Bank Guarantees and Letters of Credit on behalf of its clients. For this they charge commission to the client. This is a big source of fee based income for a bank.

Other major source for a bank is the buying and selling of foreign exchange to its clients. The margin in such trades can be high and banks do earn a lot of money this way.

Services like providing safe deposit lockers, issuance of drafts and pay orders are two other sources of fee based income. Banks also get commission on payments made through the debit cards and credit cards. The annual fee charged for these cards is also fee based income.

Many banks have become partners of insurance companies and are selling life, general and health insurance products to their customers. Many banks are also selling Mutual Fund products. In both these cases banks earn commission and is potentially a vast source of fee based income.

Some banks are offering financial planning services for a fee.

11. **Exposure Limits:** Reserve bank of India has set exposure limits for all banks. A bank cannot lend to a single entity more than 10% of its net worth. A bank cannot lend more than 15% of its net worth to a Group of companies. These limits are to be strictly monitored and followed at all times.

RBI from time to time can put exposure limits that are sectoral. Thus exposure limits can be imposed on one single sector exposure by the RBI.

3.1.2 Performance Evaluation Parameters for Banks

The performance evaluation parameters for bank are as follows:

1. Customer Base

Banks are always trying to increase their customer base. Many banks go after Current and Savings accounts as the money deposited in these two accounts are the cheapest sources of funds for a bank and they help bring down the cost of funds for a bank. Thus we see banks even offering zero balance accounts to company employees for their salary accounts. Banks believe that the account holders will have money in these accounts and that money can be profitably deployed by banks for short term gains.

Banks are also offering various services to attract customers. Some banks offer safe deposit lockers, while others offer advisory services in the field of investments to attract new customers.

Banks also try and open new branches where they find scope to attract new customers. New townships or fast developing suburbs of existing cities are prime locations for opening new branches.

While choosing measures for customer perspective of the scorecard, banks must answer two critical questions.
- Who are our target customers and market segment?
- What is our value proposition in serving them?
- Operational Excellence: Focus on low price, zero defects, convenience and no frills.
- Product Leadership: Constantly innovating to offer the best product in the market.
- Customer Intimacy: Focus on a long term relationship building through their deep knowledge of customer needs.

A bank should use the following measures to track its success, should it follow a customer intimate approach.
- **Customer knowledge:** To gauge staff knowledge of the customers the bank may measure "training hours on client products".
- **Solutions Offered:** To measure the attribute of providing an unmatched total solution banks measure "total number of solutions offered per client"
- **Penetration:** the bank should ensure that its efforts are achieving success by deep penetration of accounts
- **Customer data:** "Percentage of employees with access to customer information" may be measured to track this key differentiator of success
- **Culture of driving client success:** "Number of customer awards received" helps track this goal.

Other sources of customer measures are given below:
- **Financial objectives and measures:** Determining how they translate into customer requirements
- **The customers voice:** Using message boards and targeted sites
- **Moments of Truth:** At any point at which a customer comes in contact with a business defines a moment of truth. Mapping these moments of truth provides any bank branch with an opportunity to isolate the differentiating features offered and designing metrics to track success

2. **NPAs**

   A **Non-performing asset** (NPA) is defined as a credit facility in respect of which the interest and/or installment of principal has remained 'past due' for a specified period of time.

   Banks are required to classify their loan assets in four categories as follows:

   (a) **Standard Assets:** These assets are those loans where payment of principal repayment and interest on loans is being paid regularly.

- **(b) Sub standard Assets:** These are assets where there is a default of repayment, meaning interest or installments or both are not paid within 90 days from the due date.
- **(c) Doubtful Assets:** The sub standard assets if are not regularized within 18 months then the loan is considered doubtful loan.
- **(d) Loss Assets:** When loan remains doubtful for two years then it is classified as Loss Asset.

The bank has to make provisions for writing off the assets from its book from the time a loan gets classified as Non standard. In the first phase, 20% of the asset value is to be provided for. If the loan becomes doubtful then another 40% of the loan has to be provided for. When it is classified as Loss Asset then the balance 40% also needs to be provided for.

The provision for bad loans has to be done by debiting the amount to the Profit and Loss account of the bank. Thus higher NPAs would put pressure on the profitability of a bank. It ultimately has an impact on the Capital Adequacy Ratio of the bank as due to provisioning there is little amount left for shoring up banks reserves. When this happens the banks' ability to lend decreases. It can also have adverse impact on the bank's liquidity position and thus it is detrimental to the interests of the depositors. We have seen many banks especially smaller ones like The United Western Bank, The Sangali Bank, Global Trust Bank and scores of co-operative banks going under in the last 15 years or so. These banks had to be merged with larger banks to protect the interests of the depositors. The RBI has thus far made sure that depositors have not lost money. However in many developed economies neither the Central bank nor the governments intervene and try and save such banks. In future this may also be the practice in India.

When a bank faces a high NPA it is sure sign of the failure of control systems in the bank. When loans are made without proper scrutiny and due diligence, this happens. Banks also have to make sure that their risk is adequately covered by the security of the assets of the borrower that can be sold in case of default. We have recently seen banks suffering a staggering loss of around ₹ 7000 crores on account of loans given to King Fisher Airlines that went under. SBI and IDBI Bank suffered massive losses on this account. The security offered to and accepted by the banks proved to be inadequate to cover the losses. Some of the losses were recouped by the banks by selling the pledged shares of the parent company.

Banks have a responsibility to make sure that the borrowers use the money only for the purpose for which it has been lent. There are many cases where borrowers have diverted money lent to them by the banks. There have been numerous cases of misappropriation of bank funds. It is important that banks keep a strict vigil on its borrowers. Monitoring the loans once given is a control mechanism that is most effective. Making sure that borrowers furnish the information that they are expected to provide routines and also independently verifying this information by regularly inspecting the books of the company, verifying stock levels reported with purchase bills etc. are common control systems that good banks follow.

3. Deposits

The ratio of Bank Credit to Bank Deposits indicates the extent to which banks intermediate savings into private sector credits. It increases with the level of economic and financial sector development. While a high credit-to deposit ratio indicates high intermediation efficiency, a ratio higher than one suggests that private sector lending is funded with non deposit sources and this can results in funding instability.

Credit-Deposit Ratio: The ratio of total advances to total deposits indicates efficient utilisation of resources after meeting the statutory liquidity reserve requirements. C-D ration in backward rural and semi-urban areas, in particular, assumes greater significance in the sence that a major portion of the deposits (60%) mobilised by a branch is required to be invested in the same area.

4. ROI

Banks have to try and increase their Return on Investment as far as possible. Banks have a limitation on managing higher Net Interest margins due to increasing competition. Therefore to increase its profitability and hence ROI, the banks are now concentrating on increasing their Fee based income by selling mutual funds and insurance products or by offering investment advisory services to its clients. The Increase in fee based incomes increases the bank's profitability.

Some banks are aggressive players in treasury business. They are thus seeking to take advantage of interest rate arbitrage situations to increase their treasury income. Thus they seek to borrow money at lower rates and lend at higher rates. These banks are big players in Call Money Markets.

Some banks also aggressively deal in bond markets. Some other banks are big players in FOREX markets. However it must be understood that these markets are volatile and they can be extremely risky. The banks that wish to play in these markets must have good people and processes to minimise risks.

5. Financial Inclusion

This is the latest development in banking. India is an under banked society. Almost 50% of the population has no bank accounts. The government is planning that most Indians should have a bank account. To this the RBI is planning to have only deposit taking banks that will not lend money but all the money that they collect will be invested in government securities thus eliminating risk of default. There is a move to start Indian Posts Bank. Since most Indian villages have post offices they will in future offer banking services to the rural people.

RBI has also undertaken Correspondent banking scheme. Here some Non Banking Finance companies are allowed to offer limited banking services like depositing and withdrawing money and transfer of funds. This will be launched across the country. Technology is going to be used to make it work.

Financial inclusion is also being encouraged through Micro Finance companies in many states.

There is a proposal that is being actively discussed by the government and the RBI wherein all account holders will have an overdraft facility of ₹ 5000. This it is hoped will encourage the poor to open and operate bank accounts. It is hoped this will encourage the habit of savings amongst the poor and will also help them not to borrow money from the local moneylenders at exorbitant rates.

We still have a long way to go In this area. However if the government is going to follow Direct Bank Transfer (DBT) route to pay subsidies, pensions and scholarship etc directly in the bank accounts of the beneficiaries then this initiative is of paramount importance and urgency.

It is hoped that most Indians will have a bank account in the next five years and this will ultimately help in mobalising savings for development purposes.

6. Spread

Spreads or Net Interest margins (NIM): The bank borrows money and then lends. Naturally the rate at which it borrows money is lesser than the rate at which it lends the money. The difference between the two is known as NIM. Banks strive to maintain this NIM as their profitability depends on this.

7. Credit Appraisal

Credit appraisal means an investigation/assessment done by the bank prior before providing any loans and advances/project finance and also checks the commercial, financial and technical viability of the project proposed its funding pattern and further checks the primary and collateral security cover available for recovery of such funds. Credit Appraisal is a process to ascertain the risks associated with the extension of the credit facility. It is generally carried by the financial institutions which are involved in providing financial funding to its customers.

8. Investments

Investments of a bank: SLR is the major source of banks investments. Banks also invest money in other government securities if they do not find safe avenues for lending. Banks can invest money in the bonds issued by other banks or bonds and debentures issued by companies. Banks are also allowed to invest money in Capital markets. However, most Indian bank tend to stay away from these markets.

Banks hold their security portfolio in two categories. One is known as Held to Maturity (HTL). These securities are held till maturity by a bank. Thus the banks will not trade on these.

The second category is of the securities are known as Held for Trading (HT). The banks buy and sell securities held in this category and try and book profits. However such securities have to be marked to market by the banks. This means that any loss that even though notional in nature will have to accounted for in the P/L account of the bank. For example if banks buy a security at a price of ₹ 109 and on the day of the balance sheet if it is quoting @ ₹ 106, then bank has to book the notional loss is ₹ 3. This loss has to be accounted for. Banks Treasury departments have to be very careful about this category. The loss on account of Mark to Market (MTM) can ruin a bank's profitability.

Treasury operations in a bank are a risky operation at all times. The exposure limits have to be set up to monitor these

3.1.3 Use of Risk Management Indicators by Banks

Banks also typically use indicators of risk management to complement other financial measures.

Commonly used financial measures are tabulated below:

• Total Assets	• Earnings base = Earning Assets/Total Assets
• Total Assets/Employee	• Burden/Total Assets = (Non interest exp-Non interest income)/Total Assets
• Profits as a % of total assets	
• Return on Equity	• Efficiency ratio = Non interest exp/(Net interest income + Non interest income)
• Gross Margins	
• Net Interest Income	• Profit per employee
• Net Interest Margin	• Revenue per employee
• Equity Multiplier =Total Assets/Equity	• Return on Investment
• Interest Expense/Total Assets	• Share price
• Non-interest expense/total assets	• Cash Flows
• Provision for loan losses/Total Assets	• Credit rating
• Taxes/Total Assets	• Interest coverage ratio
• Debt equity ratio	• NPA/Total Assets
• Interest Income/Total Assets	**Capital Adequacy ratio**
• Spread = (interest inc/earning assets)-(interest expense/interest bearing liabilities)	• Advances/Total Assets
	• G-Secs/total investments
• Operating profit to average working funds	• Gross NPA's/Total Advances
	• Net NPA's/Total Advances
• Liquid assets/Total assets.	• Total Advances/Total Deposits-a measure of management efficiency

Customer perspective

While choosing measures for customer perspective of the scorecard, banks must answer two critical questions.

- Who are our target customers and market segment?
- What is our value proposition in serving them?
- Operational Excellence: Focus on low price, zero defects, convenience and no frills.
- Product Leadership: Constantly innovating to offer the best product in the market.
- Customer Intimacy: Focus on a long term relationship building through their deep knowledge of customer needs.

A bank should use the following measures to track its success should it follow a customer intimate approach.

- **Customer knowledge:** To gauge staff knowledge of the customers the bank may measure "training hours on client products".
- **Solutions Offered:** To measure the attribute of providing an unmatched total solution, banks measure "total number of solutions offered per client".
- **Penetration:** The bank should ensure that its efforts are achieving success by deep penetration of accounts.
- **Customer data:** "Percentage of employees with access to customer information" may be measured to track this key differentiator of success.
- **Culture of driving client success:** "Number of customer awards received" helps track this goal.

Other Sources of Customer Measures

- **Financial objectives and measures:** Determining how they translate into customer requirements.
- **The customers voice:** Using message boards and targeted sites.
- **Moments of Truth:** At any point at which a customer comes in contact with a business, defines a moment of truth. Mapping these moments of truth provides any bank branch with an opportunity to isolate the differentiating features offered and designing metrics to track success.
- **Look into the channels:** Each of the channels has specific processes and will entail different performance measures.
- **Working from the customer experience** and thereby unearth a number of critical measures of success for the customer and all other perspectives of the scorecard.
- **Customer Relationship management Initiatives:** The bank should track the effectiveness of the considerable investment in CRM processes.

1. A Sample of Customer Measures:

• Customer Satisfaction	• Win rate (sales closed/sales contacts)
• Customer Royalty	• Customer visits to the company
• Market Share	• Hours spent with the customers
• Customer Complaints	• Marketing cost as a % of sales
• Complaints resolved on first contact	• Number of ads placed
• Return rates	• Number of proposals made
• Response time per customer request	• Brand recognition
• Direct price	• Response rate
• Price relative to competition	• Interest and Non Interest Income
• Total cost to customer	• Share of target customer saving invested in the bank's deposits
• Average duration of customer relationship	• Volume of various types of deposits mobilized
• Customers lost	• Deposits per channel
• Customer retention	• Average customer size
• Customer acquisition rates	• Customers per employee
• Percentage of revenue from new customers	• Customer service expense per customer
• Number of customers	• Customer profitability
• Annual sales per customer	• Frequency (no of transactions converted)

Internal Process Measures

• Average cost per transaction	• Breakeven time
• On-time delivery	• Cycle time improvement
• Average lead time	• Continuous improvement
• Research and Development Expense	• Internal rate of return on new projects
• Community Involvement	• Waste reduction
• Patents pending	• Space utilization
• Average age of patents	• Downtime
• Ratio of new products to total offerings	• Planning accuracy
• Stockouts	• Time to market of new products/services
• Man Power Utilisation rates	• New product introduced
• Response time	• Number of positive media stories
• Defect percentage	• Rework
	• Customer database availability

2. Learning and Growth Perspective

This is the enabler of the other three perspectives. These measures close the gap between the current organisational infrastructure of employee skills and information system and the level necessary to achieve the results. These include

- Employee skills
- Employee satisfaction
- Availability of information

Motivated employees with the right mix of skills and tools in an enabling organisational climate are key ingredients in driving process improvements, meeting customer expectations and ultimately driving financial returns.

Measuring capabilities

- **Using core competencies to measure skill development:** The bank must identify the differentiating competencies the bank needs to achieve its strategy. The best way of doing this is to involve as many people as possible from all levels of the organisation. Focus groups and interviews can be used to assess company needs and competence gaps.
- **Using personal development planning (PDP) to boost competence holders:** The majority of personal goals in the plan should help the employee influence the achievement of the company's strategy. Goals in the plan should be measurable and should include specific action steps. Now the bank should track the percentage of employees who meet their personal development plan goals. There should be quarterly or monthly progress updates. The bank can also measure the "competency coverage ratio" which tracks the percentage of necessary skills currently possessed to meet the anticipated needs.
- **Encourage healthy lifestyles**: The bank can measure its health promotion initiatives by tracking the number of employees who take advantage of any "health promotion" programme, or gauging employee attitudes regarding lifestyle clauses.
- **Measuring employee training**: The mistakes that most banks make is that they simply look at the raw amount of training offered, for example the number of training hours per employee. Training must be linked to organisational goals and objectives and companies should measure results of the training. The trained personnel should also be encouraged to share their learning with the other employees in the bank.

    ICICI Bank has *Learning Matrix* as its e-knowledge portal which helps employees learn all the different banking and financial aspects. A fixed amount of man days is assigned on successful completion of these courses. Importance is given to the learning aspect during performance appraisal, further motivating employees to not only learn but also to spread the knowledge. The results of this knowledge drive are for all to see, in a span of 10 years ICICI Bank is the 2nd biggest bank in the country and one of the most recognized brands in the country, its not just *Hum Hain Na....Hum Har Jagah Hain* that's the motto. HR must take the lead in the development of knowledge workers; it must act on global cues and trends developing strategies to keep the workers up to date and be competitive. They must broker knowledge between different domains and SBU's to assist in the overall competitiveness of the organisation and create employees with an all round skill to handle a wide array of jobs.

- **Employee productivity**: In order to determine the value added per employee, the value of externally purchased resources should be deducted.

3. **Tracking Employee Tools**
   - **The instruments of business**: Employees must have up to date and modern equipment if the bank has to compete in today's economy.
   - **Access to information**: The bank should measure what percentage of customer-facing staff have the ability to access detailed customer information within 30 seconds of a customer interaction. The bank should determine what information is critical to employee decision making and develop a performance measure that tracks the % of employees who have this information available to them

4. **Motivation and alignment**
   - **Employee satisfaction**: Banks attempt to measure this through annual surveys and use the findings to design better ways to do things. The data is to be appropriately swiftly acknowledging areas requiring improvement and developing measures to improve them. Corporate intranets and e-mail systems can be used to gather feedback from employees semi annually or quarterly.
   - **Alignment:** A good alignment measure is simply the number of scorecards produced within he organisation. The bank needs to analyse individual scorecard and assess their degree of alignment (i.e. the percentage of measures directly relating to strategic goals). The target should be 100%.

5. **Employee learning and growth measures**

- Employee participation in professional and trade organisations	- Quality of work environment
- Training investment per customer	- Internal communication rating
- Average years of service	- Employee productivity
- % of employees with advanced degrees	- Number of scorecards produced
- Number of cross trained employees	- Health promotion

• Absenteeism • Turnover rate • Employee suggestions • Employee satisfaction • Participation in stock ownership plans • Value added per employee • Motivation index • Outstanding number of applications for employment • Diversity rates	• Training hours • Competency coverage ratio • Personal goal achievement • Timely completion of performance appraisals • Leadership development • Communication planning • % of employees with computers • Strategic information ratio • Cross functional assignments • Knowledge management • Ethics violations • Empowerment index (number of managers)

All banks face four types of risks. Identification of these risks early and putting in place a mechanism to minimise these risks or even mitigating these risks is a very important aspect of control mechanism in a bank. This is a challenging job and requires well trained manpower. They are:

(a) Credit Risk: This is the risk that mainly arises if the counter party were to default on their contractual obligations to the bank. If a borrower defaults this risk would arise. Also in a contract of buying and selling securities this risk can manifest itself.

(b) Market Risk: This risk arises when interest rates change. If interest rates increase the banks tend to benefit as the interest rates on loans go up immediately. However the interest rates on existing deposits remain same. The rates on deposits change only for new deposits or deposits that are renewed at the new rates. Thus there is a time lag that is beneficial to a bank.

However the situation is exactly opposite when interest rates decline. The interest income on loans will come down immediately while the cost of deposits will remain high till they mature.

Exchange rate risk is also a part of market risk. Changes in exchange rates can be at times favorable but at times they can be unfavorable. This will actually depend on what position the bank has taken in the future FOREX market deals. When the Indian currency sharply depreciated in 2013 many banks were caught unawares and did suffer losses.

(c) **Operational Risk:** This risk is an internal risk. This arises out of employee mistakes or frauds on one side or due to the faulty processes including software used. This is one risk that is controllable to a large extent but not fully. Making sure that employees are well trained and putting in place controls that will detect frauds or better still preventing frauds will go a long way in minimising this risk.

Since banks today use IT solutions widely keeping them up to date is imperative. We hear of many fraudulent activities in this area and banks have to take precautions in this respect. Creating adequate firewalls for on line transactions or making sure that misuse of credit cards is detected quickly thus become a priority for a bank.

(d) **Reputation Risk:** If a bank is unable to control the above three risks effectively and suffer losses because of this then the reputation of the bank itself will be at stake. The closure of Global Trust Bank, The United Western bank and The Rupee Co-operative bank are some of the examples of this kind.

It can thus be seen that banking is a complex operation. Many other operational aspects of a bank cannot be discussed here, but students will have to learn the operations of a bank to appreciate why banking is complex.

Because the complexities involves the control systems in a bank also becomes quite complex. It is not easy to learn about the control processes in a bank without knowing all the operations of a bank. That in itself is a separate subject. Therefore we have discussed only the important controls that are in force. Many of these are imposed by the Regulator i.e. Reserve Bank of India.

For the controls used by the bank on its own we have used the Balanced Score Card method to illustrate the areas where controls are necessary and have highlighted the important points that bank has to consider while designing a control system. The BSC method is a control system in itself.

3.1.4 Some More Parameters for Evaluating Bank Performance

Some more parameters for evaluating Bank Performance can be summarised as follows:
- Aggregate deposits
- Deposit break-up
    - Branch-wise
    - Employee-wise
    - Category-wise
    - Interest rate-wise
    - Maturity-wise
    - Area-wise
    - Interest on deposits as % of total expenditure / average cost
    - Bank share in total deposits
    - % terms

- % share in incremental growth
- Advances
- Advances break-up
- Category-wise
- Limit-wise
- Interest rate-wise
- Term / maturity-period-wise
- Area-wise (R / S-U / U / M)
- Branch / employee-wise
- Branch / category-wise
- Renewal schedule
- NPA classification
- Interest on advances as % of total income
- Average yield / spread
- Bank share in total advances
- % terms
- % of priority sector advances
- Share in incremental advances
- Remittances – DD / MT / TT / EFT
- Average remittances per branch
- Bills for collection
- Centre-wise data (ABC analysis) bills / remittances)
- Income from remittances
- Remittances income as % of total income
- Bank income and industry averages
- Average float / pipeline funds
- Reconciliation status
- Total cash on hand
- Average cash balance held
- Cash retention limit
- Cash remittances sent / recd.
- CRR forecast
- Total projected DTL / NDTL
- Total projected SLR (bucket)
- Central government securities
- Total state securities
- State-wise break-up
- State-wise cap, if any
- Credit-rating up-dates
- Up-coming tranche

- Investments in bonds
- Respective PSU credit-rating
- Rate-wise / maturity-wise data
- Interest accrued / received details, alongwith periodicity and due dates
- Average / comparative yield
- Market trends (appreciation / depreciation)
- Total branch net-work
- Area-wise branch network alongwith comparative position
- Comparative deposit data
- Comparative advances data
- Comparative per branch / employee data for dep. / adv.
- CRR / SLR maintained
- Total / net DTL forecast
- CRR/SLR requirements forecast
- Asset liability management
- Capital adequacy ratios
- Personnel inventory
- Productivity parameters and actuals
- Profitability details

3.2 Performance Evaluation Parameters for Retail

The term 'Retailing' is thought to be derived from an old French word 'Retailler' which, according to **Brown (1992)**, means "a piece of" or "to cup up".

Retailing can be defined as "any business that directs its marketing efforts towards satisfying the final consumer based on the organisation of selling good and services as a means of distribution".

Retailing, particularly retailing goods, encompass producers, wholesalers, retailers and consumers.

Typical functions performed by Retailers are –

- Providing an assortment of products and services.
- Breaking bulk.
- Holding inventory.
- Providing services.

The retail sector has evolved over the years and has emerged as a barometer of/for the social and economic advancement of the nations.

Retailing and retailers, over the years, have come a long way from the typical neighbourhood or Pop and Mom Stores to become global, corporate entities. Indeed, some of the corporate retailers like Wal Mart, McDonalds, Carrefour, Target, Kroger, Home Depot,

Sears Roebuck, Tesco, Metro, Albertsons, Cotsco and Mark and Spencers are among the world's bigger corporations.

With globalisation, corporatisation and the emerging competition, the retailers are being now professionally managed, with emphasis on optimisation and performance, in the same way that other corporate business organisations are managed.

The corporatised and professionally managed retailers have put in place mechanisms and ecosystem to ensure long-term strategic perspective and competitiveness as illustrated hereafter.

With the strategic ecosystem in place, the retailers have also adopted/internalised similar performance and Performance Evaluation Parameters/Indicators as are being applied by other corporate organisations.

However, in this section, we would be focussing upon the following tools/techniques/parameters with special Retail Perspective.

1. ABC analysis
2. Sell Through Analysis
3. Multiple Attribute Method
4. Gross Margin Return on Investment (GMROI)/GMROII as Gross Margin/Average Inventory at Cost.

3.2.1 ABC Analysis

In the contemporary competitive business environment, the business organisations have to control costs and must be cost-effective. Most of the business organisations, manufacturing and marketing organisations in particular, are required to maintain and manage a number of items as inventory. Inventory, however, does not come cheap or free and there are various costs involved in/with inventory management. Storage costs, carrying costs, damage/wastage costs, stock-out costs and obsolescence costs are some of the costs associated with inventory management.

Therefore, the way inventory is managed and the way inventory costs are managed and kept under control within the supply chain, becomes a critical performance evaluation parameter for a Retail Organisation.

However, it is neither desirable nor practicable to exercise the same degree of control on all items of inventory. The organisation, therefore, endeavours to pay the maximum attention to those inventory items whose value is the highest. The organisation then classifies inventory items to identify which items deserve to receive the most attention and efforts in controlling and managing inventory.

The organisation, therefore, has to be selective and analytical in its approach to control investment in various types of inventories, depending upon the significance, importance and criticality of the respective inventory items.

This analytical approach is known as the ABC Analysis.

What is ABC Analysis?

"ABC Analysis is a widely-used classification/categorisation technique to identify various items of inventory for purposes of inventory control".

"ABC Analysis is an Inventory Categorisation Method which consists in dividing items into three categories, viz. A, B and C, and tends to measure the significance of each item of inventory in terms of its value and in order of its perceived/estimated importance".

'A' category items are **very important** as they are of high value and involve the largest investment. The Annual Consumption Value of 'A' items is the highest. While 'A' category items generally account for around 65-70% of the Annual Consumption Value, such items typically account for around 5-10% of total inventory items. Further, "A" items call for very tight control and accurate records and warrant the most attention of/from the management. Hence, inventory control for 'A' category items should be the most rigorous and intensive and the most sophisticated inventory control techniques should be applied to these items.

'B' category items are **important.** However, such items are in between or midway items as they are **relatively less important than 'A' items but more important than 'C' items**. 'B' category items have a medium Annual Consumption Value of around 15-25%, 'B' items, therefore, are less tightly controlled, compared to 'A' items, need good records and require reasonable attention of management. 'B' items can also be controlled by employing less sophisticated techniques.

'C' category items are of **marginal importance**. 'C' items represent relatively low/least value and the Annual Consumption Value is around 5-10%. Such items involve relatively small investments, although the number of items is fairly large, around 70%. 'C' items can be kept under simple controls and require **minimal** records.

While there cannot be any category-wise specific/standard stipulated quantity or threshold limit for the A, B and C inventory items, the conventional proportion of break-down pattern for the A, B and C items can be illustrated as follows –

Item Category	% Share in Total Inventory	% Share of Annual Consumption Value
A	5-10%	70%
B	25-30%	25%
C	60-70%	5%

{Annual Consumption = (Annual Demand) × (Item Cost Per Unit)

Sometimes, instead of Annual Consumption Value, the total cost of such items can also be considered.}

Another observed category-wise break-down of the inventory is,

Item Category	% in Total Inventory	% in Total Cost/Value
A	10%	66.6%
B	20%	23.3%
C	70%	10.1%

It may be noted that the ABC Analysis is also known, or referred to, as, Selective Inventory Control (SIC), Control by Importance and Exception (CIE) or Proportional Value Analysis (PVA).

These terms are used as the ABC Analysis focuses/concentrates on the Critical Few rather than Trivial many, and the items are classified in accordance with the importance of their relative values.

ABC Analysis: Implementation Process/Steps

Having discussed the basics of ABC Analysis, let us now note the steps involved in the implementation of the ABC Analysis in an organisation.

1. Classify the inventory items, determining the expected use in units and the price per unit for each item.

2. Determine the total value of each item by multiplying the expected units by its unit price.
3. Rank the items in accordance with the total value, in descending order (First Rank to the item having highest total value).
4. Calculate the percentage/ratios of number of units of each item to total units of all items and the ratio of total value of each item to total value of all items.
5. Combine items on the basis of their relative value to form the 'A', 'B' and 'C' categories.

Importance of ABC Analysis

From the Managerial and Retail Management view/perspective, the ABC Analysis is found to be useful and helpful in the following ways –

1. ABC Analysis can help the organisation keep costs under control within the supply chain.
2. ABC Analysis can help in choosing appropriate order pattern and avoid excess stock.
3. ABC Analysis can help the management undertake effective value analysis and initiate appropriate measures/actions to ensure better control of high value and high priority items.
4. ABC Analysis helps draw the manager's attention on the 'Critical Few 'A' category' items, rather than on the 'Trivial Many 'C' Category items and facilitates Control by Exception.
5. ABC Analysis can facilitate more efficient Cycle Counts.
6. ABC Analysis can help Supply Chain Management identify Inventory Hot Pots and separate them from the rest of the items, especially those that are numerous but not profitable.
7. ABC Analysis helps provide a mechanism for identifying items that will have a significant impact on overall inventory cost and initiate suitable measures.
8. ABC Analysis provides a mechanism for identifying different categories of stock that will require different management and controls, by taking into account the volume, usage, cost and the annual consumption value of the relative/respective inventory item.
9. ABC Analysis helps the Retail Management, in particular, in the areas of merchandise, category and stock management.

For Retail Sector, the ABC Analysis helps taking decisions as regards

(a) Items that should **never be out of stock.**
(b) Items that can be **out-of-stock occasionally.**
(c) Items that should be **deleted from the stock selection.**

For Retail Organisations, in particular, rather than just the percentage in stock and annual consumption value, the ABC Analysis could emphasise contribution to sales, as shown below.

A = 5% items contributing 70% of sales.
B = 10% items contributing 20% of sales.
C = 65% items contributing 10% of sales.
D = 20% items contributing 0% of sales.

3.2.2 Sell Through Analysis

Sell Through Analysis is an important performance evaluation parameter for retail. It is important because it provides a composite measure of sales and inventory. It can be used by both – the Retailers and the Vendors – for evaluating sales performance of a product / item. Sell Through is also a leading indicator and can be used for predictive analysis.

Sell Through, is not to be understood or interpreted as 'Sales' only. However, it allows the retailer to understand the velocity with which inventory is being consumed, as it relates to sales.

Sell Through is about how many products/units/items the Retailer has sold, from the stock/inventory it originally started from the point of view of Supply Chain, Sales, Merchandise/Category Management. It is also important from the perspective of Inventory Management, Control and Turnover.

Sell Through: Definition

1. "Sell Through is a calculation commonly represented as a percentage, comparing the amount of inventory a retailer receives from a vendor against what is actively sold to the consumer".
2. "Sell Through is the ratio of the quantity of goods sold by a retail outlet to the quantity distributed to it wholesale".

The Sell Through can be calculated as follows –

$$\text{Sell Through} = \frac{\text{Units Sold}}{\text{(Units on Hand + Units Sold)}}$$

Why and How to Evaluate Sell Through?

Any inventory that is not sold through is at a risk for mark down or return, depending upon the contract between the vendor and the retailer. As such, there is a need to evaluate and track Sell Through. Both, the Vendor/s and the Retailers always have the goal to have as high a Sell Through as possible.

While evaluating the Sell Through, it is considered useful and desirable to group/bunch together products which have been selling for a similar period of time and/or which are sold into the similar store types.

In most cases, Sell Through is compared for/in recent periods like current week and previous/last week. It can, however, be compared in aggregate across several previous months or even a year.

With the advent of Information Technology, however, Sell Through is now typically evaluated on a daily basis for fast moving items and weekly basis for slower-moving or replenishment-based products.

Most Retail Buyers (Stores) have pre-determined or pre-set Sell Through percentage ratio. They use this parameter to judge vendors, based upon store, department or product category. As such, it is important for vendors to discuss the Sell Through expectations with the Retailer/Buyer in order to align with those objectives.

What Does the Sell Through Indicate?

If Sell Through is low, it indicates either poor sales or too much inventory.

If Sell Through is high, it indicates that the Retailer's Sales Velocity is good/high and the Retailer's inventory is forecasted/worked out appropriately and optimally.

A High Sell Through is, of course, better and desired.

Sell Through Analysis and Decision-making"

Some of the illustrative areas, where Sell Through Analysis helps the managerial decision-making in retail are follows –

1. It helps understand what is selling, in what Configuration, Category, Department, Store, Item and Season-wise.
2. It helps track the size and movement at/of the market place.
3. It helps optimise product assortments and fine tune supply chain linkages with the vendors.
4. It helps track product life cycle and product launches.
5. It helps identify and uncover new market opportunities.
6. It helps determine what is driving market growth.
7. It helps evaluate, and adjust/weak marketing and advertising messages.
8. It helps support product Design and Development.
9. It helps working out competitive strategy (Pricing, Marketing, Product Design and Development) and helps position products against competition, competitively.
10. Helps drive revenues and improve profitability.

3.2.3 Multiple Attribute Method

There was a time when Henry Ford could say that 'My customers can have any colour of the car, as long as it is black", and get away with it.

At that time, being in a monopoly/seller's market, customers would purchase the car because of its availability, the only attribute the buyer/customer was interested in.

Today, however, when a customer wants to purchase a car, it is not availability alone, but for the customer other factors/attributes like price, comfort, colour, performance, fuel efficiency, reliability, size, style, safety, brand image, technology, operating / running costs, warranty and service centre network etc. are equally important.

Similar dilemma is faced by the organised corporate retail organisation as the products the organisations are going to purchase from vendors and going to sell to customers have to be evaluated in the context of multiple attributes. The dilemma, the decision-makers in the retail face is because of the multiple attributes they have to consider before taking decisions pertaining to retail business, encompassing, inter alia, vendors, products, customers, merchandise, category, store, store size, location and season, among others.

If there is only a single criterion/parameter/attribute (like say cost), then the decision can be made implicitly by determining the alternative with the best value of the single criterion/attribute/aggregate measure.

Many times, however, situations arise where there are many factors/parameters/attributes to be considered, before taking decisions. Alternatively, it may also happen that the number of criterion and alternative is finite and the alternatives are given explicitly. When there is a finite number of attribute/criterion, but the number of feasible alternatives, which meet the decision requirement, is infinite, the problem becomes more complex.

Problems of this type are called multi-attribute decision-making problems and it is here where the multiple attribute/criteria method/model enters the scenario.

Multiple Attributes Method

There are various methods used for making decision based on the multiple attributes.

Basically, these methods could **EITHER**

1. Help "choose" the best alternative, from a set of available alternatives, **OR**
2. Help "choose" a small set of alternatives, **OR**
3. Help find all efficient alternatives.

There are Multiple Attribute Methods which require the Decision Maker's preference information at the beginning of the process and are said to operate by "Prior Articulation of Preferences".

There are other methods based on estimating a value function or using the concept of "OUTRANKING RELATIONS".

There are also methods based on decision-rules and there are interactive methods or methods that require "Progressive Articulation of Preferences".

According to Janos Fulop (Introduction to Decision-Making Models), there could be the following Multiple Attribute Methods

1. **Elementary Methods**
    - Pros and Cons Analysis
    - Maximin and Minimax Methods
    - Conjunctive and Disconjunctive Methods
    - Lexicographic Methods

2. **MAUT (Multi Attribute Utility Theory) Methods**
    - Simple Multi Attribute Rating Technique (SMART)
    - Generalised Means
    - Analytical Hierarchy Process (AHP)
3. **Outranking Methods**
    - The ELECTRE Methods
    - The PROMETHEE Methods
4. **Group Decision Making Methods**
5. **Sensitivity Analysis:**

   The various multiple attributes methods are stated as follows:
    - Aggregate Indices Randomisation Method (AIRM)
    - Analytical Hierarchy Process (AHP)
    - Analytical Network Process (ANP)
    - Conjunctive and Disconjunctive Methods
    - Data Envelopment Analysis
    - Disaggregation - Aggregation Approaches (UTAII/UTADIS)
    - Dominance-based Rough Set approach
    - ELECTRE
    - Evidential Reasoning Approach
    - Fuzzy VIKOR Method
    - Generalised Means
    - Grey Relational Analysis (GRA)
    - Inner Product of Vectors (IPU)
    - Lexicographic Methods
    - Maximin and Minimax Methods
    - Measuring Attractiveness by a Categorical Based Evaluation Technique (MACBETH)
    - Multi Attribute Global Inference of Quality (MAGIQ)
    - Multi Attribute Utility Theory (MAUT) Methods
    - Multi Attribute Value Theory (MAVT)
    - New Approach to Appraisal (NATA)
    - Non-Structured Fuzzy Decision Support System (NSFDSS).
    - Potentially All Pairwise Rankings of all Possible Alternatives (PAPRIKA)
    - PROMETHEE methods
    - Pros and Cons Analysis
    - Simple Multi Attribute Rating Technique (SMART)
    - Superiority and Inferiority Ranking Method (SIR)

- Technique for the Order of Preference/Prioritisation by Similarity of Ideal Solution (TOPSIS)
- Value Analysis (VA)
- Value Engineering (VE)
- VIKOR Method
- Weighted Product Method (WPM)
- Weighted Sum Model (WSM)

3.2.4 Gross Margin Return on Investment (GMROI)

The Gross Margin Return on Investment (GMROI), also known as the Gross Margin Return on Inventory Investment (GMROII) is a useful measure/parameter for Retail Performance Evaluation. It is useful as it helps the Management/Investors see the average amount that the inventory returns above its costs.

It may be noted that in our discussions, we would be using the terms GMROI and GMROII interchangeably.

It is one way to determine how valuable the Retailer's/ Seller's inventory is, and describes the relationship between Total Sales, Total Profit from Total Sales, and the amount of resources invested in the inventory sold. In the Retail sector/industry, the GMROI is now accepted as the standard inventory statistics by many retailers as it reflects the movement of inventory relative to profitability, rather than to sales. The GMROI/GMROII is considered to be a better measure of inventory performance because retailers are more interested in profitability than sales.

What is 'GMROI'?

"The Gross Margin Return on Investment (GMROI) is an Inventory Profitability Evaluation Ratio that analyses a Retail Firm's ability to turn inventory into cash, above the cost of inventory".

The GMROI can also be said to be "a Ratio that describes a seller's income on every unit of currency spent on inventory". The GMROI answers the question: "For each unit of currency at cost, how many units of currency of gross profit will the Retailer/Seller generate in one year?"

'GMROI': Computation

The GMROI is traditionally calculated by using one year's gross profit against the average of 12 to 13 units of inventory at cost.

More specifically, the GMROI is calculated by dividing the gross margin by the average inventory cost, as illustrated.

$$\begin{aligned} \text{GMROI} &= \text{Gross percentage} \times \text{Sales-to-Stock Ratio} \\ &= \frac{\text{Gross Margin}}{\text{Net Sales}} \times \frac{\text{Net Sales}}{\text{Average Inventory at Cost}} \\ &= \frac{\text{Gross Margin}}{\text{Average Inventory Cost}} \end{aligned}$$

It may please be noted that "**Gross Margin** is the difference between the selling price and the cost of the product, **LESS** reduction for mark downs, shrinkage and employee discounts".

What is the Desired GMROI?

A GMROI ratio higher than 1 means the retail firm is selling the merchandise for more than what it costs the retail firm to acquire/procure it.

If the GMROI ratio is below 1, then the opposite is true.

Here, it would be interesting to note that –

(a) The minimum standard for GMROI in most retail operations is expected to be 200%. Anything less is considered to be unprofitable.

(b) A heuristic rule of thumb in the retail industry is that for the retail business to break even, the GMROI should be at least 3.2.

Inventory Costs

Every firm would like to minimise investments in inventory as maintaining inventory involves costs.

For our purpose, inventory costs, apart from the cost of merchandise, would include:

(a) Ordering or acquisition or set-up costs, and

(b) Carrying costs

    (i) Storage costs

    (ii) Insurance costs

    (iii) Obsolescence costs

    (iv) Theft and Pilferage costs

    (v) Opportunity cost of funds

GMROI in Retail

Retailers usually drive their business based on sales or margins.

However, in a retail organisation, where budgets and bonuses are based on sales, employees often tend to achieve the budgets/sales by lowering the margins or putting too much stock in stores. It can also happen, it is observed, that in case of items with high sell-offs (e.g. Fashionable items in vogue), the final stock level on hand might tend to fall towards zero. Such items, therefore, might appear better business than items with constant inventory supplies and regular sales.

The GMROI becomes particularly important for the retail organisations facing such situations where Stock Turn (i.e. Sales Units/Average Inventory Units) and Gross Margin Percent (i.e. margin) may/can vary widely/heavily by items, store, location, week or season.

The GMROI can act as the main driver for retailers to analyse their product and store offering by getting an insight into the real margins.

A high GMROI indicates a good balance of sales, margin and inventory cost.

While on GMROI and Retail, it may be noted that some retailers prefer to use Average Weekly GMROI, instead of the annual one. This is done as the weekly GMROI enables the retailer to look at similar types of numbers, regardless of how many weeks are being looked at.

The weekly GMROI is worked out as follows:

$$\text{Average Weekly GMROI} = \frac{\text{Profits for the Total Time Period}}{\text{Sum of each week-ending Inventory Cost Value}}$$

Illustrative Examples of Evaluation Parameters currently prevailing among the Retail Organisations

Level of Organisation	Output	Input	Performance Measure (Output/Input)
Merchandise management (measures for a merchandise category)	Net sales	Inventory level	Gross Margin (Return on Investment (GMROI)
	Gross margin	Markdowns	Inventory turnover
	Growth in sales	Advertising expenses	Advertising as a percentage of sales*
		Cost of merchandise	Markdown as a percentage of
* These productivity measures are commonly expressed as an input/output.			

Examples of Performance Measures used by Retailers:

Level of Organisation	Output	Input	Performance Measure (Output/Input)
Store operations (measures for a store or department within a store)	Net sales	Square feet of selling areas	Net sales per square foot
	Gross margin	Expenses for utilities	Net sales per sales associate or per selling hour
	Growth in sales	Number of sales associates	Utility expenses as a percentage of sales*
* These productivity measures are commonly expressed as an input/output.			

Illustrative Productivity Measures used by Retailing Organisations:

Level of Organisation	Output	Input	Performance Measure (Output/Input)
Corporate (chief executive officer)	Net profit	Owners' equity	Net profit/Owners' equity = Return on owners' equity
Merchandising (merchandise manager and buyer)	Gross margin	Inventory *	Gross margin / Inventory* = GMROI
Store operations (director of stores, store manager)	Net sales	Square foot	Net sales / Square foot
* Inventory = Average inventory at cost.			

To Conclude

It is submitted that the Multi Attribute Methods should be used as Decision Support Tools and not as the means for deriving final answer.

The Multi Attribute Methods should be treated only as "Indication" to what may be the best answer. As there cannot be a single best / unique solution for the complex situations, the Multi Attribute Methods should be seen / treated more as a Mechanism facilitating / enabling WHAT IF ANALYSIS, rather than as Performance Evaluation Measure / Parameter.

Multi Attribute Methods/Models are "Selector Models" and are to be used for evaluating, ranking and selecting the most appropriate alternative/option from among the alternatives available.

Points to Remember

- **Capital Adequacy Ratio (CAR):** Banks are required to have capital in proportion to its assets.
- **Asset Liability Management (ALM):** Banks have liabilities that have a certain maturity period.
- **Priority Sector lending:** All banks in India have to adhere to the guidelines of RBI towards priority sector lending. They have to make sure that out of their loan assets 40% loans are given to this sector.
- Statutory liquidity ratio (SLR) refers amount that the commercial banks require to maintain in the form of gold or govt. approved securities before providing credit to the customers.
- **Cash Reserve Ratio (CRR):** Every commercial bank has to keep certain minimum cash reserves with RBI.

- Bank rate is the rate at which RBI lends or refinances a bank. This is also known as benchmark rate.
- Non-Performing Assets are loans that are not repaid in time or interest on loans is not paid regularly.
- Spreads or Net Interest margins (NIM): The bank borrows money and then lends. Naturally the rate at which it borrows money is lesser than the rate at which it lends the money. The difference between the two is known as NIM. Banks strive to maintain this NIM as their profitability depends on this.
- Credit appraisal means an investigation/assessment done by the bank prior to providing any loans and advances/project finance and also checks the commercial, financial and technical viability of the project proposed its funding pattern and further checks the primary and collateral security cover available for recovery of such funds.
- ABC Analysis is an Inventory Categorisation Method which consists in dividing items into three categories, viz. A, B and C, and tends to measure the significance of each item of inventory in terms of its value and in order of its perceived/estimated importance.
- Sell Through is a calculation commonly represented as a percentage, comparing the amount of inventory a retailer receives from a vendor against what is actively sold to the consumer.
- The Gross Margin Return on Investment (GMROI) is an Inventory Profitability Evaluation Ratio that analyses a Retail Firm's ability to turn inventory into cash, above the cost of inventory.

Questions for Discussion

1. What is the importance of Capital Adequacy ratio?
2. Why are controls in a bank on two levels –External and Internal?
3. What are the risks that are faced by a bank?
4. What should be the financial goals of a bank?
5. Why is learning and growth one of the most important aspects of a bank's control system?

Project Question

Study the Balance Sheet of a nationalized bank and one Private bank. Compare the two and note the areas of differences.

Chapter **4**...

Performance Evaluation Parameters for Projects and for Non-Profit Organisations

Contents ...

- 4.1 Performance Evaluation of Projects
    - 4.1.1 Introduction
    - 4.1.2 Definition of Project
    - 4.1.3 Attributes of a Project
    - 4.1.4 Project Management Cycle
    - 4.1.5 The Project Control Process
    - 4.1.6 Variance Analysis: Schedule Variance vs. Cost Variance
    - 4.1.7 Control Points in a Project
    - 4.1.8 Performance Evaluation Parameters for Project
    - 4.1.9 Risks in Projects
- 4.2 Performance Evaluation of Non-Profit Organisations
    - 4.2.1 Introduction
    - 4.2.2 Meaning of Non-profit Organisation
    - 4.2.3 Features of Non-Profit Organisations
    - 4.2.4 Types of Non-Profit Organisations
- 4.3 Performance Evaluation Parameters for Non-Profit Organisations
    - 4.3.1 Fund Accounting
    - 4.3.2 Governance
    - 4.3.3 Product Pricing
    - 4.3.4 Strategic Planning and Budget Preparations
    - 4.3.5 Social Audit
- • Points to Remember
- • Questions for Discussion

Learning Objectives ...
- Understand what project is
- Understand what is involved in a project
- Understand Steps of Project Management cycle
- Understand Control measures for a project
- Understanding PERT and CPM
- Understand different types of risks in a project
- Understand features of non-profit organisations
- Understand the parameters for evaluation of non-profit organisations

4.1 Performance Evaluation of Projects

4.1.1 Introduction

Projects are of different kinds and all projects are normally unique in nature. Projects require planning and execution. Most projects are complex in nature and thus they require constant monitoring and controls to make sure that they are executed properly within budgets and time allotted to them.

Most of the projects that are undertaken by companies are derived from the company's long term goals and strategies. Projects are a way of implementing the strategies and they are normally executed at the SBU level of the organisation.

Companies would undertake projects for: (a) Expansion, (b) Diversification or (c) Acquisition.

There are other types of projects as well. A company may have expertise in implementing projects for other companies. Companies like L&T, Gammon India, HCC to name a few are in this field. The owner of the projects gives the contract of project execution to such companies. The owner will define the scope of the project and will also finance it, while the contracting company will execute the contract. Some of these projects can be Turnkey Projects. In such projects the contractor is responsible for Designing, Procuring, Inspection, erection, testing and commissioning of a project. From this it can be clear that the scope of such projects is very vast and they are bound to be complex in nature.

Another type of project that are in vogue these days and their importance is likely to grow in coming years are projects that fall under the category of Public – Private - Partnership, Projects popularly known as (PPP) projects. In these types of projects, the government or its department or a corporation of government joins hand with one or a consortium of private sector companies to build infrastructure. Such projects have a huge financial outlay and are of long duration. Some examples of these projects are building national highways, power plants, airports and ports etc.

We can see many such projects across the country at present. In these projects the private sector companies bring in money and expertise. Government can participate in bringing in equity in the company. The government does not pay for the facilities created by such projects. The companies that build them are given a period in which they can recover their entire investment wit pre-determined profit from the cash flow generated by the project. Thus we have to pay toll for roads or user charges at the airport.

4.1.2 Definition of Project

- An endeavour in which human, material and financial resources are organised in a novel way to undertake a unqiue scope of work, of given specification, with constraints of cost and time, so as to achieve benefical change defined by qualitative and quantitative objectives.
- A Project is a planned set of action actitvities meant to achieve specific objectives using allocated scared resources. These activities are to be performed within a specified period of time.
- A temporary endeavour undertaken to create a unique product or service.
- A project is a process aimed at achieving specified objectives. The term project refers to a process and not the end product or result.
- A process can be defined as a series of actions or operations directed toward particular result. For example, a completed human rights commisssion office block is not the project but is the product of the project.
- The product of the process usually has a life well beyond the process. E.g. adopting a human rights culture, attitudinal change.

4.1.3 Attributes of a Project

A project involves a number of charateristics or attributes which include:

- **Unique:** That is it is a once off discrete undertaking and normally not repeated in the same way.
- **Finite:** That is it time bound, has a start and end point. It is also finite in content that is activities, objectives and organisations.
- **Multiple resources:** Each project has a mix of skills, technologies and resources human and non human which are brought together for a specific objective.
- It requires team work which usually cuts acrosss conventional lines of authority and organisational structures.
- **Change:** Project intends to create change.

4.1.4 Project Management Cycle

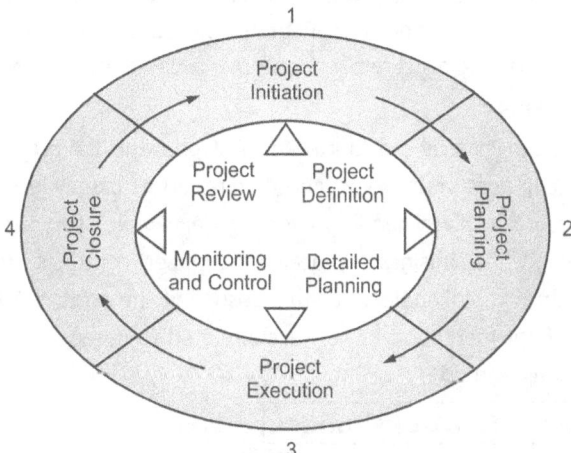

Fig. 4.1

1. **Project Initiation Phase**

   The Project Initiation Phase is the first phase in the Project Management Life Cycle, as it involves starting up a new project. You can start a new project by defining its objectives, scope, purpose and deliverables to be produced. You'll also hire your project team, setup the Project Office and review the project, to gain approval to begin the next phase. The Project Initiation Phase is the most crucial phase in the Project Life Cycle, as it's the phase in which you define your scope and hire your team. Only with a clearly defined scope and a suitably skilled team, you can ensure success.

2. **Project Planning Phase**

   The Project Planning Phase is the second phase in the project life cycle. It involves creating a set of plans to help guide your team through the execution and closure phases of the project. The plans created during this phase will help you to manage time, cost, quality, change, risk and issues. They will also help you manage staff and external suppliers, to ensure that you deliver the project on time and within schedule. The Project Planning Phase is often the most challenging phase for a Project Manager, as you need to make an educated guess of the staff, resources and equipment needed to complete your project.

3. **Project Execution Phase**

   The Project Execution Phase is the third phase in the project life cycle. In this phase, you will build the physical project deliverables and present them to your customer for signoff.

The Project Execution Phase is usually the longest phase in the project life cycle and it typically consumes the most energy and the most resources. To enable you to monitor and control the project during this phase, you will need to implement a range of management processes. These processes help you to manage time, cost, quality, change, risks and issues. They also help you to manage procurement, customer acceptance and communications.

4. Project Closure Phase

The Project Closure Phase is the fourth and last phase in the project life cycle. In this phase, you will formally close your project and then report its overall level of success to your sponsor. Project Closure involves handing over the deliverables to your customer, passing the documentation to the business, cancelling supplier contracts, releasing staff and equipment, and informing stakeholders of the closure of the project. After the project has been closed, a Post Implementation Review is completed to determine the projects success and identify the lessons learned.

4.1.5 The Project Control Process

Control is the process of comparing actual performance against plan to identity deviations, evaluate possible alternative courses of actions, and take appropriate corrective action. The project control steps for measuring and evaluating project performance are presented below.

1. Setting a baseline plan.
2. Measuring progress and performance.
3. Comparing plan against actual.
4. Taking action.

Each of the control steps is described in the following paragraphs.

Step 1: Setting a Baseline Plan

The baseline plan provides us with the elements for measuring performance. The baseline is derived from the cost and duration information found in the work breakdown structure (WBS) database and time-sequence data from the network and resource scheduling decisions. From the WBS the project resource schedule is used to time-phase all work, resources and budgets into a baseline plan.

Step 2: Measuring Progress and Performance

Time and budgets are quantitative measures of performance that readily fit into the integrated information system. Qualitative measures such as meeting customer technical specifications and product functions are most frequently determined by on-site inspection or actual use. Measurement of time performance is relatively easy and obvious, That is, is the critical path early, on schedule, or late: is the slack of near-critical paths decreasing to cause new critical activities? Measuring performance against budget (e.g. money, units in place, labour hours) is more difficult and is not simply a case of comparing actual versus budget, Earned value is necessary to provide a realistic estimate of performance against a time-phased budget. Earned value (FV) is defined as the budgeted cost of the work performed.

Step 3: Comparing Plan against Actual

Because plans seldom materialise as expected, it becomes imperative to measure deviations from plan to determine if action is necessary. Periodic monitoring and measuring the status of the project allow for comparisons of actual versus expected plans. It is crucial that the timing of status reports be frequent enough to allow for early detection of variations from plan and early correction of courses. Usually status reports should take place every one to four weeks to be useful and allow for proactive correction.

Step 4: Taking Action

If deviations from plans are significant, corrective action will be needed to bring the project back in line with the original or revised plan. In some cases, conditions or scope can change, which, in turn, will require a change in the baseline plan to recognise new information.

4.1.6 Variance Analysis: Schedule Variance vs. Cost Variance

Variance analysis is the key to success of any project. When businesses place bids to win contracts, projected schedules and costs are required. They key to win the project is presenting the best bid; the key to winning future projects – not to mention earning a good reputation within your industry – is keeping the project on time and within budget. Variance analysis quickly shows project managers where the project is running astray.

(a) Schedule Variance (Time Over-runs)

Keeping a project on schedule is not only important from a time standpoint but also to avoid future cost overages. When a project loses site of its scheduled work, overtime – or even double-time – often is required to finish the project by the completion date. This can run project costs significantly over budget. Keeping a project on schedule is also important when sending the client project status reports. The client wants to know two things: Is the project on schedule, and is the project under budget? Schedule variance analysis shows the project manager whether the project is on schedule and, if not, how far it has fallen behind schedule. The manager can then correct the scheduling issue and present the solution with the status report, demonstrating to the client that the situation is already under control.

Calculating Schedule Variance

To calculate schedule variance, accountants take the project's planned value and subtract it from the project's earned value. A project's earned value takes the scheduled amount of work and compares that with the actual work completed to date; planned value assesses the cost of the scheduled work budgeted in comparison to the cost of the work actually completed to date. So, earned value looks at hours, and planned value looks at costs. A positive result, which is when the project hours do not exceed the project costs to date, present a schedule variance that indicates the project is on schedule. A negative result, which is when the project costs exceed the project hours, present a schedule variance that indicates the project is behind schedule because the amount of work actually paid for exceeds the amount of scheduled work performed.

(b) Cost Variance (Cost Overruns)

Cost variance analysis is equally important to schedule variance analysis because project costs obviously need to stay within the budget. It is disastrous for both the company and its client if project costs exceed budgeted values. Unless there is a good explanation for the overage, the client is left with a poor impression of the company it hired to complete the project – not to mention less money in its pocket. Cost variance analysis compares the budgeted costs of the project to the actual costs of the project by line item. This can quickly tell a project manager the portion of the project budget that is over the original estimated amount. For example, if the company budgeted a certain amount of money to cover the project license and permit costs and the country in question raised the fees unexpectedly, the "License and Permits" budgeted line item will show a cost variance that is over budget.

Calculating Cost Variance

Cost variance is much easier to calculate as the accountant simply takes the earned value of a line item and subtracts the actual cost of the line item. Taking the license and permit costs example discussed previously, if the company projected this line item at ₹ 50,000 and the actual costs were ₹ 55,000, the cost variance for this line item in the budget would be negative ₹ 5,000, showing this budgeted line item is ₹ 5000 over the projected costs. If the budgeted permits and licenses actually cost ₹ 45,000, the cost variance would show a positive ₹ 5,000, showing the actual cost was ₹ 5000 under budget – a result any client would appreciate.

4.1.7 Control Points in a Project

Now that we have broadly seen what a Project consists of we can now look at the different control points in a Project:

Broadly following are the things/activities that are crucial to a project and hence the control system has to be focused on these parameters.

Time is of immence importance and the pre-decided timelines for execution and completion of a project are very crucial. This will include

(a) Deployment of Right Quality of People on the Project: A project manager is overall in charge of a project. He should be given a team that must include people who have experience in similar projects. Quality of people goes a long way in making a project a success or a failure. A project manager must be a good team leader and he should be able to carry the entire team with him. He must therefore discuss frequently with his team members and keep himself appraised of what is happening. Many times several tasks are being performed simulteneously, at such times co-ordination becomes a key area of control. A brain storming session allows team memebers to express their views freely about the happenings. It will also bring in goal congruence and that will help the team in its task.

(b) PERT/CPM: These are scientific tools of project management and are used globally. PERT is an activity chart that puts a time line to all the tasks that are required to be performed. The interdependency of tasks is highlighted here. It helps in starting time and finishing time of each task.

4.1.8 Performance Evaluation Parameters for Project

Three most important techniques for project scheduling and control are:
1. Gantt chart
2. Project Network
    (a) Critical Path Method (CPM)
    (b) Programme Evaluation and Review Technique (PERT)
3. Financial and Budgetary Control

1. Gantt Chart:
- Graph or bar chart with a bar for each project activity that shows passage of time.
- Provides visual display of project schedule.

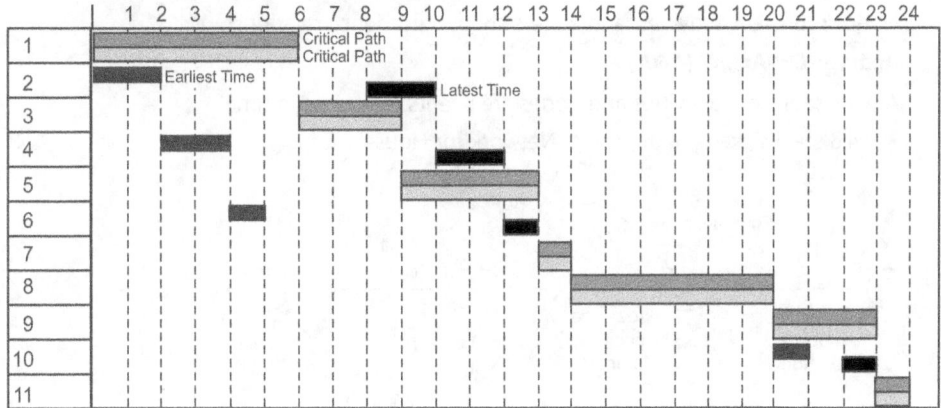

Fig. 4.2

2. Project Network

- Network analysis is the general name given to certain specific techniques which can be used for the planning, management and control of projects.
- Use of nodes and arrows.

  Arrows: An arrow leads from tail to head directionally.
  - Indicates ACTIVITY, a time consuming effort that is required to perform a part of the work.

  Nodes: A node is represented by a circle.
  - Indicate Event, a point in time where one or more activities start and/or finish.

- **Activity:**
  - A task or a certain amount of work required in the project.
  - Requires time to complete.
  - Represented by an arrow.

- **Dummy Activity:**
  - Indicates only precedence relationships.
  - Does not require any time of effort.

- **Event:**
  - Signals the beginning or ending of an activity.
  - Designates a point in time.
  - Represented by a circle (node).

- **Network:**
  - Shows the sequential relationships among activities using nodes and arrows.

- **Activity-On-Node (AON)**

  Nodes represent activities, and arrows show precedence relationships.

- **Activity-On-Arrow (AOA)**

  Arrows represent activities and nodes are events for points in time.

  Fig. 4.3 shows example of Project Network for House.

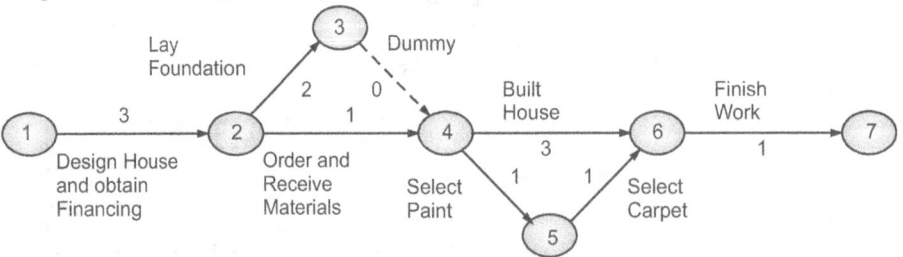

Fig. 4.3: Example of Project Network for House

Situations in Network Diagram:

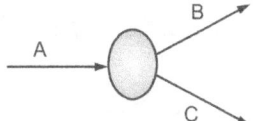

A must finish before either B or C can start

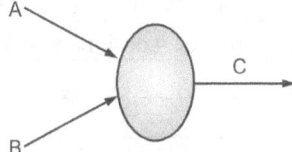

Both A and B must finish before C can start

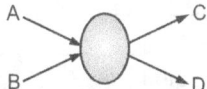

Both A and C must finish before either of B or D can start.

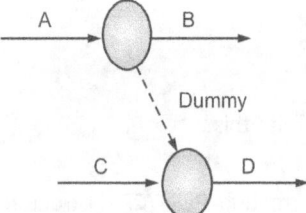

A must finish before B can start
Both A and C must finish before D can start

Fig. 4.4

Example of Concurrent Activities:

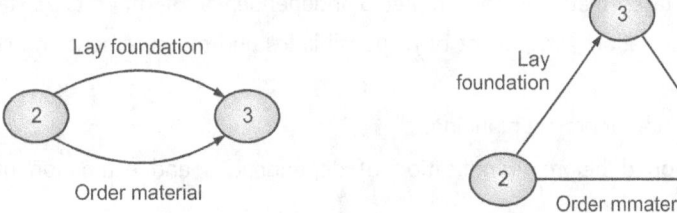

Fig. 4.5: Example of Concurrent Activities
(a) Incorrect precedence relationship, (b) Correct precedence relationship

Network example:

The key question is: How long will it take to complete this project?

Activity number		Completion time (weeks)
1	Redesign product	6
2	Redesign packaging	2
3	Order and receive components for redesigned product	3
4	Order and receive material for redesigned packaging	2
5	Assemble products	4
6	Make up packaging	1
7	Package redesigned product	1
8	Test market redesigned product	6
9	Revise redesigned product	3
10	Revise redesigned packaging	1
11	Revise redesigned packaging	1

Questions to be asked to prepare activity network:
- Is this a Start Activity?
- Is this a Finish Activity?
- What Activity Precedes this?
- What Activity Follows this?
- What Activity is Concurrent with this?

Work Breakdown structure:
- This is the first step in creating PERT/CPM structure. We need to break down the activities in the project and put a timeline for completing those activities.
- A method of breaking down a project into individual elements (components, subcomponents, activities and tasks) in a hierarchical structure which can be scheduled and cost.
- It defines tasks that can be completed independently of other tasks, facilitating resource allocation, assignment of responsibilities and measurement and control of the project.
- It is foundation of project planning.
- It is developed before identification of dependencies and estimation of activity durations.
- It can be used to identify the tasks in the CPM and PERT.

a) CPM calculation:

- **Path**
    - A connected sequence of activities leading from the starting event to the ending event.
- **Critical Path**
    - The longest path (time); determines the project duration.
- **Critical Activities**
    - All of the activities that make up the critical path.

Forward Pass:

- Earliest Start Time (ES)
    - Earliest time an activity can start.
    - ES = maximum EF of immediate predecessors
- Earliest finish time (EF)
    - Earliest time an activity can finish.
    - Earliest start time plus activity time.

EF = ES + t

Backward Pass

- Latest Start Time (LS)

Latest time an activity can start without delaying critical path time.

LS = LF − t

- Latest finish time (LF)

Latest time an activity can be completed without delaying critical path time.

LS = minimum LS of immediate predecessors.

CPM Analysis:

- Draw the CPM network.
- Analyse the paths through the network.
- Determine the float for each activity.
    - Compute the activity's float.
        Float = LS − ES = LF − EF
    - Float is the maximum amount of time that this activity can be delay in its completion before it becomes a critical activity, i.e., delays completion of the project.
- Find the critical path is that the sequence of activities and events where there is no "slack" i.e. Zero slack.
    - Longest path through a network
- Find the project duration is minimum project completion time.

b) PERT:

- PERT is based on the assumption that an activity's duration follows a probability distribution instead of being a single value.
- Three time estimates are required to compute the parameters of an activity's duration distribution:
  - **Pessimistic time (t_p):** The time the activity would take if things did not go well.
  - **Most likely time (t_m):** The consensus best estimate of the activity's duration.
  - **Optimistic time (t_o):** The time the activity would take if things did go well.

PERT analysis:

- Draw the network.
- Analyse the paths through the network and find the critical path.
- The length of the critical path is the mean of the project duration probability distribution which is assumed to be normal.
- The standard deviation of the project duration probability distribution is computed by adding the variances of the critical activities (all of the activities that make up the critical path) and taking the square root of that sum.
- Probability computations can now be made using the normal distribution table.

PERT Example:

Activity	Immediate Preceding	Optimistic Time (Hr.)	Most Likely Time (Hr.)	Pessimistic Time (Hr.)
A	--	4	6	8
B	--	1	4.5	5
C	A	3	3	3
D	A	4	5	6
E	A	0.5	1	1.5
F	B, C	3	4	5
G	B, C	1	1.5	5
H	E, F	5	6	7
I	E, F	2	5	8
J	D, H	2.5	2.75	4.5
K	G, I	3	5	7

Benefits of CPM/PERT
- Useful at many stages of project management.
- Mathematically simple.
- Give critical path and slack time.
- Provide project documentation.
- Useful in monitoring costs.
- CPM/PERT can answer the following important questions.
- How long will the entire project take to be completed? What are the risks involved?
- Which are the critical activities or tasks in the project which could delay the entire project if they were not completed on time?
- Is the project on schedule, behind schedule or ahead of schedule?
- If the project has to be finished earlier than planned, what is the best way to do this at the least cost?

Limitations to CPM/PERT
- Clearly defined, independent and stable activities.
- Specified precedence relationships.
- Over emphasis on critical paths.
- Deterministic CPM model.
- Activity time estimates are subjective and depend on judgement.
- PERT assumes a beta distribution for these time estimates, but the actual distribution may be different.
- PERT consistently underestimates the expected project completion time due to alternate paths becoming critical.

Thus it can be seen that PERT and CPM are very effective tools of control in projects. They also help in cash flow estimations. The PERT will tell the project Manager when he can claim money from the client since payments may be linked to milestone achievements. Sometimes payments are made on monthly progress basis. How much monthly billing can be achieved can be judged from the targets in PERT.

3. **Financial and Budgetary Control:**

This is to be done through a budget. A budget for the entire project has to be in place with provision for contingencies. A tight control has to be excercised on budget.

A company decides to undertake a project only after it is sure that in can raise the financial resources that are required for the project. The company can raise money either through equity or by borrowing or by utilising its internal accruals to finance the project.

The concepts like Capital Budgeting are used to find out the projects' financial feasibility. Net Present Value (NPV), Payback Method, and Internal Rate of Return (IRR) are some of the tools used for this.

A overall budget is prepared to finance the entire project cost. While doing so costs are attributed to engineering design and drawing, purchases, labour cost for erection and expenses that many have to be incurred for testing and commissioning the project.

The cost of interest can be a major head of expense if a lot of money is required to be borrowed to finance the project. At times a company may also require working capital to execute the project. This is especially true of company who are in the business of doing third party projects like L&T, GMR, GVK, Gammon etc.

Risk Management:

All projects have inherent risks. Such risks have to be identified right at the beginning and then they have to be managed properly. Some risks can be transfereed and they will have to be transferred. Other risks will have to be managed by the Project Managment team as they arise. Some of the risks are impossible to predict. These risks will have to be dealt with if they do arise. The experience of the Project Manager and his team members is valuable in this.

4.1.9 Risks in Projects

There is a probability or chance that a thing will not turn out as planned. This is always the possibility. In spite of all the meticulous planning, a risk may still manifest itself.

High certainty of outcome means less risk and vice versa.

Once we recognise that all projects have inherent risks some of them can be identified while others we may not be able to identified. We have to identify and quantify as many risks as possible.

Since large sums of money (or effort converted to money) over a period of time are involved in Projects. Once these sums are deployed it is virtually impossible to take out the money. Many Projects embody a firm's strategic intent.

Lenders are interested in the Project's ability to service the debt. Lenders actually take on the financial risk of the project. Since their money is involved they have to make sure that the projects they are going to finance should have proven feasibility. Otherwise a lender will not be able to recover his money.

Risks in Projects stem from

1. Technical uncertainties/ constraints.
2. Schedule uncertainties.
3. Cost uncertainties.

High certainty of outcome depends on knowledge and experience in prior projects.

Unique or first time projects have higher element of risk- It must be remembered that every project is unique. Many projects are similar but they are always unique because similar projects have a tendency to be uniquely different as many conditions vary from project to project.

Risk is a fact of life in Projects: It's reduction by anticipation and contingency planning is the objective of Risk Management.

Risk Management: Main elements

- Risk identification.
- Risk assessment.
- Risk response planning.

4.2 Performance Evaluation of Non-Profit Organisations

4.2.1 Introduction

So far, our discussions had been moving around the business organsiations where the primary objective is to earn profits, add value and create wealth. Indeed, it is said that "the business of business is earning profits". As the focus of the business organisations is on profits, as a survival condition, all the other discussions centered around performance measurement and evaluation which was aimed at maximising profits and thereby add value to the firm.

However, every organisation does not aim at profits alone. There are other organisations which work in economic domain, build, assets, add value but are non-profit organsiations. Such organisations in the private sector are more popularly known as non-governmental organsiations or NGOs.

These organisations, rather than focusing upon profit earning and profit-maximisation, are more concerned about social welfare at large, and operate in the larger interests of society. Today, such non-profit organisation have emerged as an important instrument for social and good and welfare.

Indeed, such non-profit organisation, NGOs in particular, have emerged as a major economic and financial entities and a force to be reckoned with. In this context, it would be interesting to note that around 41,844 NGOs were registered under the Foreign Contribution Regulation Act (FCRA) by 2013. The foreign donations not to mention the domestic mobilisation of resources in India by the NGOs over the past few years, beginning from F.Y. 2006-2007, have been in the range of ₹ 10,000/- to ₹ 11,000/- crores as per data available from Ministry of Home Affairs, Government of India (*Times of India, 01/07/2014*).

Indeed, some claim that it is good business to set-up a NPO/NGO!

As such organisation command, and are in possession of huge resources, let us now discuss as to what is a non-profit organisation, their features as also related issues like Fund Accounting, Governance, Product Pricing, Strategic Planning and Budget Preparation.

We will also discuss the concept of 'Social Audit later.

4.2.2 Meaning of Non-profit Organisation

A non-profit organisation can be said to be one whose mandate is to operate for/in the interests of the society. Its funding comes from grants, donations, contributions made by founders or endowments or by way of income from sale of products/services.

A non-profit organisation can create assets and earn income, but it cannot distribute asset or income to or for the benefits of its members, office-bearers or directors. It can, however, pay to personnel employed by its discharging its goals and promoting its activities.

Such an organisation can earn income and have surplus.

These organsiations, however, cannot distribute the surplus earned by them, unlike profit-oriented or for-profit organisations who can distribute profits by way of dividends.

The non-profit organsiations basically earn income by way of donations, contributions, grants, sale of goals/services etc. They may also raise loans for the attainment of their purpose. However, being non-profit organsiations, they do not have to pay Income Tax. Indeed, subject to the legal provisions, the donations/contributions to such organisations are eligible for Income Tax rebate/exemptions. In most cases, such organisation do not have to pay Income Tax at all.

The principal goal is of the non-profit organisation is defined by their vision/mission. The mission is basically the social mission and might pertain to socially relevant areas encompassing inter alia, education, health-care, HIV/AIDS awareness, children and women healthcare/welfare, rural development, agricultural, extension/development activities, promotion of literature, science or fine arts, diffusion of useful knowledge, protection and improvement of the natural environment, sports, medical relief, provision for facilities for recreation or other leisure time occupation (when the facilities are provided in the interest of social welfare and public benefit etc.)

4.2.3 Features of Non-Profit Organisations

Having discusses the basic concept of what a non-profit organisation is, let us now note the features of non-profit organisation.

1. The NPOs generally tend to be service organsiations. Hence, they usually tend to be service-oriented and developmental in nature.
2. The NPOs mostly have the funds contributed by grants, donations, contributions and endorsements. Further they have specific sources/support for funds.

3. The NPOs receive 'Contributed Capital' and have no shareholders.
4. The deployment/usage of funds may be restricted or specifically directed by the donors for specific pre-determined purposes.
5. As the sources of funds more or less, captive, the NPOs may not be dependent on service/product users/customers for financial support.
6. The NPOs tend to be set up/managed by professionals from belonging to varied or respective field/area/disciplines. As such, there might exist differences in management.
7. The people managing NPOs could be committed to their cause. But, in the process, managerial skills might be undervalued or underestimated. This may lead to management operating sub-optimally.
8. When the NPOs are registered under the laws of the land, they will have to follow the related provisions to illustrate, a NPO/NGO registered under the Societies Regulation Act, 1860 or the Maharashtra Public Trusts Act, 1950 or an act applicable in the State, by operating modalities as stipulated in the respective Acts.
9. The NPOs are not subjected to market mechanism. Hence, these organisations, more often that not, may not fed or face the pressure of competitive forces.
10. The NPOs, except and Governmental NPOs, tend to be aligned to or owe alligance to specific social causes/activities. They may also be aligned to religion or political thought.
11. There is no profit motive. As such, financial performance would not be the dominant goal.
12. Financial or monetary performance measures may not be significant applicable.
13. As such, the output or performance evaluation parameters' would tend to be more qualitative and non-monetary in nature. Identification of measures or parameters of performance, therefore, tends to be interpretive and judgemental.

4.2.4 Types of Non-Profit Organisations

Non-profit organisations can be classified into the following types:
1. Government organisations.
2. Non-government organisations.
   (a) Commercial organisations
   (b) Charitable Institution (Societies/Trusts)

1. Government Organisation

These organisations, set up and/or sponsored by the Government, cover the normal functions of the State. Some of such organisations could be Municipal Corporations, Municipalities, Gram Panchayats. Entities like Khadi and Village Corporation, Council for

Scientific and Industrial Research, IITs, IIMs and AIIMS and such other organisation can also be included in this category type:

2. **Non-government Organisation**

   (a) **Commercial Organsiations:** These organisations, although engaged in commercial activities, do not aim at earning profits but provide goods/services where they face competition and operate in the market place.

   (b) **Charitable Institutions:** These organisations are registered under the Societies' Registration Act, 1860 or the Public Trust Act (as applicable to the respective State) and have a clear focus and social mission.

The entities are funded by diverse and diversified donors, both domestic and foreign. Quite a few of these organisations more popularly known as NGOs, tend to be activist or developmental organisations, dedicated to a particular course.

4.3 Performance Evaluation Parameters for Non-Profit Organisations

Performance evaluation parameters for non-profit organisations include:

1. Fund Accounting
2. Governance
3. Product Pricing
4. Strategic Planning and Budget Preparations
5. Social Audit.

4.3.1 Fund Accounting

The funds for the NPOs come from various sources. The funds can be provided by the Government, or the funds could come in by way of sales of goods/services, contributions and donations from munificent donors. The donors, again, could be domestic or foreign. The donors, again, could be domestic or foreign. The donors could be individual or institutional.

While the basic accounting norms and procedure as laid down by the regulatory/legal authorities would need to be adhered to, the accounting reports and audited statement accounts should be devised in such a manner that the requirements, if any of the donors is also taken care of.

The accounting norms laid down are known as 'Fund Accounting'. While the Western countries the U.S.A. and U.K. in particular, have provided for mandatory accounting standards for 'Fund Accounting', Accounting Standards prevalent in India are rather ambivalent.

However, before we specify the Accounting Procedure and Practices in India for Fund Accounting, let us keep in mind that 'Fund Accounting Products for NPOs should be designed with a view to facilitating the monitoring and controlling function, as the fact remains that 'Funds' are 'Resources' and, therefore, have to be managed effectively and efficiently.

Accounting Stipulations

The basic stipulations as regards accounts as laid down by the Indian Trusts Act, 1882 are 2 that a trustee is bound:

(a) To keep clear and accurate accounts of the trust property, and

(b) At all reasonable times, at the request of the beneficiary to furnish him with full and accurate information as to the amount of State of the trust property.

According to the Maharashtra Public Trusts Act, 1950, the following major stipulations have been laid down:

1. Every Trustee of a public trust shall keep regular accounts.
2. Such accounts shall be kept in such form as may be approved by the Charity Commissioner and shall contain such particulars as may be prescribed.
3. The accounts kept shall be balanced each year on the thirty-first day of March or such other day, as may be fixed by the Charity Commissioner.
4. The accounts shall be avoided annually by a person who is a qualified Chartered Accountant or is so authorised by the State Government. The Auditor should not take any interest in or connection with the Public Trust.
5. The Trustees shall make all the documents and records available to the Auditor.
6. A special audit can be ordered by the Charity Commissioner, if considered necessary.

The following records, related with accounts, is required to be maintained:

(a) Account Books
(b) Receipts
(c) Day Book
(d) Stock Book
(e) Bank Correspondence File.

4.3.2 Governance

The Governance structure, as applicable to the non-profit organisations, is stipulated by the Societies Regulation Act, 1860 and the Public-Trusts Act, 1950 (as applicable to the respective states).

These provides for Trustees, Management Committees, Board of Directors, etc. The duties and powers of the Trustees, Committees etc. are also provided for.

4.3.3 Product Pricing

Product pricing is critical one of the most important decision-areas not duly for corporates but also for non-profit organisation.

For the profit-oriented corporates, pricing is important as sales volume itself depends upon the price. Pricing is also a key to profits as the margin depends upon the cost-price difference. Pricing is also the key to the organisations resources.

Corporates, therefore, have been following various pricing strategies like cost-based strategies, demand-based strategies, competition-based strategies on product-mix/line pricing strategies. Indeed, the profit-centric corporates have to follow pricing strategies as mistakes in pricing may make:

(a) Public perception

(b) Competitiveness and

(c) Organsiation's business

Although the non-profit organisation do not face the same dilemma that the corporates face, the pricing decisions for product/service offered by them is equally crucial for the non-profit organisations as well as product/service pricing decisions are crucial for the non-profit organisations as these decisions would determine the continuity and sustainability of the non-profit organisations.

The non-profit organisations can follow a differential pricing policy for the products/services provided by it. While in case of certain products/services considered public goods or essential for the NPO's mission, it may not be charge any price (viz. Pulse Polio Campaign) as it may be able to mobilise substantial grants or subsidy from the Government or donations from the donors.

If, however, there is no grant, subsidy or donation available, the non-profit organisation may resort to a full pricing.

If the prices are set lower than the full cost, the NPO may end up with deficits/losses. On the other hand, if prices are changed at a level higher than full cost, it may result in creating surplus or generating profits which goes against the very DNA of the non-profit organisation.

If the non-profit organisation is a single product/service organisation, then it has to be a full-cost pricing.

However, if the NPO has multiple products/services, the NPO can engage into differential pricing - certain products/services can be changed a price that is higher than the full cost, while certain other products/services may be charged at a price that is below the full costs incurred. However, the NPO must be able to recover the full cost for the organisation as a whole, to ensure financial viability, continuity and sustainability.

To summarise, the pricing of NPOs should be based upon:
(a) Allocative efficiency.
(b) Keeping transaction costs in control/lower.
(c) Keeping administrative costs in control/lower.

The NPOs, because of the issues mentioned earlier, can effectively act as a force in the market to keep prices under check for the society at large.

4.3.4 Strategic Planning and Budget Preparations

Strategic planning is important in non-profit organisations as it facilitates transformation of an organisation from "what it is" to "what it ought to be" in future. The process of strategic planning involves environmental analysis, SWOT analysis and leveraging the strengths of the NPO to accomplish its social mission.

The Trustees or Board of Directors of the NPO may undertake SWOT analysis and review and revise the existing goals and their relative priorities. The strategic planning exercise would also enable the Trustees/Board of Directors to identify constraints and problems and facilitate seamless accomplishment of the organisational goals with a long-term perspective.

Notwithstanding the imperative for any organisation, it is generally observed that strategic planning as a formal system has been formally institutionalised in corporate organisations, with all the elements for Strategic Management ecosystem in place.

The NPOs, it is observed, do not usually have well-developed, formal strategic planning in place.

However, majority of the NPOs do have budgeting process in place. The budget preparation focuses upon quantifying the operational contents of each specific objective and also plan for the specific tasks and their backward forward linkage. The budget components need to be closely and seamlessly integrated with specific objectives, with the strategic goals. While preparing the budget it should be ensured that there is goal and congruence between personal and NPO goals. Towards ensuring goal congruence, it is important that the budgetary goals are understood and internalised by all concerned the trustees as well as managers and all other employees.

In case of the NPOs which are Trusts/Societies, there is a statutory obligation to prepare the budget and submit it to the Charity Commissioner. As per the Public Trust Act, a Trustee of a Public Trust, which has annual income exceeding the prescribed amount shall atleast one month before the commencement of each accounting year, prepare and submit a budget showing the probable receipts and disbursement of the trust during the following year.

Each such budget shall make adequate provision for carrying out the objects of the trust, and for the maintenance and preservation of the trust property.

4.3.5 Social Audit

Social Audit concepts are now becoming increasingly popular and relevant. The demand for social audit has grown in recent years due to the steady shift in devolution of resources - Governmental, Corporate or NGOs and functions relating to socio-economic projects/ schemes.

The vital role of social audit for ensuring the local stakeholders role in grass root level implementation of the Government, Corporate or NGOs socio-economic programmes/ initiatives, verification of deliverables and ensuring end-use of resources has now been accepted. Apart from this, the critical role of social audit is fixing accountability of implementing agencies as also providing safeguard against mis-use, corruption and frauds, has been duly recognised.

However, the origin of social audit goes back to almost over sixty years. The first use of the term 'Social Audit' is generally attributed to George Goyder in the 1950s.

The roots of the idea lay within the perceived need at that time to make business more accountable to the community and to ensure that impact of business - both beneficial and non-beneficial - are understood by the society. Earlier, in the past, controls and influence were exerted by local communities over local companies operating locally. **Goyder** linked the growing importance of Social Audit to the need for society to be able to exert the controls and influence over the corporate organisations as they globalise. **Goyder** in his book "The Responsible Company (1961)' emphasised that in an economy of 'Big Business', there was clearly as much need for a Social Audit as for a Financial Audit.

Later, **Charles Medawar** is credited to have further accelerated the concept of Social Audit in 1972 with the application of the idea in medicine policy, drug safety issues and on matters of Government, Corporate and professional accountability.

According to **Medawar**, the concept of Social Audit starts with the principle of a democracy, the decision-makers should account for the use of their powers, which should be used as far as possible with the consent and understanding of all concerned.

In mid-1970s, in Europe and UK, the team Social Audit emerged to describe evaluation that focussed on the likely impact on jobs, the community and the environment, if a particular enterprise/industry were to close or relocate. These evaluations used the term Social Audit to clearly make the point that they were concerned with the 'social' and not the 'economic' consequences of a particular action.

Today, the Government, Corporates and the NGOs have experienced resource crunch, and have realises the imperative need to ensure the efficient and effective management of resources. Today, the economies and finance have attained social dimension and hence Social Audit has become important.

It has become important for Governmental Agencies as there is devolution of Government Funds for socio-economic schemes.

Social Audit has also been carried out by some NGOs as a means of understanding their impact on society and to see whether they are catering to peoples needs.

The concept of Social Audit has evolved among corporates as tool for reporting their contribution to society and obtaining people's feedback on their activities to supplement their market and financial performances. In today's era, corporates are often expected not just to deliver value to consumers and shareholders, but also to meet environmental and social standards deemed desirable by some vocal members of the general public.

Social Audit can help Governmental and corporates organisations and NGOs create, improve and maintain a positive public relations image.

Let us now, note the definitions of Social Audit.

Social Audit: Definitions

Having discussed the origin and evolution of the concept of Social Audit, let us note a few definitions of Social Audit.

1. "Social Audit is a formal review of an organisation's endeavours in social responsibility".
2. "Social Audit is a process of reviewing official records and determining whether the reported expenditure reflects actual monies spent on ground".
3. "Social Audit looks at factors such an organisation's record of charitable giving, volunteer activity, energy use, transparency, work environment and worker pay and benefits to evaluate what kind of social and environmental impact a company is having in the locations where it operates".
4. "Social Audit is the process of evaluating a firm's various operating procedures, code of conduct and other factors to determine its effect on the society.

    The goal is to identify, what, if any, actions of the firm have impacted the society in some way".
5. "Social Audit can be understood, in a broader sense, as a continuous process of public vigilance to ensure public accountability in the implementation of projects, laws and policies by the community as a whole".

Principles of Social Audits

The foremost principle of Social Audit of course is to achieve continuously improving performance relative to the chosen social objectives.

There are eight specific principles, identified from Social Auditing practices around the world. The principles are as listed below:
1. Multi-perspective/Polyvocal
2. Comprehensive
3. Participatory
4. Multi-directional
5. Regular
6. Comparative
7. Verified
8. Disclosed.

Benefits of Social Audit

The major benefits of Social Audit can be summarised as follows:
1. Enhances organisation's reputation.
2. Alerts policy makers to stakeholders trends.
3. Increases accountability.
4. Assists in re-orienting and re-focussing priorities.
5. Facilitates positive organisational change.
6. Provides increased confidence in social areas.
7. Helps strengthen decentralisation and deepen process of democracy.
8. Helps improve organisational cohesiveness and improve it image within society.

Uses of Social Audit

The managerial of Social Audit can be stated as follows:
1. Helps capture the broader, social, community and environmental benefits.
2. It can be used as an instrument to provide critical and specific inputs.
4. Helps monitor the social and ethical impact and performance of the organisation on the social well-being of the citizens.
5. Helps assess the social costs and measure the social benefits accrued consequent upon programme implementation.
6. Provides a basis for shaping and designing management strategy in a socially responsible and accountable manner.
7. Facilitates the Strategic Management of Government/Corporate organisation with special reference to their impact/influence on community and environment.
8. Facilitates communication/information as regards resource allocation to the public, community and other organisations.

9. Facilitates organisational learning on how to improve social performance.
10. It is a powerful tool for Programme Audit and monitoring by the beneficiaries and stakeholders.
11. It plays a crucial role in implementation of social sector programmes and even in ensuring Corporate Social Responsibility
12. It provides an opportunity to plug long felt gap in Audit Process and techniques.
13. It provides the strongest and irrefutable direct evidence for inputs, processes, financial and physical reporting, compliance, physical verification, assurance against misuse, fraud and misappropriation and utilisation of resources and assets.
14. It provides a forum for strengthening the democratic process in governance and grievance redressal.
15. Social Audit helps to create, improve and maintain a positive public image. This can have a positive impact on the corporate's bottom line.

A Comparative Overview of Social, Financial and Operational Audits

Financial and Operational Audits are based on the conventional accounting principles and practices. These audits centre on financial viability, profitability and performance/productivity of the individual economic enterprise.

Social Audit is better understood as a reaction against the conventional audits. Social Audit proposes a broader financial and economic perspective, reaching far beyond the individual enterprise.

While the operational and financial audits take cognisance of financial profitability and operational efficiency, social audit posits other goals as well. To illustrate, social audit attempts to embrace not only economic and monetary variables, but also social ones. Some of these social variables may not be amendable to quantification in monetary terms, as pointed out by M. Gedders (1992).

While operational and financial audit looks at quantitative performance parameters, Social Audit examines performance vis-à-vis the organisations stated core values in the light of community values and the distribution of benefits among different social group reached through good governance principles.

Let us now briefly and succinctly compare Financial, Operational and Social Audits.

Financial Audit	Operational Audit	Social Audit
Directed towards recording, processing, summarising and reporting of financial data.	Establishing standards of operations, measuring performance against standards, examining and analysing deviations, taking corrective actions,	Social Audit provides an assessment of the impact of a organisation's non-financial objectives, through systematic and regular monitoring on

| | and re-appraising standards based on experience are the main focus. | the basis of the views of its stakeholders. |

To conclude, social audit needs to be understood, in a broader sense, as a continuous process of public vigilance to ensure public accountability in the implementation of social sector projects/programmes, laws and policies by the community as a whole.

Let us also remember that although found to be desirable and useful social audit, as of now, is optional.

Points to Remember

- A Project is a planned set of action actitvities meant to achieve specific objectives using allocated scared resources. These activities are to be performed within a specified period of time.
- **Phases in Project Management Cycle**
    1. Project Initiation Phase
    2. Project Planning Phase
    3. Project Execution Phase
    4. Project Closure Phase
- **Project control process involves following steps:**
    1. Setting a baseline plan
    2. Measuring progress and performance
    3. Comparing plan against actual
    4. Taking action
- Schedule variance analysis shows the project manager whether the project is on schedule and, if not, how far it has fallen behind schedule.
- Cost variance analysis compares the budgeted costs of the project to the actual costs of the project by line item.
- Three most important techniques for project scheduling and control are:
    1. Gantt chart
    2. Project Network
        (a) Critical Path Method (CPM)
        (b) Program Evaluation and Review Technique (PERT)
    3. Financial and Budgetary control
- **Network analysis** is the general name given to certain specific techniques which can be used for the planning, management and control of projects

- **A non-profit organisation** can be said to be one whose mandate is to operate for/in the interests of the society. Its funding comes from grants, donations, contributions made by founders or endowments or by way of income from sale of products/services.
- **Non-profit organisations** can be classified into the following types:
    1. Government organisations.
    2. Non-government organisations.
        (a) Commercial organisations
        (b) Charitable Institution (Societies/Trusts)
- **Performance evaluation parameters** for non-profit organisations include:
    1. Fund Accounting
    2. Governance
    3. Product Pricing
    4. Strategic Planning and Budget Preparations
    5. Social Audit
- The accounting norms laid down are known as 'Fund Accounting'.
- **Social Audit** is a process of reviewing official records and determining whether the reported expenditure reflects actual movies spent on ground.

Questions for Discussion

1. What are the steps in project initiation?
2. Explain PERT and CPM and why they are control systems in a project?
3. Explain the different risks that may impact a project.
4. Why environmental issues need to be dealt with in a project?

Chapter 5...

Audit Function as a Performance Measurement Tool

Contents ...

5.1 Audit
    5.1.1 Meaning
    5.1.2 Objectives of Audit
    5.1.3 Advantages of Audit
    5.1.4 Basic Principles and Practices of Audit

5.2 Types of Audit
    5.2.1 Statutory Audit/ Financial Audit
    5.2.2 Internal Audit
    5.2.3 Cost Audit
    5.2.4 Management Audit

- Points to Remember
- Questions for Discussion

Learning Objectives ...

- Understand the concept and objectives of Audit
- Understand the need for conducting Audit
- Understand various types of Audit viz. Financial Audit, Internal Audit, Statutory Audit, Cost Audit, Management Audit
- Understand and be aware of Measures for Performance Management

5.1 Audit

5.1.1 Meaning

In simple words, the term Audit indicates the verification and examination by an independent person of the books of accounts and records of an organisation with the intention to confirm that the financial statements drawn there from give true and fair view of the financial status of the organisation as on any given date and the profitability of the organisation for any given duration of time.

The above description of the term Audit indicates that the process of auditing is restricted to the verification and examination of the financial records of the organisation. To some extent, it is the fact also. However, considering today's competitive circumstances, the term auditing is extended to non-financial and technical areas as well. Today, we come across the terms like systems audit, energy audit, management audit etc. Crux of the term Audit lies in the fact that it is verification and examination carried out by an independent person who is not a part of decision-making process for the organisation. As a result, the auditor is able to view the operations of an organisation as a third party.

Origin of the audit may be traced to the increasing size and complexities in the operations of the business organisations and the separation of the ownership from managership which is the specific feature of a company form of organisation. In the earlier period, when the size of the organisation was small, it was possible for the owner to exercise proper control over the various affairs of the organisation, including financial affairs. With the increasing size of the organisation, it became difficult for the owners to exercise proper control on the regular financial affairs.

Due to the emergence of joint stock companies, where the ownership is with the shareholders and managership is in the hands of board of directors, it was difficult for the shareholders to participate in the affairs of the company on a regular basis. In such a case, need was felt for an independent professional who can protect the interests of the shareholders. Auditor took over the role of such an independent professional with the primary intention to protect the interest of the shareholders or the owners.

5.1.2 Objectives of Audit

Basic objective of auditing is to prove true and fairness of results presented by profit and loss account and financial position presented by balance sheet. Its objectives are classified into two groups which are given below:

(a) Primary Objectives of Audit

The main objectives of audit are known as primary objectives of audit. They are as follows:

(i) Examining the system of internal check.
(ii) Checking arithmetical accuracy of books of accounts, verifying posting, costing, balancing etc.
(iii) Verifying the authenticity and validity of transactions.
(iv) Checking the proper distinction of capital and revenue nature of transactions.
(v) Confirming the existence and value of assets and liabilities.
(vi) Verifying whether all the statutory requirements are fulfilled or not.
(viii) Proving true and fairness of operating results presented by income statement and financial position presented by balance sheet.

(b) Subsidiary Objectives of Audit

These are such objectives which are set up to help attain the primary objectives. They are as follows:

(i) Detection and Prevention of Errors

Errors are those mistakes which are committed due to carelessness or negligence or lack of knowledge or without having vested interest. Errors may be committed without or with any vested interest. So, they are to be checked carefully. Errors are of various types. Some of them are:

- Errors of principle.
- Errors of omission.
- Errors of commission.
- Compensating errors.

(ii) Detection and Prevention of Frauds

Frauds are those mistakes which are committed knowingly with some vested interest on the direction of top level management. Management commits frauds to deceive tax, to show the effectiveness of management, to get more commission, to sell share in the market or to maintain market price of share etc. Detection of fraud is the main job of an auditor. Such frauds are as follows:

- Misappropriation of cash.
- Misappropriation of goods.
- Manipulation of accounts or falsification of accounts without any misappropriation.

(iii) Under or Over Valuation of Stock

Normally such frauds are committed by the top level executives of the business. So, the explanation given to the auditor also remains false. So, an auditor should detect such frauds using skill, knowledge and facts.

(iv) Other Objectives

- To provide information to income tax authority.
- To satisfy the provision of Company Act.
- To have moral effect

5.1.3 Advantages of Audit

1. Interests of the shareholders or members who are unable to take part in the day-to-day business operations of a company are properly safeguarded.
2. Audited financial statements are the base for the tax authorities to evaluate the tax liability of a taxpayer.

3. For the purpose of evaluating the financial status of a prospective borrower of funds, audited financial statements are insisted upon by the banks or the financial institutions.
4. Audited financial statements may be the basis for negotiations with the employees in respect of their various demands.
5. Audited financial statements may be the basis for valuation of shares and goodwill in case of the take over bids.
6. Audited financial statements prepared on uniform basis are the best tool available to the management to evaluate its own performance on annual basis and to take the corrective actions wherever necessary.
7. The weaknesses and drawbacks located during the course of audit may provide the basis to the management for evolving proper management information and control systems.
8. The knowledge of the fact that the records and documents are subjected to audit may prove to be a tool to control the errors and frauds committed by the management.
9. Errors and frauds can be detected at an early date and if the financial statements are subjected to regular audit, occurrence of such frauds and errors can be restricted.
10. In case of the partnership firms, audited financial statements may help the settlement of the share of deceased or retiring partner.

5.1.4 Basic Principles and Practices of Audit

During the last two three decades, efforts have been made to bring the harmony in the profession of accounting and auditing all over the world. Formation of the International Accounting Standards Committee (ISAC) in 1973 was the first step in that direction. Till today ISAC has issued about 34 accounting standards in various areas.

In 1977, International Federation of Accountants (IFAC) was formed to bring the harmony in the accounting profession worldwide. International Federation of Accountants constituted a number of committees one of which is International Auditing Practices Committee (IAPC) which is re-christened as International Auditing and Assurance Standards Board (IAASB). The Institute of Chartered Accounts of India and The Institute of Cost & Works Accountants of India are members of both ISAC as well as IAASB. IAASB has issued number of standards which are known as "International Auditing Standards."

In Indian circumstances, The Institute of Chartered Accountants of India constituted the Accounting Standards Board (ASB) in 1977. Till today, ASB has issued about 40 accounting standards in order to bring the uniformity in accounting policies and practices in India. In September 1982, The Institute of Chartered Accountants of India constituted Auditing

Practices Committee (re-christened as Auditing and Assurance Standards Board - AASB) to harmonise the auditing practices in India. AASB has issued various standards on Standard Auditing Practices. Since 1st April 2008, AASB re-categorised and re-numbered the Auditing and Assurance Standards on the lines followed by IAASB. Following Auditing and Assurance Standards have been issued by AASB.

1. Basic principles governing an audit – SA 200
2. Objectives and scope of the audit of Financial Statements – SA 200A
3. Documentation – SA 230
4. The Auditor's responsibility relating to Fraud in an audit of financial statements – SA 240
5. Audit Evidence – SA 500
6. Relying upon the work of an Internal Auditor – SA 610
7. Audit Planning – SA 300
8. Using the work of an expert – SA 620
9. Using work of another auditor – SA 600
10. Written representations – SA 580
11. Responsibility of Junior Auditors – SA 299
12. Audit Materiality – SA 320
13. Analytical Procedures – SA 520
14. Audit Sampling – SA 530
15. Going Concern – SA 570
16. Quality Control for Audit Work – SA 220
17. Auditing Accounting Estimates including Fair Value Accounting Estimates and related disclosures – SA 540
18. Subsequent Events – SA 560
19. Knowledge of Business – SA 310
20. Consideration of Law and Regulations in an Audit of Financial Statements – SA 250
21. Initial Engagements opening balances – SA 510
22. Related Parties – SA 550
23. Audit considerations relating to entities using Service Organisations – SA 402
24. Comparatives – SA 710
25. Terms of Audit Engagement – SA 210
26. Communication with those charged with Governance – SA 260
27. The Auditor's Report on Financial Statements – SA 700
28. External Confirmations – SA 505
29. Audit Evidence – Additional considerations for specific items

The gist of above statements issued by the Institute of Chartered Accountants of India is summarised in the following paragraphs –

1. The auditor should be honest and sincere towards his work. He should be fair and impartial while carrying out his audit. He should not be biased and should be objective in his approach. The auditor should maintain confidentiality about the information which he acquires during the course of his audit. The audit should be conducted by the persons having sufficient experience, skills and competence to carry out the audit.

2. The objective of audit of financial statements is to enable the auditor to express his opinion about the financial statements. The opinion given by the auditor helps the determination of the true and fair view about the financial status and financial performance of an organisation. However, the opinion given by the auditor should not be taken as an assurance about the future viability of the organisation or effectiveness with which the management has conducted the affairs of an organisation.

3. The auditor should maintain sufficient documentation and working papers to justify that the audit was carried out according to the basic principles. Working papers help the auditor to carry out the audit work as per the plan, facilitate the review of the audit work and prove to be the evidence of the work performed by the auditor in order to arrive at the final conclusion.

4. As stated earlier, detection of frauds and errors is the basic responsibility of the management and not of the auditor. However, the auditor should try to obtain reasonable assurance that the frauds or errors which are material to the financial information have not taken place and if they have taken place, the same have been properly reflected in the financial information or the same have been properly corrected.

5. The auditor is required to obtain sufficient appropriate evidence to enable him to draw conclusions required to give his opinion about the financial information. The term sufficient refers to the quantum of information to be checked by the auditor. If the volume of information is very large, the auditor may apply the test check while checking the information. However, while applying the test check, the auditor should ensure that the selected sample is representative of the financial information. The term appropriate refers to the reliability of the information. In this connection, it should be noted that the external evidence is always preferred as compared to the internal evidence. Similarly, evidence in the form of written documentation and representations is always better than the oral explanations.

6. It is the basic responsibility of the management to maintain proper accounting systems and incorporate proper internal control measures to exercise control over

the affairs of an organisation. However, the auditor should ensure that the accounting system is adequate. Further, he should study and evaluate the internal control measures implemented by the company, as his opinion will be based upon the effectiveness of these internal control measures.

7. During the course of audit, the external auditor may depend upon the work performed by the internal auditor. However, before relying upon the work performed by the internal auditor, the external auditor should carry out the evaluation of the work done by internal auditor to decide the extent upto which he can rely upon the work done by the internal auditor. However, the external auditor has the sole responsibility of his report and in the event of some problems arising due to this reliance, he cannot plead that while preparing his report he has relied upon the work done by the internal auditor.

8. An audit carried out in a well-planned manner enhances the quality of audit work. A properly planned audit work ensures that there are no slips and omissions in the checking process.

5.2 Types of Audit

The term audit can be viewed basically from three angles:
1. Statutory Audit (which in some cases is referred to as External Audit).
2. Internal Audit.
3. Cost Audit.
4. Management Audit.

We would first discuss Financial Audit, Internal Audit, Cost Audit, Management Audit and later study Secretarial Audit, Statutory Audit and Tax Audit.

5.2.1 Statutory Audit/ Financial Audit

Section 224 contains the various provisions in respect of the audit of the company form of organisation. We will discuss these provisions under the following heads –

(A) Appointment of Auditors

(a) **Appointment of First Auditor:** Section 139 provides that the first auditor of the company shall be appointed by the Board of Directors of the company within 30 days from the date of registration of the company. The first auditor of the company holds the office till the conclusion of the first Annual General Meeting of the company. The company, at the Annual General meeting of the company, shall appoint an individual or a firm as the auditor of the company who shall hold the office till the conclusion of the sixth Annual General Meeting. It means that the same individual or the firm can not be the auditor of the company for more than five years. The provision is based on the fact that in some of the financial frauds committed by some companies, auditors of the company were found involved.

Before such appointment is made, the company shall obtain the written consent of the auditor for such appointment. After the appointment is made, the company shall inform the auditor concerned of his appointment and also file as notice with the Registrar of Companies of such appointment within 15 days of the meeting in which the appointment is made.

If the Board of Directors fails to appoint the first auditor, he can be appointed by the general meeting of the company.

(b) Casual Vacancy: Section 138(8) of the Companies Act, 2013 provides that the casual vacancy in the office of the auditor can be filled in by the Board of Directors within 30 days and the auditor appointed in the casual vacancy shall hold the office till the conclusion of the next Annual General Meeting. It is further provided that if the casual vacancy is caused by the resignation of the auditor, the vacancy can be recommended by the Board of Directors, but the same is required to be approved by the general meeting within three months of the recommendation of the Board of Directors.

Though the term casual vacancy is not defined in the Act, the vacancy caused by the validly appointed auditor ceasing to act in that capacity may be termed as the casual vacancy which may take place on account of death or disqualification of the auditor.

(B) Remuneration of the Auditor

Section 142 of the Companies Act, 2013 provides that the remuneration of the first auditor of a company may be fixed by the Board of Directors. Remuneration of the other auditors shall be fixed at the Annual General Meeting of the company. In practical circumstances, the shareholders or members may authorise the Board of Directors to decide the remuneration of the auditors.

(C) Removal of the Auditor

An auditor can be removed before the expiry of his term by the company only by a special resolution after obtaining the previous approval of the Central Government. Approval of the Central Government is required to be taken before effecting the removal.

(D) Qualifications of the Auditor

Section 141 of the Companies Act, 2013 provides that a person cannot be appointed as auditor of a company unless he is a chartered accountant. However, a firm of chartered accountants may be appointed as the auditor in the name of the firm if all the partners are qualified for appointment as the auditor.

Following persons are not qualified for appointment as the auditor
(a) A body corporate.
(b) An officer or an employee of the company
(c) A person who is a partner or who is in employment of an officer or employee of the company.
(d) A person who is indebted to the company for an amount exceeding ₹ 1,000 or who has given any guarantee with the indebtedness of a person to the company for an amount exceeding ₹ 1,000.
(e) A person holding any security (i.e. an instrument carrying the voting rights) of the company.

(E) Right of the auditor to attend the meetings

Section 146 of the Companies Act, 2013 provides that every notice and communication related to the meetings which have to be sent to the members should also be sent to the auditors of the company. The auditors are also entitled to attend any general meeting and is also entitled to be heard on any business that concerns him as the auditor.

(F) Auditor's Report

Report under Section 143(1) of Companies Act, 2013

According to this section, the auditor is required to enquire into the matters stated therein. The auditor is not required to report on these matters unless he has special comments to make on any of these matters. As such, in respect of all these matters, the auditor has to make the enquiry and he has to report on these matters only if he is satisfied with the results of his enquiry. The matters which are specified in this section are as below –

(a) Whether the loans and advances made by the company on the basis of the security are properly secured and whether the terms on which they are made are prejudicial to the interests of the company or its members. This takes care of the possible situations that the company makes the advances to the interested parties at no interest or low interest and without taking proper security for the same and on such terms which may be detrimental to the interests of the company.

(b) Whether the transactions of the company which are represented merely by the book entries are prejudicial to the interests of the company.

(c) Whether assets of the company representing shares, debentures and other securities have been sold at a price which is less than at which they were purchased. This takes care of the possible situations where the company sells the shares, debentures and other securities at the low rate with the intention to book the losses fictitiously.

(d) Whether the loans and advances made by the company have been shown as deposits. This takes care of the possible situation that the company gives the loans and advances to the interested parties and discloses them as the deposits with the intention to avoid further scrutiny of such transactions by the members and the others. Usually the term deposits indicates that the amounts kept by the company with the banks or the Government departments or the public authorities which are repayable after the purpose for which such deposits are made is over. The term deposit conveys the safety connected with the amount deposited.

(e) Whether personal expenses have been charged to revenue account. This takes care of the policy followed by the company to debit the personal expenses to Profit and Loss Account.

(f) Where it is stated in the books and papers of the company that shares have been allotted for cash, whether the cash has been actually received in respect of such allotment and if no cash has actually been so received, whether the position stated in the account books and the balance sheet is correct.

Report under Section 143(3) of Companies Act, 2013

According to this section, the auditor's report is required to state:

(a) Whether he has obtained all the information and explanations which to the best of his knowledge and belief were necessary for the purpose of his audit and if not the details thereof and the effect of such information on the financial statements

(b) Whether in his opinion proper books of accounts as required by the law have been maintained by the company as far as it appears from his examination of those books and proper returns adequate for the purpose of his audit have been received from the branches not visited by him.

(c) Whether the report on the accounts of any branch office of the company audited by a person other than the company's auditor have been sent to him and the manner in which he has dealt with it in preparing his report.

(d) Whether the company's balance sheet and profit and loss account dealt with in the report are in agreement with the books of accounts.

(e) Whether in his opinion, the financial statements comply with the accounting standards.

(f) The observations or comments on financial transactions or matters which have any adverse effect on the functioning of the company

(g) Whether any director is disqualified from being appointed as a director

(h) Whether the company has adequate internal financial control systems in place and the operating effectiveness of such controls.

5.2.2 Internal Audit

Usually, following three terms are used interchangeably to convey the same meaning, though these terms differ from each other:

(a) Internal Control

(b) Internal Check

(c) Internal Audit

(a) Internal Control

The Statement of Standard Auditing Practices issued by the Institute of Chartered Accountants of India defines Internal Control as all the methods and procedures adopted by the management of an organisation to assist in achieving management's objective of ensuring:

- Orderly and efficient conduct of the business, including adherence to the management policies.
- Safeguarding of assets
- Prevention and detection of frauds and errors
- Accuracy and completeness of accounting records
- Timely preparation of reliable financial information

Internal control is a prerequisite for the effective and efficient conduct of management of any organisation. Every management will be interested in establishing proper internal control procedures in order to comply with the above stated objectives. The auditor will like to study the internal control procedures established by the organisation. The auditor will carry out selective checking of all those areas where the internal control procedures are effective whereas he will concentrate maximum in those areas where the internal control procedures are weak.

Other two terms viz. Internal Check and Internal Audit are the important constituents of Internal Control procedures.

(b) Internal Check

In Internal Check, the work done by one person is checked by another person on a continuous basis so that the errors and frauds can be detected at an early stage. Thus, the primary requirement of internal check is to ensure that the allocation of duties is done in such a way that no single individual has the total control on all the operations involved in a transaction.

For example, if you go to your bank for withdrawing the money from your account, you hand over the cheque or the withdrawal slip to the clerk on the savings counter who in turn issues a token to you. The clerk on the savings counter checks the balance in your account and makes the entry in your account in the savings ledger. The details of the cheque are entered in the scroll book marinated by the clerk. The accountant checks the entry in the ledger as well as in the scroll book. The actual payment of cash is done by the cashier against the token presented by you to the cashier. Thus, the system is designed in such a way that no single official has the complete control of the transaction in totality. The work done by one official is checked by another official so that if some error or fraud is to be committed that will not be possible unless all the involved officials collide together.

(c) Internal Audit

Due to the increasing volume and complexities of business operations, it may not be possible for the statutory auditor to go into the details of each and every transaction in details. Further, propriety of various transactions and the compliance with the various procedures while carrying out various transactions may not be within the purview of the statutory auditor. Internal Audit plays an important role here as a control system. Internal Auditor is supposed to check the details of each and every transaction entered into by the organisation, study the procedures followed by the organisation in respect of every transaction and if there are any lacunas, suggest the measures to overcome these lacunas.

Internal Audit indicates the examination and evaluation of the adequacy and effectiveness of the organisation's system of internal control and quality of performance in carrying out assigned responsibilities.

Scope of Internal Audit

Internal Audit is the process which is not necessarily confined to the financial activities of the organisation. It is concerned with the non-financial activities as well. According to the Institute of Internal Auditors, Internal Audit is concerned with the following areas:

(a) **Reliability and integrity of Information:** Whether the financial or non-financial information is reliable.

(b) **Compliance with the policies, plans, procedures, laws and regulations:** Whether the organisation is complying with the plans and policies and various legal provisions which have a significant impact on the operations of the organisation.

(c) **Safeguarding of assets:** Whether the operations of the organisation are safeguarding the assets of the organisation in a proper manner.

(d) **Economic and efficient use of available resources:** Whether the organisation is using the available resources in an effective manner.

(e) **Compliance with the established goals and objectives of the organisation:** Whether the operations of the organisation are complying with the goals and objectives of the organisation.

As per the provisions of Section 138 of the Companies Act, 2013, Internal Audit has been made compulsory for the following class of companies –

(a) Every Listed Company

(b) Every Unlisted Public Limited Company having –
- Paid up share capital of ₹ 50 crores or more during the preceding financial year or
- Turnover of ₹ 200 crores or more during the preceding financial year or
- Outstanding loans or borrowings from banks or public financial institutions exceeding ₹ 100 crores or more at any point of time during the preceding financial year or
- Outstanding deposits of ₹ 25 crores or more at any point of time during the preceding financial year

(c) Every Private Limited Company having
- Turnover of ₹ 200 crores or more during the preceding financial year or
- Outstanding loans or borrowings from banks or public financial institutions exceeding ₹ 100 crores or more at any point of time during the preceding financial year

Section 138 of the Companies Act, 2013 provides that the Internal Auditor shall be a Chartered Accountant or a Cost Accountant or any other professional as may be decided by the Board of Directors. As a result, the Board of Directors has been given the freedom to appoint any professional as the Internal Auditor of the company who may be or may not be the employee of the Company.

The scope or functions of the Internal Auditors has not been defined by the Companies Act, 2013. It means that the scope or functions of the Internal Auditor can be decided by the Audit Committee of the Board of Directors.

Characteristic Features of Internal Audit

The nature of Internal Audit will be further clear on the basis of following characteristic features of Internal Audit:

(a) Internal Audit is not a legal requirement for all the companies. It is carried out by the management on its own in order to evaluate its own control mechanism on the various operations of the company. The appointment of internal auditor, terms of references given to him, remuneration to be paid to the internal auditor etc. are decided by the company on its own.

(b) Internal Audit is not restricted to the financial transactions alone. It may be concerned with the financial as well as non-financial matters.

(c) Internal Audit is a part of Internal Control procedures.

(d) As the purpose of internal audit is to confirm the effectiveness of the operations of the company, it is more detailed in nature. Similarly, to be more effective internal audit is carried out on continuous basis so that the lacunas located by the internal auditor can be rectified by the management on regular basis.

(e) The work done by the internal auditor does not replace the work of the statutory auditor. In fact, it supplements the work done by the statutory auditor. In practical circumstances, the statutory auditor may use the report given by the internal auditor in order to arrive at his own conclusions.

Internal Audit vs. Statutory Audit

The nature of Statutory Audit is entirely different from that of the Internal Audit. The areas of difference between the two can be stated as below –

1. The Statutory Auditor is appointed by the shareholders or members in the Annual General Meeting, except under certain circumstances which are already discussed where the statutory auditor can be appointed by the Board of Directors of the Central Government. The Internal Auditor is appointed by the management.

2. Appointment of Statutory Auditor is obligatory as per the provisions of Companies Act, 2013 and the same is independent of nature of operations and size of operations of the company. Appointment of Internal Auditor is not obligatory as per the Law. In this connection, it should be noted that as per the provisions of Manufacturing and Other Companies (Auditor's Report) Order, 1988, the statutory auditor is supposed to comment in his report whether the company is having internal audit system commensurate the nature and size of operations of the company if the paid up share capital is more than ₹ 50 Lakhs or if the average turnover of the company during the three preceding financial years is greater than ₹ 2 Crores.

3. The Statutory Auditor is required to comply with the requirements of Section 141 of the Companies Act, 2013 in respect of the qualifications. The said section does not apply to the Internal Auditor. As a result, the Internal Auditor need not be a Chartered Accountant.

4. Statutory Auditor is not the employee of the company. He is supposed to be an independent professional. Internal Auditor is the employee of the company.

5. The scope of work, rights and duties of the Statutory Auditor are determined as per the provisions of Companies Act, 2013. The scope of works, rights and duties of the Internal Auditor are determined by the management.

6. The Statutory Auditor is supposed to submit his report to the shareholders or members of the company. The Internal Auditor is supposed to submit his report to the management.

7. The remuneration of the Statutory Auditor is fixed by the shareholders or members in the Annual General Meeting, though in practical circumstances the same duty is delegated to the Board of Directors of the company. Remuneration of the Internal Auditor is decided by the management.

8. Statutory Auditor can be dismissed before the expiry of his term only by the shareholders or members at the Annual General Meeting after obtaining approval of Central Government. Internal Auditor can be removed by the management.
9. The basic objective of the Statutory Auditor is to decide whether the financial statements of the company are properly drawn up as required by the law and whether the same disclose true and fair view about the financial status of the company and the profitability of the company. Detection of errors and frauds is the secondary objective of the statutory audit. The basic objective of the Internal Audit is to make the suggestions to the management to facilitate the efficient conduct of the business so as to maximise the profitability. Detection of errors and frauds is the primary duty of the Internal Auditor.
10. Considering the nature of statutory audit, it is customary to find in the practical circumstances that the statutory audit is not able to carry out the verification of records and documents to the extent of 100%. The statutory auditor usually applies test check during the course of his checking. Internal Auditor is more detailed in nature.
11. The conduct of statutory audit is usually periodical, usually quarterly or annual. The conduct of Internal Audit is continuous in nature.
12. Statutory Auditor has the right to attend the meetings of the shareholders. Internal Auditor does not have such a right.

5.2.3 Cost Audit

According to The Institute of Cost and Works Accountants of England, Cost Audit is the verification of the correctness of the cost accounts and of the adherence to the cost accounting plans. The purposes of Cost Audit can be enumerated as below –

(a) To verify the arithmetical accuracy of the cost accounting records.
(b) To verify whether the cost accounting records have been properly maintained according to the cost accounting principles in the respective industry.
(c) To verify whether the cost statements are properly drawn up and whether they give true and fair view of the cost of production.

Cost Audit in the Indian circumstances

According to Section 148 of the Companies Act, 2013 the prescribed class of companies shall be required to maintain the cost accounting records. Further it is provided that if the Central Government feels, the audit of cost accounting records of such companies having the prescribed net worth or the prescribed turnover may be conducted by a cost accountant in practice who shall be appointed by the Board of Directors of the company. Principally, this section is applicable to the companies from strategic, regulated and the sectors where the public interest is involved.

Section 148 further provides that the Cost Auditor is required to furnish his report to the Board of Directors of the company. The company, within 30 days from the date of receipt of this report, shall furnish the same to the Central Government.

For the non-compliance of the provisions of this section, the company, every officer of the company in default and the cost accountant in practice shall be punishable with the fine.

Distinction between Financial Audit and Cost Audit

(a) Financial Audit is compulsory as per the provisions of Companies Act, 2013 for all types of companies. Cost Audit is applicable in case of the companies falling under certain specific categories of industries and for those companies who have been asked by the Central Government to maintain the cost accounting records and get these cost accounting records audited as per the provisions of Section 148 of the Companies Act, 2013.

(b) The objective of financial audit is to ensure that the financial statements of an organisation give true and fair view about the financial status and financial performance of the organisation.

(c) During the course of his audit, Financial Auditor does not go into the details of the cost accounting records maintained by the company. Cost Auditor does go into the details of cost accounting records maintained by the company with the intention to locate errors and manipulations in the cost accounting records.

(d) The appointment of the financial auditor is done by the shareholders or members in the Annual General Meeting. Similarly, he sends his report to the members of the company. Cost Auditor is appointed by the Board of Directors

(e) Financial Audit is concerned with the financial aspects of a company, while the Cost Audit is concerned with the cost aspects of the company.

(f) Financial Audit primarily protects the interests of the shareholders, while the Cost Audit primarily protects the interests of the management.

5.2.4 Management Audit

Audit, as we all know, is an "Attestation Function", that is, an audit basically checks and verifies whether the specific activities related to Internal Accounts, Cost Accounts, Finance as the case may be – are carried out according to the laid down standards or parameters or not. An audit attempts to asses the compliance with reference to a specific task or function. As such Internal Audit, Cost Audit, Statutory Audit and Financial Audit are activity or function-specific and that too with more focus on the operational aspect.

As regards, these functional/operational audits, there used to be a very interesting quip by operating personnel. General Managers generally do not manage, Assistant General

Managers neither assist nor generally manage, Managers are damages but Accountants are held accountable!!".

As the business environment underwent dramatic changes and businesses became more competitive both, locally and globally, it was realised that apart from ensuring compliance at the operational level, it was imperative to critically evaluate if the leadership of the organisations was responsive or dynamic or not, and whether the top leaders/managers were navigating their organisations efficiently and effectively or not. It was soon realised, and accepted, that not only the operational, but even the tactical and strategic management also needs to be tracked and monitored.

It was in this dynamic perspective that Management Audit emerged on the scene.

The term Management Audit is commonly used for examination and appraisal of the efficiency and effectiveness of management in carrying out its activities.

Let us now look at some of the definitions of the Management Audit.

Definitions

(a) It is a systematic assessment of methods and policies of an organisation's management in the administration and the use of resources, tactical and strategic planning and employees and organisational improvement.

(b) A Management Audit is a periodic manager (or by external experts/consultants) to determine the effectiveness or efficiency of business operations. The Management Audit would test a variety of business functions, including production, operations, resource procurement, employee hiring practices and financial reporting/performance.

(c) **According to William Leonard**, "Management Audit is a comprehensive and constructive examination of an organisation, the structure of a company, institution or branch of Government or of any component thereof, such as division of department and its plans, objectives, its means of operations and its use of human and physical facilities.

(d) Management Audit is the analysts and assessment of competencies and capabilities of a company's management in order to evaluate their effectiveness, especially with regard to the strategic objectives and policies of the business.

(e) Management Audit is an investigation of a business from the higher level downwards in order to ascertain whether sound management prevails and throughout, thus facilitating the most effective relationship with the outside world and the most efficient and smooth running internally.

(f) Management Audit is an objective and independent appraisal of the effectiveness of managers and the effectiveness of the corporate structure in the achievement of company objectives and policies. Its aim is to identify existing and potential management weaknesses within an organisation and to recommend ways to rectify these weaknesses. (Chartered Institute of Management Accountants)

(g) Management Audit is a systematic examination of decisions and actions of the management to analyse the performance. Management Audit involves the review of managerial aspects like organisational objective, policies, procedures, structure, control and system in order to check the efficiency or performance of the management over the activities of the company. Management Audit mainly examines the non-financial data to audit the efficiency of the management.

Objectives of the Management Audit

The objectives of the Management Audit can now be stated as follows:

(a) To evaluate the performance of the Management Team in relation to their competition and undertake a SWOT Analysis of the structure of the organisation, management team as well as the corporate culture.

(b) To assess the process of strategy formulation and its efficiency.

(c) To assess the relevance and reality connect of the strategy, vision, mission and objectives.

(d) To assess whether strategy, vision, mission and objectives are properly communicated throughout the organisation and whether the same is understood, accepted and internalised at all levels.

(e) To help management accomplish the most efficient administration of its operations and assess the functional utility and relevance of the organisational structure.

(f) To check and verify the provision, existence and adequacy of appropriate control mechanism/system at different levels in the organisation and its effectiveness in accomplishing the goals of the organisation.

(g) To identify any deficiencies or irregularities, in the areas/elements examined and to suggest the possible/desired requisite corrective action/s to achieve the optimum result/performance.

(h) To be a "Friend, Guide and Philosopher" to the Management Team in ensuring the efficient and effective performance.

(i) Suggest improvements/modifications as also lay down standards for future performance.

(j) Enable the organisation to gain, retain and sustain competitive advantage in today's competitive battlefield to succeed, survive and prosper.

Pre-requisites of a Team Conducting Management Audit:

The Management Audit can be conducted by internal managers or employees or by external auditors or management consultant. Irrespective who is conducting the Management Audit, the following pre-requisites have to be ensured.

(a) The Management Audit has to be conducted by a team seasonal/veteran professionals with proven track record and expertise.

(b) As Management Audit encompasses every aspect of the organisation/managerial function, the Auditors must follow an Interdisciplinary and System Approach, viewing the organisation.

(c) The Management Audit Team may include management experts, professional accountants, operations research and such other functional experts and even social scientists.

(d) The Management Audit Team Members must possess analytical and diagnostic approach/attitude based on facts/data.

(e) The Team Members must have the ability to "look into" and "see through" as also the ability to view the management function from "out of box" perspective.

(f) The Team Members must be properly groomed and trained and they must possess thorough knowledge of Management, Management Science alongwith familiarity and insight into various/peculiar features of various functional and organisational issues.

(g) It is imperative that the team members have appropriate corporate exposure and experience and they must understand the industry and business of the organisation for which they would be conducting Management Audit.

(h) The Management Audit Team must thoroughly acquaint itself with the culture strategy and organisational structure of the organisation.

(i) To be able to undertake and complete the Management Audit, the Management Audit Team must possess the requisite authority as also support from the Top Management of the organisation for which they would be conducting the Management Audit.

Areas Covered by Management Audit/Scoped Management Audit

The Management Audit, as we have realised by now, is not a routine, periodic, functional audit. Indeed, as stated in Envelope of Management Audit is a process of systematically examining, analysing and appraising management's overall performance, as regards efficiency and effectiveness of management in carrying out its functions/activities.

The Management Audit, therefore, focuses on results and performance, evaluating the effectiveness and suitability of controls, put in place, by challenging underlying existing rules, procedures and methods. Generally, Management Audit are conducted internally. At times they tend to be both - "compliance reviews" and "goals-and-effect-analysis". However, if performed correctly, and in the right spirit, Management Audits can potentially be the most useful evaluation and learning method, leading to positive and significant changes, for the business organisations.

The Management Audit, therefore, encompasses an assessment of a broad spectrum of areas/functions, examined in historical, competitive and futuristic context.

The areas which could be covered while conducting Management Audit are:

(a) Economic Contribution Analysis
(b) Appraisal of Planning Analysis
(c) Appraisal of Objectives Analysis
(d) Corporate/Organisational Structure
(e) Appraisal of Control
(f) Systems and Procedures
(g) Research and Development
(h) Functional Evaluation/Analysis/Review
(i) Board/Directors Analysis
(j) Executive/Management Evaluation

Let us now discuss these areas/function in more details.

(a) Economic Contribution Analysis

This analysis would evaluate if and how, the organisation is contributing to the economy and what is the importance of the company to the economy. The value of the company would be determined after taking cognisance of what the company is doing, what services/products it is selling and how the company going about its business in value-based and ethical ways.

It would also encompass the company's reputation (Brand/Image/Good Corporate Citizen) as also the management view of the purpose of the company.

This analysis would also attempt to review the measures initiated by the company to face and survive the dynamics of Business Cycle and Business Environment, Comparative Market Place, Management Development and the company's brand equity/reputation. Company's prospects of creating wealth and adding value could also be considered.

(b) Appraisal of Planning Analysis

The following issues can be taken into account:

(i) Does the company use Strategic Management Concept?
(ii) Is there a formal mechanism/framework in place to undertake scanning and analysis of Business Environment.
(iii) Is the environmental analysis factored/leveraged at the time of Strategy Formulation?
(iv) Is the Business Environment Analysis an ongoing activity/function or is it Ad Hoc?
(v) Is the Strategic Planning undertaken for short-term or long-term?

(vi) Is a clear strategy/vision/mission laid out?
(vii) Is the strategy/vision/mission communicated across the organisation?
(viii) Is it understood and internalised by all?
(ix) Is strategic planning taken seriously and is it the point of reference as well as the starting point for all business decisions down the line?
(x) Is the strategy clearly breakdown into Corporate Strategy, Strategic Business Unit (SBU) strategy and functional strategy and is it communicated to understood and internalised by all?
(xi) Do managers at all levels plan effectively?
(xii) Is there a mechanism for mid-term/periodic review of strategy/vision/mission and are suitable modifications/revisions made, if so required?

(c) Appraisal of Objectives Analysis

The following issues can be considered:
(i) Is there any co-relation between the strategy/vision/mission and objectives or not?
(ii) Are the objectives stated and communicated in a clear and specific manner?
(iii) Are the objectives understood and owned by all?
(iv) Is there a review mechanism to evaluate objectives and revise them, if so required?
(v) Are the objectives incorporated and reflected in the annual budget.
(vi) Are the objective measurable?
(vii) What is the extent of commitment and sanctity accorded to the objective/budgets? How seriously are they taken?

(d) Corporate/Organisational Structure

The review of corporate structure/organisation would look into the following:
(i) Is the organisational structure through which the management seeks to realise its strategic goals, effective and appropriate?
(ii) Does it ensure effective decision-making or are there too many layers, leading to unwarranted and avoidable delays?
(iii) Is it a micro-managed or empowered structure?
(iv) What is the degree of meaningful delegation?
(v) Are the managers wiling to delegate authority and do they delegate authority well?
(vi) Are clear lines of authority established and is there a well-defined, formal organisational chart?
(vii) Are there any instances of conflict or break-down in the acceptance of authority?
(viii) What is the nature of superior-peer-subordinate relationship in general?

(ix) Are there any potential issues?

(x) How /what is the organisational culture? Is it paternal, fraternal, collegial, formal, informal, professional, lackadaisical or highly competitive and result-oriented?

(e) Appraisal of Control

The following issues would need to be taken into account:

(i) Is there a sync between strategic control, tactical/management controls and operational controls?

(ii) What is the relationship between strategy objectives and controls?

(iii) What is the Control Philosophy? Is it based on Theory X and Theory Y or Theory Z?

(iv) How effective is the Control Mechanism?

(v) Are the controls cost-effective and speedy?

(vi) Are the control parameters clearly laid down, communicated and understood?

(vii) Are controls equated between Budgeted and Actual Goals and arriving at the 'Variances' only?

(viii) Are the controls acceptable to the various levels of management?

(ix) Are the controls static or dynamic? Are they reviewed and revised periodically?

(x) Are the controls related to reward and recognition systems?

(xi) Is the control and reward mechanism effective? (Frauds, Misappropriation, Attrition, Income Leakages, etc.)

(f) Systems and Procedures

The following aspects could be looked into:

(i) Are these well-designed systems and procedures?

(ii) Are the systems/procedures followed/implemented universally and diligently across the organisation?

(iii) Are the systems and procedures activity oriented or process-oriented.

(iv) Are the job profiles, job descriptions and job specifications clear?

(v) Is there proper documentation of the systems and procedures?

(vi) Are employees imparted training as regards systems and procedures? Do they have 'ownership' and 'trustee' spirit about the systems and procedures?

(vii) Is a perioding/ongoing review of the costs, benefits and efficiency of the systems and procedures undertaken?

(viii) Are the systems and procedures transparent and related to the changing technology and dynamic business environment?

(ix) When was the last time a system/procedure reviewed, revised or revamped?

(x) Is the I.T. and MIS in place? Is there a CIO/CTO in place?

(xi) What is the Systems Security Environment?

(xii) Is Business Strategy and I.T./Systems Strategy in sync?

(xiii) Are employees trained and skilled in leveraging I.T. capabilities for competitive advantage?

(g) Research and Development

In today's Business Environment, there is great emphasis on a company reinventing itself and being innovative. Research and Development, therefore, has become imperative, indeed critical. It is the R & D which is now often responsible for a company's growth and improving competitiveness, in view of the emerging Intellectual Property Rights (IPR) regime.

The Management Audit would not only look into the R & D spend, but would focus more upon new ideas/products/services introduced and taken to market. It would also assess management's willingness and desire to leverage R & D for future growth and sustainable competitiveness. Management Audit can also attempt to determine what part of the company's progress can rightly be attributed to R & D and how well could R & D policies and performance prepare the company for future.

(h) Functional Evaluation/Analysis/Review

While the functional evaluation would not be like an internal audit, the evaluation would take into account the firm's performance and procedures in the overall industry/macro perspective and would cover all the functional areas. Some of the Illustrative functional areas would be:

- Corporate Planning
- Finance, Accounts and Audit (Compliances)
- Legal and Secretarial Practices (Compliances)
- Research and Development
- Production
- Marketing
- Distribution
- Personnel H.R.
- Corporate Communication/Public Image

The review/analysis/evaluation would be mainly from the Strategy Policy Perspective to enable the organisation to be competitive.

Some of the specific issues addressed in illustrative functional areas are presented hereafter.

Functional Area	Issues Looked Into
(i) Production Function	- Purchases - Production Planning and Control - Inventory/Storage - Production/Capacity Utilisation - Inspection - Rejection/Wastage/Re-work - Quality Standards and Quality Systems followed - Technology (Modernisation and Replacements).
(ii) Marketing Function	- Marketing Strategy - Segmentation (Targeting and Positioning) (STP) - Adhrence to Marketing Principles 4Ps or 7Ps) - Brand equity - Market share (Incremental/Absolute) - Market Research - New Product Launches - Share of New Products - Managing Product Life Cycle - Customer Relationship Management (CRM) - CRM Strategy and Initiatives - Internet/Web Marketing
(iii) Finance Function (Evaluate the investment, financing and dividend decisions)	- Project Management (Cost/Time over run or on schedule compaction) - Sources of Funds - Cash Flow/Funds Flow - Liquidity and Profitability - Receivables/Payables - Pricing and Costing Strategies and Competitiveness - EPS/Market Cap - RROI/ROE/ROCE - Value creation and EUA - Asset Utilisation - Operating yields - Debts/Expenses

(i) Board/Directors Analysis

At times, the Management Audit, when carried out by external consultants, may undertake Board/Directorate Analysis. Such an analysis would mainly cover and focus upon, the quality and effectiveness of the Board of Director, and would cover

(i) The assessment of quality of each director alongwith the quality and quantity of the contributions made by the Director to the Board.

(ii) Evaluate and assess as to how well the Board of Directors worked together as a team.

(iii) Assess the directors to determine if they have really rated as trustees for the company and have acted in the best interest of the shareholders and other stakeholders.

(iv) It would be also assessed whether them has been a conflict of interest between the company executives and its owners and public.

(v) The Management Audit may review the composition of Board of Directors as regards Non-executive and independent directors and their core and value-added.

(j) Executive/Management Evaluation

As we have seen, the Management Audit goes beyond the conventional audit and undertaken a comprehensive and critical review of all organisational activities with broader perspective and interdisciplinary and systems approach. The Management Audit evaluated the efficiency of the management itself and hence, executive evaluation is one of the most important aspect/quality of Management Audit.

The other functions/areas discussed earlier, indirectly evaluate the management, as they reflect and represent the assets of management's decisions and actions.

The Executive Evaluation function addresses the quality of the executives and their management philosophy.

The Management Audit assesses the ability, industry and integrity of the executives. It also endeavours to ascertain whether they provide the leadership and whether they are transactional or transformational leaders. It also looks into the policies of executive selection, development, advancement, replacement as well as succession planning.

This is important as it is observed that most of the times the basic problem is leadership deficit or leadership crisis.

To conclude

We must remember that Management Audit is not a typical audit undertaken to find out gaps and faults.

Management Audit, no doubt, does identify the gaps, omissions and deficiencies. But it is not an audit to find fault and crucify/penalise people. It critically looks into the nature and quality of decision making responsiveness, performance and results and comes out with suggestions/solutions not for the sake of compliance alone, but to ensure that the firm/company/organisation realises its potential and ensures survival, success and sustainability into today's competitive battlefield.

Points to Remember

- Audit indicates the verification and examination by an independent person of the books of accounts and records of an organisation with the intention to confirm that the financial statements drawn there from give true and fair view of the financial status of the organisation as on any given date and the profitability of the organisation for any given duration of time.
- Internal Audit indicates the examination and evaluation of the adequacy and effectiveness of the organisation's system of internal control and quality of performance in carrying out assigned responsibilities.
- Cost Audit is the verification of the correctness of the cost accounts and of the adherence to the cost accounting plans.
- Management Audit is a systematic assessment of methods and policies of an organisation's management in the administration and the use of resources, tactical and strategic planning and employees and organisational improvement.

Questions for Discussion

1. What is Audit? State its Objectives.
2. State the Advantages of Audit.
3. Explain the Basic Principles and Practices of Audit.
4. What is Internal Audit? State its scope and characteristics.
5. What is Management Audit? State its scope and characteristics.
6. Write short notes on:
   (a) Cost Audit
   (b) Financial Audit
   (c) Auditor's Report
   (d) Internal Audit Vs. Statutory Audit
   (e) Internal check.

CASE STUDIES

Case Study 1: L&T

In May 08 L & T India's most respected diversified company announced that it was restructuring its business. This exercise will result in creation of a dozen "Operating Companies" under the guidance of a separate Board of Directors. From July 1st, 08 this will lead to L & T becoming the umbrella organisation, with a board to look after the overall performance of all businesses and the ownership of the L & T brand that is estimated to be $ 2 billion.

Experts say that this move will help the company unlock shareholders value by listing all these companies in future.

Company's CFO says that the creation of operating companies will help L & T have more focused operations in the market place. These separate companies can concentrate more on their businesses and their customers. The boards of the operating companies will help them take decisions expeditiously. However he made it clear that operating companies will not be separate legal entities.

Giving reasons for this move the company has stated that the recent growth in the Indian economy has not only created opportunities for the company but has also raised the expectations from various stakeholders such as investors and customers. This move is therefore thought to be imperative so that the company gears up its organisational structure and processes to meet the enhanced expectations of all stakeholders.

What all this is likely to lead to is:

- Creation of a dozen operating companies under the guidance of a new board. L & T will become an umbrella body with a board to look after overall performance and brand ownership.
- Operating companies will come up in the following businesses-Buildings and Factories, Infrastructure, Metallurgical, Material handling and water, Electrical Projects and Gulf Operations.
- These companies will have independent support functions as finance and accounts and HR. They will look after the businesses of nearly 60 special business units of the diversified conglomerates.

From the above it is clear that L & T will be structured on Profit Center basis functionally. This is a good example of how companies with diverse interests and large size need to look after their businesses.

1. Discuss the company's strategy of converting its SBUs into separate companies.
2. Find out how the HO will exercise ownership and control on these companies.

Case Study 2: The Case of Leon Horn

Johnson Manufacturing Company was a large producer of manufactured parts like stampings, machined castings and machine parts for various manufacturers nationwide. These parts were used in final products like automobiles, refrigerators and home appliances. The company had 32 manufacturing plants. The annual sales were approximately $ 1 billion.

For many years the company had no formal control system for its manufacturing plants. The plants had an actual cost-accounting system and monthly reports were submitted to the central office. No action was taken on these reports, as long as the managers met their production schedules.

In the late 80s the competition became fierce. This resulted in the decline of profit margins. The management responded by asking its central control group to install system for the control of manufacturing costs in each of its plants. The result was the installation of a standard cost system for manufacturing and strong cost and employment controls over discretionary expenditures in plants.

The new system was able to reduce the manufacturing costs significantly. This was possible as plant managers and supervisors became very sensitive to cost control since it became the predominant measure of performance in plants.

Now let us see a problem that arose in one of the plants after some years.

The Cherry Hill Plant problem:

This plant produced machined parts and assemblies for the automobile industry. At about the time of implementation of the new system a new plant manager Leon Horn was hired to manage this plant. He was recruited from a competitor where he had acquired a reputation as a "no frills ", "no – nonsense "production manager.

Horn was shocked to see the fat that accumulated at this plant. His response was to begin an ongoing program of cost cutting. His first budget for the plant was 15% below actual expenses of the previous year. He managed the budget continuously and was able to hold actual costs to 95% of the budget. Leon was promptly rewarded by the management with a large bonus and he was signalled out for praise at the company's annual awards banquet for plant managers.

This emboldened Leon to cut costs further. His budget for the second year was approximately 10% below the actual costs of the previous year.

Horn's initial cuts were savings that were realised as a consequence of reduction in direct costs. These cuts were largely a by-product of the new standard cost system. The more recent cuts were however form the indirect cost cuts. These included employment reduction in manufacturing and industrial engineering, production control, purchasing, training, and maintenance. Horn's budget for the second year was approximately 50% lower in the overhead category than it was when he assumed the charge at the plant. Moreover, Horn's actual cost performance was under budget well into the second year.

There were very few design changes in the parts produced at Cherry Hill during Horn's first year. The same parts were produced with only minor modifications. The second year was much different. Every large automobile producer made changes in its specifications for the assemblies, which were manufactured at Cherry Hill. To make matters worse, the automobile producers made numerous design changes to the parts as the year unfolded. Because of staff reductions in the engineering, purchasing, production supervision and production control areas, Horn was unable to respond rapidly to these new and changing designs and missed a number of scheduled commitments. As a result, the Cherry Hill plant lost much of its business, as manufacturers became important and sought out other sources of supply. Profits turned to big losses. The management of Johnson reacted by firing Horn.

Case Study: Tata Business Excellence Model (TEBM)

Many organisations have developed their own performance evaluation systems which are broadly based on the Baldrige and BSC models. The Tata group is in the forefront of this development in India. The Godrej group has also developed its own performance evaluation system that is based on the principal of EVA in consultation with Stern and Stewert. Here we will have brief look at the TEBM.

Business Excellence Tata's have defined it as follows:

Business Excellence: A state of long-term sustained competitive success, which an organisation aspires to achieve by creating and balancing value for all its stakeholders - shareholder, customers, employees, suppliers and the society at large.

The task at hand is: "How to **establish a convention**, within our organisations, to create and balance **stakeholder value**, focused on achieving **long-term sustained competitive success**?"

How does a company assess, evaluate and drive business excellence?
- Behaviours /Practices
- Norms / Processes
- Beliefs / Culture
- Values

Core Values and Concepts
- Common in high-performing organisations
- Foundation for integrating key business requirements

Values Enabling Business Excellence
- Visionary Leadership
- Customer Driven Excellence
- Organisational and Personal Learning
- Focus on Future
- Agility
- Management by Fact
- Valuing Employees and Partners
- Focus of Results and Creating Value
- Managing of Innovation
- Social Responsibility
- System Perspective

A Framework for Business Excellence
- Values---Processes----Approach
- Processes---Practices----Deployment
- Practices----Outcomes---Results.

The Tata's have allocated marks to different criterions as below:

Leadership	125
Strategic Planning	85
Customer & Market Forces	85
HR Focus	85
Process Management	80
Information & Analysis	90
Business Results	450
Total Marks	**1000**

The Journey to Business Excellence
The steps in this journey are:
- Early Development
- Early Results
- Early Improvements
- Good performance
- Emerging Industry Leader
- Industry Leader
- Benchmark Leader
- World class Leader

Scoring System:

Approach	Deployment	Result
Appropriate	Extent	Outcomes
Effective		Current performance
Systematic	Addressing item requirements	Relative performance
Integrated	Appropriate work units	Rate, breadth, importance of performance outcomes
Alignment		Linkage to measure.
Fact Based		
Innovative		

Case Study: The Accounts that brought down GTB

The Reserve Bank of India (RBI) clearly knew how bad things were at Global Trust Bank (GTB) as far back as 1999-2000. Let's now look at how the annual inspection report of the Department of Supervision (DOS) had touched on every single issue that contributed to its doom. Why then was GTB allowed to spin out of control? Our documents show that it was because senior officials of the RBI's Hyderabad office (many had children working in GTB) worked hard to tone down words like 'ever-greening' or "NPA investments" to help suppress bad loans.

Many dubious cases, including loans to Ketan Parekh, Shankar Sharma's First Global, and those to diamond traders, were specifically discussed by relegation to the annexure. Although the inspection was completed in September 2000, the report was released only in January 2001, because RBI's officials wanted to help GTB bag an insurance licence. It almost got it too, except that Scam 2000 also crashed GTB's high-flying reputation.

Here are some issues flagged in the inspection. First, it drew attention to 'serious irregularities' in the accounts of 18 firms of the Ramesh Gelli group, and specifically "suspected money laundering". The DOS had concurred with the seriousness of doubts raised and referred it to the central office for action. There is no evidence of corrective action.

Instead, as Sridhar Subashri, GTB's former executive director recently wrote to a newspaper, "any one in the banking sector would be aware" that even after Gelli stepped down from GTB in 2001 "he continued to guide decisions of the bank through his sister,

Parimala Anand" (a director) and his son Girish Gelli who became a director in November 2003.

They were connected with many of the 18 companies mentioned above. Bankers insist that even Sudhakar Gandhe, who took over as GTB's Executive Director was close to Gelli.

Yet, RBI benignly swallowed Gelli's fiction of having distanced himself from the bank. While Gandhe tells the media that he ensured massive loan recoveries, the bad loans are estimated at a huge ₹ 1,500 crore and could be as high as ₹ 2,500 crore according to banking sources. GTB tried to engineer a quick merger with UTI Bank to bury the problem but failed to push it through.

One of the first danger signals should have been the infamous preferential allotment of 148 lakh shares worth ₹ 125.80 crore in 2000. The shares were allotted to mixed bunch of entities. On one hand there were four institutions — IFC Washington, Sun F&C, Kotak Mahindra Finance and Prudential ICICI Trust. The others included the infamous Nishkalp Investments, which brought down Tata Finance.

Nishkalp, which turned out to have extremely close connections with a crony of Ketan Parekh was the single biggest investor with a ₹ 50 crore allotment. Interestingly, it also had an overdraft facility of exactly ₹ 50 crore from GTB, which was also rolled over several times. Did this over-draft finance the subscription? What was the relationship with Nishkalp? Instead of investigating this, RBI supervisors wanted the inspection report to delete specific names and replace them with generic references.

Other big allottees were Ketan Parekh entities Nakshatra Software and Chitrakut Computers. Three others, Palm Print Textiles, AMA Real Estate and M.F. Properties, were unknown Ghaziabad-based companies.

The last two owned 1.2 and 1.4 per cent respectively of GTB's equity until 2003. Interestingly, on December 22, 2000, former chairman Ramesh Gelli, in reply to a query, had explained with a flowchart how Chitrakut and Nakshatra had funded their purchase of preferential shares. Both were funded through money from Madhavpura Cooperative Bank and Bank of India among others.

If the RBI central office were more alert in its supervision, it would have questioned the two banks (as in the 1992 scam) and discovered Ketan Parekh's crooked nexus well before the bubble burst.

RBI's Hyderabad office had unearthed clear evidence of 'self dealing' in the bank's shares by the promoter group, through a pattern on clean short-term clean loans to a range of brokers. This too was never investigated.

Consequently, when the bank was placed under moratorium on July 24, Ketan Parekh's outstanding dues to the bank were estimated at nearly ₹ 240 crore, without including bad loans to crony industrialists.

Two sets of industry groups were flagged by the inspection for their special relationship with GTB in 2000. One was the problem exposure of ₹ 150 crore to several Balaji group companies such as Balaji Distilleries, Balaji Hotels, Balaji Industrial Corporation, Jayaswal Neco, and a further loan of ₹ 46 crore to Pearl Distilleries (60 per cent owned by the Balaji group).

GTB allowed these companies to recklessly run up bad loans, divert funds within the group to pay off creditors and it even subscribed to their Preference Shares and Non Convertible Debentures, in order to help 'evergreen' the loan accounts.

A single account called Petro Energy Products Company India (PEPCO) is worth a mention. In 1999-2000, GTB wrote off a hefty ₹ 82 crore as bad loans. Of this, exactly half (₹ 41.23 crore) was on account of PEPCO. The company was allowed to remit money abroad for a second-hand refinery, although the land for the project was not acquired. Also, the technology was obsolete and the project feasibility doubtful.

The RBI inspector noted that the beneficiary of the remittances abroad needed to be investigated, because the bank had hurriedly written off the money without making any serious effort to recover its dues. The inspection report listed 10 other companies where GTB had written off loans within a year, without serious recovery efforts. Banking sources say that many of these loans smack of political funding.

It was never investigated. Another large term loan flagged by the report was to diamond merchant Bharat Shah's company Rhiday Real Estate (₹ 43 crore) to finance a ₹ 72.49 crore commercial complex in Mumbai (Trambak Court). The bank flouted all prudential guidelines to lend money to the rich Mr. Shah and the loan had already turned bad by 2000. It had a huge exposure to Bharat Shah's companies such as Beautiful Diamonds (₹ 46 crore default), B. Vijay Kumar & Co (₹ 131 crore exposure in 2000) and crystal Gems, while the security cover on these loans was abysmal.

Many of these loans had turned bad even then. Clearly, GTB was killed by the crooked lending of its own management and a regulator who deliberately ignored jangling alarm bells until it was too late.

This is an article written by Sucheta Dalal on GTB. From this article and the information that you have about this issue you are to point out the deficiencies in the control mechanism of the bank internally as well the externally. Also try and create a Balanced Scorecard for the banking industry.

Case Study 5: Critical Chain by Dr Eliyahu Goldratt

The book Critical Chain is a guide for project management. A brief summary of that book is given below:

- The critical chain of a project is the set of dependent tasks that define the expected lower limit of a project's possible lead time.
- Dependencies used to determine the critical chain include both logical hand-off dependencies (where the output of the predecessor task is required to start the successor), and resource dependencies (where a task has to wait for a resource to finish work on another task).

In Critical Chain scheduling, uncertainty is primarily managed by:

- Using average task duration estimates.
- Scheduling backwards from the date a project is needed (to ensure work that needs to be done is done, and it is done only when needed).
- Placing aggregate buffers in the project plan to protect the entire project and the key tasks.
- Using buffer management to control the plan.

The key tasks are those on which the ultimate duration of the project depends, also known as the Critical Chain.

- Reduce activity duration estimates by 50%. Activity durations are normal estimates, which we know to be high probability and contain excessive safety time.
- Eliminate resource contentions by levelling the project plan. The Critical Chain can then be identified as the longest chain of path and resource dependencies after resolving resource contentions.
- Insert a Project Buffer at the end of the project to aggregate Critical Chain contingency time. (initially 50% of the critical chain path length)
- Protect the Critical Chain from resource unavailability by Resource buffers. Resource buffers are correctly placed to ensure the arrival of Critical Chain resources.
- Size and place Feeding Buffers on all paths that feed the Critical Chain. Feeding buffers protect the Critical Chain from accumulation of negative variations, e.g. excessive or lost time, on the feeding chains. This subordinates the other project paths to the Critical Chain.
- Start gating tasks as late as possible. Gating tasks are tasks that have no predecessor. This helps prevent multitasking.

- Ensure that resources deliver Roadrunner performance. Resources should work as quickly as possible on their activities, and pass their work on as they complete.
- Provide resources with activity durations and estimated start times, not milestones. This encourages resources to pass on their work when done.
- Use buffer management to control the plan. Buffers provide information to the project manager, for example, when to plan for recovery and when to take recovery action.
- Using the Critical Chain Method, projects can be completed more quickly and with greater scheduling reliability. The difference between traditional and Critical Chain scheduling is in how uncertainty is managed. In traditional project scheduling, uncertainty is managed by padding task durations, starting work as early as possible, multi-tasking, and focusing on meeting commitment dates. The following bullet points illustrate some of the problems associated with traditional project scheduling.
- Padding task durations (providing worst-case estimates) is done to ensure a high probability of task completion. The knowledge that there is so much safety time built into tasks results in various time wasting practices, e.g., waiting until the last moment to complete a task. As a result, all the safety time can be wasted at the start of the task so that, if problems are encountered, the task over-runs.
- Starting work as early as possible, even when not scheduled, is a response to worst-case estimates. When workers give worst-case estimates, they don't expect to stay busy with just one task – so they multi-task, working on several tasks at once by switching between them. The result is that everything takes a long time to complete and very little completes early.

  With the focus on meeting commitment dates (start and finish), output from a task completed early will rarely be accepted early by the next person needing this output. So, any effort spent in finishing early will be wasted. Early delivery of one task can't be used to offset lateness on another. Lateness, however, is always passed on and the lost time can't be made up without cutting the specifications or increasing resources allocated to subsequent tasks, if possible

- Drum-Buffer-Rope for Process Control
    - **Drum:** The Pace Setting Resource - constraint
    - **Buffer:** The amount of protection in front of the resource
    - **Rope:** The scheduled staggered release of material to be in line with the Drum's schedule.

A Pull System:

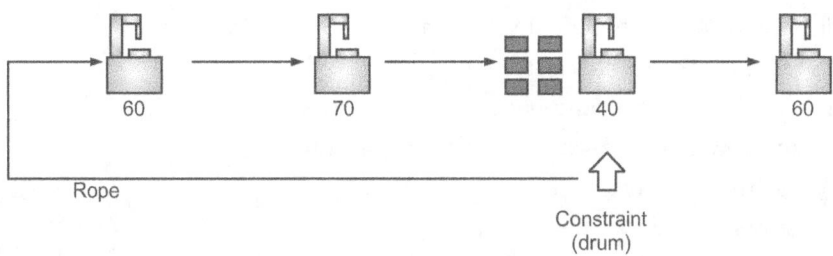

Questions:
1. What are your learnings from the Critical Chain?
2. Can these measures be implemented in a project?

***

MULTIPLE CHOICE QUESTIONS

1. All Responsibility Centres are structured as Profit Centres. True/False.
2. Responsibility Centres are created for ......
   (a) decentralisation of functions
   (b) to relieve top management of day to day activities
   (c) for better control
   (d) all of the above
3. The right way of calculating EVA is ......
   (a) NPOAT-WACC
   (b) NOPAT + Depreciation – Interest
   (c) NOPAT + Interest – WACC
4. Discretionary expenses are expenses ......
   (a) that do not create value
   (b) that do not hamper the operations immediately
   (c) that are completely unnecessary
5. Revenue Centres Managers are good if they ......
   (a) spend the budget fully but do not meet revenue targets
   (b) they spend more than the budget but also meet their revenue target
   (c) they spend within the budget but over achieve their revenue target
6. Profit Centre's profit is calculated ......
   (a) before debiting Corporate overheads
   (b) after debiting corporate overheads
   (c) without considering corporate overheads
7. Higher EVA will lead to higher MVA. True/False.
8. The four perspectives of BSC are interrelated but financial performance is the most important one. (True/False)
9. BSC is important for ......
   (a) creating strategy
   (b) controlling strategy
   (c) evaluating the performance of a strategy
10. Hours spent with customers should be ......
    (a) to get payments
    (b) to assess future requirements
    (c) to inform about new innovations made by the company

Enterprise Performance Management | Multiple Choice Questions

11. In financial performance measurement most important these days is ......
    (a) EVA
    (b) ROI
    (c) Profit margin
12. Strategy implementation is done by ......
    (a) corporate office
    (b) SBU
    (c) both Corporate office and SBU
13. Transfer price impacts the profits of the entire organisation. True/False.
14. Two step transfer prices depend on ......
    (a) ROI requirement.
    (b) profit requirement
    (c) corporate profit requirement
15. Market based transfer prices include a charge for ......
    (a) marketing expenses
    (b) bad debt provisions
    (c) indirect taxes
    (d) none of the above
16. While setting transfer prices the profitability of the profit center is more important than that of the Corporate. True/False
17. MNCs set transfer prices considering ......
    (a) manufacturing units' profitability
    (b) buying centre's requirement
    (c) tax structure in two countries' involved
18. The capital adequacy ratio to be maintained by banks in India is ......
    (a) 8%
    (b) 10%
    (c) 12%
19. Operational risk is ......
    (a) created by the fluctuations in interest rates
    (b) created by people and processes of a bank
    (c) created by reputation of a bank
20. SLR/CRR are used by RBI to ......
    (a) to manage liquidity in the system
    (b) to fight inflation
    (c) both of the above
    (d) none of the above
21. Fee based income is important for a bank because ......
    (a) it is an additional source of income
    (b) it is risk free by nature
    (c) both of the above
    (d) none of the above

22. Registration of charge while giving the loan is the responsibility of the ......
    (a) borrower
    (b) bank
    (c) both
23. An asset becomes Non Performing ......
    (a) after default of 180 days
    (b) after default of 60 days
    (c) after default of 90 days
24. A project may face the following risks ......
    (a) completion risk (b) financial risk
    (c) technology Risk (d) all of the above
25. PERT/CPM have to be used for proper control of all projects. (True/False)
26. All Projects are unique in nature. (True/False)
27. Arrange in the order of priorities.
    (a) Financial (b) Idea
    (c) Manpower (d) Location
28. Which of the following pair about Paradigm Shifts in the contemporary Business Environment is incorrect?
    (a) Control to Decontrol (b) Competition to Opening Up
    (c) Production to Marketing (d) Volume to Profit
29. Which of the following pair of changes in the Organisational Changes in the 20th Century and 21st century is incorrect?
    (a) Goal-directed to Vision-directed (b) Bureaucratic to Entrepreneurial
    (c) Compliance to Commitment (d) Efficient to Stable
30. Today's organisations are not changing internally as regards ......
    (a) structure (b) systems
    (c) culture (d) leadership in Market
31. The Six Essential Dimensions of Performance does not include which of the following?
    (a) Innovation (b) Re-Engineering
    (c) Speed (d) Quality
32. Today's Market Place is described as "Competitive Battlefield" by ......
    (a) C. K. Prahlad (b) Michael Porter
    (c) Peter Drucker (d) Philip Kotler

33. Performance Management is ......
    (a) Strategic Tool
    (b) Re-Engineering Tool
    (c) Business Process
    (d) Strategic Management Tool
34. The Enterprise Performance Management core processes does not include which of the following?
    (a) Financial Planning
    (b) Operational Planning
    (c) Business Analytics
    (d) Consolidation and Reporting
35. Entrprise Performance Management should not be seen as a ......
    (a) Corrective Action
    (b) Post-Mortem
    (c) Critical Success Factor
    (d) Key Performance Indicator
36. Which of the following is not one of the methodologies used for ensuring effective Enterprise Performance Management?
    (a) Six Sigma
    (b) Activity Based Costing
    (c) Total Quality Management
    (d) Control by Exception
37. Which of the following is not one of the four types of Performance Indicators?
    (a) Quantitative Indicators
    (b) Qualitative Indicators
    (c) Laggard Indicators
    (d) Lead Indicators
38. The SAVI Indicators does not include which of the following?
    (a) Speed Indicators
    (b) Accuracy Indicators
    (c) Velocity Indicators
    (d) Investment Indicators
39. Responsibility Accounting ...... accounting and financial reporting with management and lines of authority and responsibility.
    (a) provides
    (b) integrates
    (c) separates
    (d) diagnoses
40. Which of the following is not one of the steps for installing Responsibility Accounting System?
    (a) Create a set of financial performance goals
    (b) Measure and report actual performance goals
    (c) Evaluate based on comparison of Actuals with Budgets
    (d) Initiate corrective actions.
41. Which of the following is not one of the three types of Responsibility Accounting Systems?
    (a) Process-based Responsibility Accounting System.
    (b) Functional-Based Responsibility Accounting System.
    (c) Activity-based Responsibility Accounting System.
    (d) Strategic-based Responsibility Accounting System.

Enterprise Performance Management — Multiple Choice Questions

42. Return on Assets (ROA) Ratio is given by which of the following?
    - (a) Net Income / Sales
    - (b) Sales / Total Assets
    - (c) Net Income / Total Assets
    - (d) Gross Margin / Net Sales

43. Which of the following is not a component of Market Value Added (MVA)?
    - (a) Invested Capital
    - (b) Current Operations Value (COV)
    - (c) Future Growth Value (FGV)
    - (d) Net Present Value (NPV)

44. The Financial Performance Evaluation Parameters only give ......
    - (a) "Position as at"
    - (b) "Competitive Position"
    - (c) "Position as regards Six Sigma"
    - (d) "Position in Market"

45. Which of the following is not a Non-Financial Performance Evaluation Parameter?
    - (a) Productivity
    - (b) Quality Rejection
    - (c) Cost to Company
    - (d) Market Share

45. The Malcolm Baldrige Award is awarded by the Government of ......
    - (a) Japan
    - (b) Russia
    - (c) U.K.
    - (d) U.S.A

46. Which of the following areas is not covered under the Baldrige Award?
    - (a) Education
    - (b) Health Care
    - (c) Small Business
    - (d) Multi National Corporation (MNC)

47. Which of the following is not one of the criterion for the Baldrige Award?
    - (a) A set of expectations or requirements.
    - (b) Application of ISO 2000-2003 Guidelines.
    - (c) A Structured approach to Performance Management.
    - (d) A Framework for a Systems View of Performance Management.

48. Which of the following is the "odd man out" entity with reference to the Baldrige Criteria / Framework?
    - (a) Team Focus
    - (b) Customer Focus
    - (c) Operations Focus
    - (d) Work Force Focus

49. Given below are the Point Values allotted to various Baldrige Criteria. Which of them is incorrect?
    - (a) Operation Focus (85)
    - (b) Customer Focus (85)
    - (c) Leadership (100)
    - (d) Results (450)

50. The Strategic Business Unit (SBU) evolved from ......
    - (a) Hierarchy-based structure of organisation
    - (b) Function-based structure of organisation
    - (c) Territorial structure of organisation
    - (d) Divisional structure of organisation

51. The Strategic Business Unit (SBU) evolved during the ......
    (a) 1970s & 1980s
    (b) 1990s
    (c) 1960s
    (d) 21st Century

52. Which of the following statement about the Strategic Business Unit (SBU) is TRUE?
    (a) SBUs are not tightly controlled.
    (b) SBUs are not separate business set-up.
    (c) SBUs are held responsible for their own Results / Performance.
    (d) SBUs are evolved from Matrix Structure.

53. A Strategic Business Unit is a ......
    (a) Cost Centre
    (b) Revenue Centre
    (c) Profit Centre
    (d) Investment Centre

54. Which of the following is not a Financial Performance Measure?
    (a) Opening Cash Flow
    (b) Return on Assets (ROA)
    (c) Market Cap
    (d) Market Share / Growth

55. Find the odd statement out:
    (a) The Strategic Business Units (SBUs) are the "Natural Groupings" of part of a Corporation
    (b) The Strategic Business Units (SBU's) strategy is the same as the Corporate Strategy
    (c) The Strategic Business Units (SBUs) have an external Market Focus
    (d) The Strategic Business Units (SBUs) allow Corporates to respond quickly to changes taking place

56. Which of the following is not a Customer-related Performance Measure?
    (a) Market Share
    (b) Customer Volume
    (c) Customer Satisfaction
    (d) New Customers

57. "A projected state of affairs that a person, a system or an organisation, plans or intends to achieve is ......".
    (a) Strategy
    (b) Mission
    (c) Vision
    (d) Goal

58. "A process where the actions people are led to take in accordance with their perceived self-interest are also in the best interest of the organisation" is known as ......
    (a) Synergy
    (b) Synchronisation
    (c) Congruence
    (d) Integration

59. Which of the following is not one of the typical functions performed by the Retailers?
    (a) Breaking Bulk
    (b) Holding Inventory
    (c) Providing Service
    (d) Providing Single Product / Service

60. The selective and analytical approach to control investment in various types of inventories is known as ......
    (a) ABC Analysis
    (b) Gross Margin Return on Investment(GMROI)
    (c) Multiple Attribute Method
    (d) Sell Through Analysis

61. Which of the following is not one of the steps involved in implementation of ABC Analysis?
    (a) Classify Inventory Items based on expected use in units
    (b) Rank the items in accordance with total value of each item
    (c) Determining the Annual Consumption Value
    (d) Combine items on the basis of their relative value to form the ABC Categories.

62. The Sell Through Analysis is not about ......
    (a) Sales
    (b) Inventory / Sales Turn Over
    (c) Sales Velocity
    (d) Merchandise Management

63. Poor Sales or Too Much Inventory is indicated by Sell Through Ratio which is ....
    (a) High
    (b) Medium
    (c) Low
    (d) Exponential

64. While calculating the Gross Margin Ratio on Investment (GMROI), the TWO important aspects are:
    (a) Stock on Hand and Stock-Outs incidents
    (b) Gross Margin and Average Inventory Cost
    (c) Gross Revenue and Stock on Hand
    (d) Carrying Costs and Stock-Out Costs

65. The Retailer is selling the merchandise for more than it costs the Retailer to acquire it, then the GMROI Ratio would be ......
    (a) Higher than 1
    (b) Equal to 1
    (c) Less than 1.
    (d) 3.2

66. The Elementary Methods, The MAUT Methods and the Out-Ranking Methods refer to the technique of ....
    (a) Inventory Classification Method
    (b) Sell Through Analysis
    (c) MAL
    (d) GMROI Analysis

67. The Non-Profit Organisation focus more on ....
    (a) Social Welfare / Interests
    (b) Surplus Generation
    (c) Funds Mobilisation
    (d) Governance

68. Which of the following statement about Non-Profit Organisation is incorrect?
    (a) It can create assets and earn income
    (b) It can get donations from abroad
    (c) It cannot distribute assets to members/directors
    (d) It cannot earn income by sale of goods / services.

69. Which of the following statement about NPOs is not true?
    (a) The NPOs generally tend to be service organisations
    (b) The NPOs receive "Contributed Capital" and have no shareholders
    (c) The sources of funds for NPOs are more or less captive
    (d) The NPOs are subjected to Market Mechanism.

70. The stipulations as regards maintenance of accounts of of/by the NGOs / NPOs are stipulated by which of the following?
    (a) The Societies Registration Act   (b) The Public Trust Act
    (c) The Companies Act   (d) The Indian Trust Act

71. The first use of the term "Social Audit" is generally attributed to ....
    (a) Peter Drucker   (b) George Coyder
    (c) Charles Medawar   (d) Amartya Sen

72. An Audit, carried out as a means of understanding an organisation's impact on society is known as ....
    (a) Environmental Audit   (b) Special Audit
    (c) Social Audit   (d) Performance Audit

73. Which of the following is not one of the eight specific principles of Social Audit?
    (a) Comprehensive   (b) Comparative
    (c) Multi-directional   (d) Non-Participatory

74. Which of the following statement is incorrect?
    (a) Management Audit is Systematic Assessment
    (b) Management Audit is Periodic Assessment
    (c) Management Audit is Statutory.
    (d) Management Audit is Comprehensive and Constructive.

75. Which of the following area is specifically covered by Management Audit?
    (a) Economic Contribution Analysis   (b) Cost-Benefit Analysis
    (c) Social Cost-Benefit Analysis.   (d) Sensitivity Analysis

76. Which of the following is not covered by Management Audit?
    (a) Systems and Procedures
    (b) Board's / Directors' Analysis
    (c) Research and Development
    (d) New Product Development Cycle Time

77. Management Audit mainly looks into ....
    (a) Non-Compliance by Management
    (b) Efficiency and Effectiveness of Management
    (c) Act of Commission of/by Management
    (d) Act of Omission of/by Management

ANSWERS

1. False	2. (d)	3. (c)	4. (b)	5. (c)	6. (b)	7. False	8. False
9. (c)	10. (b)	11. (a)	12. (b)	13. True	14. (c)	15. (d)	16. False
17. (c)	18. (c)	19. (b)	20. (c)	21. (c)	22. (a)	23. (c)	24. (d)
25. True	26. True	27. (b), (d), (a), (c)	28. (b)	29. (d)	30. (d)	31. (d)	32. (a)
33. (c)	34. (c)	35. (b)	36. (d)	37. (c)	38. (c)	39. (b)	40. (d)
41. (a)	42. (c)	43. (d)	44. (a)	45. (c)	46. (d)	47. (d)	48. (b)
49. (a)	50. (a)	51. (d)	52. (a)	53. (d)	54. (d)	55. (b)	56. (a)
57. (d)	58. (c)	59. (d)	60. (a)	61. (c)	62. (a)	63. (c)	64. (b)
65. (a)	66. (c)	67. (a)	68. (d)	69. (d)	70. (d)	71. (b)	72. (c)
73. (d)	74. (c)	75. (a)	76. (d)	77. (b)			

www.ingramcontent.com/pod-product-compliance
Lightning Source LLC
Chambersburg PA
CBHW080924180426
43192CB00040B/2708